ENEMY
OF THE
DISASTER

Enemy of the Disaster

Selected Political Writings of Renaud Camus

Edited with an Introduction by Louis Betty

Translated by Louis Betty and Ethan Rundell

VAUBAN
BOOKS

.

26   25   24   23   1   2   3   4

ISBN 979-8-9887399-0-6 (paperback)

Library of Congress Control Number: 2023942821

Front cover illustration, Renaud Camus, *Le Jour ni l'Heure*, self-portrait in the garden, Monday, March 8th, 2010, 13:21:41

Vauban Books
P.O. Box 508
Blowing Rock, NC 28605
www.vaubanbooks.com

Contents

Acknowledgements

The present book represents the culmination of a genuinely collective effort stretching over the better part of a year. Among the many who assisted us along the way, several deserve our particular thanks. The author of one of the only sympathetic English-language portraits[1] to appear in the avalanche of recent publications devoted to the work of Renaud Camus, Nathan Pinkoski was there from the start, making connections and encouraging us along. In Paris, François Bousquet, director of La Nouvelle Librairie, played a crucial role in our first contacts with Camus and was unstinting in helping us assemble the materials needed to begin work on this volume. As we negotiated the form this book would ultimately take, Quentin Verwaerde proved an invaluable intermediary, advising us on how best to approach what often proved to be delicate editorial questions. Above all, we wish to thank Renaud Camus for the confidence he has shown in this fledgling venture and for his stubborn determination to remain, come what may, that rare thing: an *honnête homme*.

LB and ER

---

1. Nathan Pinkoski, "The Man Behind the 'Great Replacement," Compact Magazine, May 21, 2022, https://compactmag.com/article/the-man-behind-the-great-replacement.

Through trackless, through unknown territory has ventured the restlessness of men, and behind them came their wives and children and parents stricken in years. Some of them, driven about in their long wanderings, did not choose their goal deliberately, but through weariness settled at the nearest place; others by force of arms established their right in a foreign country. Some tribes were drowned while they sought unknown regions; others settled where they were stranded by running out of supplies. They did not all have the same reason for abandoning one homeland for another. Some, escaping the destruction of their cities by enemy attack, were driven to other territory when they lost their own; some were banished by civil strife; others were sent out to relieve the burden of overpopulation; others fled from disease or constant earthquakes or some intolerable deficiencies in their barren soil; others were tempted by the exaggerated report of a fertile shore. Different reasons aroused different peoples to leave their homes; but this at least is clear, nothing has stayed where it was born.

Seneca, Consolation to Helvia[1]

National divisions and conflicts between peoples increasingly disappear with the development of the bourgeoisie, with free trade and the world market, with the uniform character of industrial production and the corresponding circumstances of modern life.

The rule of the proletariat will make them disappear even faster.

Marx, The Communist Manifesto[2]

---

1. Seneca, *On the Shortness of Life* (New York, Penguin, 2005), pp. 42-43.
2. Karl Marx, *Late Political Writings*, ed. Terrell Carver (Cambridge, Cambridge University Press, 1996), pp. 17-18.

Introduction: *Renaud Camus, Enemy of the Disaster*[3]

Renaud Camus, born in 1946 to a provincial bourgeois family in Auvergne, made his entry into the world of French letters in the 1970s. An acolyte of Roland Barthes, France's most influential literary critic of the second half of the twentieth century, Camus was to center his own work on *bathmology*, or the study of levels of language and discourse, a notion that Barthes had described very much in passing in his 1975 book *Roland Barthes par Roland Barthes*.[4] Camus' first published works, which heavily owed to Barthes' influence, were highly formalistic in content and execution as suited the *Nouveau Roman* sensibilities of the time: very loosely defined as novels, his *Eglogues*, beginning with *Passage*[5] in 1975, were a cycle of polyphonic texts built largely on ironizing quotations of other authors and later on those of Camus himself. Because modern literature could say nothing new, its work, as the Barthesian line of thinking went, was inescapably referential and ironizing; originality lay simply in eliminating the quotation marks.[6] *Buena Vista Park*,[7] which appeared in 1980, was an aphoristic illustration of bathmology exploring how identical words and statements could have different meanings, or could mean differently, that is, depending on when and by whom they were uttered. More similarity could exist between a *yes* and a *no* than between a *yes* and a *yes*; two speakers might agree with a proposition for wildly different reasons,

---

3. Camus often uses the term "friends of the disaster" to refer to French cultural and political authorities who favor what he deems to be disastrous immigration and educational policies. Insofar as he opposes such policies, one can consider Camus an "enemy of the disaster." Hence our choice of title for this book.
4. Roland Barthes, *Roland Barthes par Roland Barthes* (Paris, Seuil, 1975).
5. Renaud Camus, *Passage* (Paris, Flammarion, 1975).
6. See Force, Pierre and Dominique Jullien, "Renaud Camus," in *After the Age of Suspicion: The French Novel Today*, ed. Charles A. Porter, *Yale French Studies* special issue (1988), pp. 285-289.
7. Renaud Camus, *Buena Vista Park* (Paris, Hachette/P.O.L., 1980).

) others disagree with it over the slightest of details. In the
g spiral of meaning, Camus argued, *yes* always means *yes*
....ways *no*, but never in exactly the same way, even for the same
speaker.

Camus also established his reputation beginning in the late 1970s
as a prominent homosexual writer. His 1979 book *Tricks*,[8] the only
of Camus' works to have enjoyed translation into English, described
in detail the writer's numerous gay sexual encounters and was prefaced by Roland Barthes. Camus' writings on homosexuality attracted
the attention of American scholars, perhaps most notably Lawrence
Schehr,[9] and in 1996 Camus gave an interview to *Yale French Studies*
for its issue on gay and lesbian writing in France.[10] In addition to his
contributions to gay literature (which feature Camus' neologism for
the word *gay*, *achrien*), Camus has also authored a number of historical
novels, at least a dozen books on topography, a dozen and a half books
on political subjects, and half a dozen elegies. Camus has published
a personal journal every year since 1980 that typically runs over 500
pages. His four volumes of *Vaisseaux brûlés* [Burned Vessels], another
of his intensely formalistic projects, come to over 1300 pages. When
one includes his lengthy interviews,[11] his writings on art, a piece of
theater, works of philosophy and numerous other miscellaneous texts,
Camus has published some 150 books numbering in total many tens of
thousands of pages. With the possible exceptions of Michel Onfray and
Alain de Benoist, Renaud Camus may be France's most prolific living
writer, a man of Balzacian ambition in terms of quantity and scope,
whose lack of financial success[12] is made up for, at least artistically, by
sheer variety and immensity of production. Camus' prolixity is such

---

8.   Renaud Camus, *Tricks* (Paris, Mazarine, 1979).
9.   See Lawrence Schehr, *The Shock of Men: Homosexual Hermeneutics in French
     Writing* (Palo Alto, Stanford University Press, 1995).
10. Bruno Vercier, Charles A. Porter and Ralph Sarkonak, "Interview with Renaud
     Camus," in *Same Sex/Different Text: Gay and Lesbian Writing in French*, Yale
     French Studies 90 (1996), pp. 7-21.
11. Camus' extended interview, *La Dictature de la petite bourgeoisie: entretiens avec
     Marc Saune* (Toulouse, Privat, 2005), employs a false narrator. In this respect, it
     mimics a Platonic dialogue.
12. For a consideration of Camus' "failure" as a writer, see Jan Baetens, Études camu-
     siennes (Amsterdam, Rodopi, 2000), pp. 22-25.

that one wonders if it will be possible for a future doctoral student to make a thorough study of his work or, for that matter, an established scholar to produce an edition of his complete works. As one scholar has commented (facetiously but just barely, perhaps), "Camus' productivity [. . .] is making him into an author that no one will study."[13]

The great irony, then, in the case of this prolific native of Chamalières is that his name has become synonymous, nearly to the exclusion of everything else in his vast opus, with one of our age's most ideologically charged terms: the Great Replacement. In the formulation that has come to us from the manifestos of mass shooters, *great replacement* refers to a conspiracy, typically on the part of left-wing governments if not shadowy cosmopolitan mandarins often imagined as Jews,[14] to replace the indigenous white populations of western countries, either to secure electoral advantages for leftist parties who believe they have greater appeal for minority voters, or to dilute and dissolve nation states and other recalcitrant identities in favor of one-world government. Understood in this sense, *Great Replacement Theory* has become a centerpiece of contemporary white supremacist rhetoric, which, from Charlottesville, Virginia, to Christchurch, New Zealand, lurks online only to erupt in horrendous spasms of violence against perceived racial enemies or race traitors. The term receives regular, emphatic denunciation in the legacy anglophone press whenever it is invoked, as happened in Buffalo, New York in 2022, as a motivation for the perpetration of lethal racist violence.[15]

How did the Frenchman Renaud Camus, once a gay literary icon and, moreover, an avowed pacifist, come to be associated with the noxious fulminations of racist identitarianism in the English-speaking world? Camus is, to be sure, the originator of the term *great replacement*; he

13. See Hugo Frey, "Contradiction without End: Renaud Camus and the Parti de l'In-nocence" in *Les Spirales du sens chez Renaud Camus*, ed. Ralph Sarkonak (Amsterdam, Rodopi, 2000), p. 224.

14. During the white supremacist demonstrations in Charlottesville, Virginia, in 2017, demonstrators alternately chanted "You will not replace us" and "Jews will not replace us."

15. See, for example, Shane Goldmacher and Luke Broadwater, "Republicans Play on Fears of 'Great Replacement' in Bid for Base Voters, *New York Times*, 16 May 2022, https://www.nytimes.com/2022/05/16/us/politics/republicans-great-replacement .html?searchResultPosition=1.

claims to have invented it after a visit during the mid-1990s to several villages in southwestern France whose populations were, at least visibly, mostly of North African rather than European origin. Beyond mere observation, however, Camus' understanding of *replacism* departs radically from its subsequent white supremacist formulation. Camus has consistently rejected the claim that a conspiracy is afoot to replace the native populations of Europe; he refers to the imputation of conspiracy theorizing to his thought as the "conspiracy theory theory." Population replacement is, rather, a matter of observation, Camus has written, the reasons for which are multiple, complex, and hardly attributable to a plot on the part of globalist overlords, let alone Jews. As for replacism in the North American case, Camus claims that immigration to the United States has forced politicians to pander to recently naturalized citizens, whose sentimental loyalties toward their ethnic cohort abroad lead them to demand more open immigration policies at home. He says nothing about a conspiracy, arguing instead that the country's independence is degraded when politicians are forced to factor foreign ethnic sympathies into their electoral calculi.[16]

Camus has only ever advocated political solutions to population replacement. His small political party, the Party of In-nocence (a play on the Latin verb *nocere*, which means *to harm* and from which English receives the word *nuisance*) is critical of *nocence* – of harm, of nuisance – in all its forms and has, for instance, condemned the occasional vandalizing of the tombs of Muslim soldiers who died fighting in French wars.[17] Camus' commitment to non-harm places him much more in the camp of John Stuart Mill than in that of ethnic identitarians,[18] and he has never claimed that only ethnic Europeans can truly become French (or German or English, etc.), only that it is impossible for Europe to assimilate *peoples*. In fact, by far the worst solution to the Great Replacement, Camus insists, is an increase in the

---

16. See Renaud Camus, *Le Grand Remplacement: introduction au remplacisme global* (Paris, La Nouvelle Librairie, 2021), pp. 23-24.
17. See, for example, https://www.renaud-camus.net/journal/2015/02/05.
18. Nathan Pinkoski makes a similar observation in his article "The Man Behind the 'Great Replacement,'" *Compact Magazine*, 21 May 2022, https://compactmag.com/article/the-man-behind-the-great-replacement.

white European birth rate; his ecological sentiments, which include non-nocence as an environmental principle, lead him, if anything, to favor a policy of population degrowth. Nor should replacism be combatted by a reinvigoration of Europe's ancestral religion, Christianity. Rather, European identities are best preserved, in Camus' telling, by a recommitment to the teaching and promulgation of high culture in society at large, beginning with France's decrepit public education system. A people that knows its classics, Camus has repeated, does not let itself be replaced.

These observations are not intended to exonerate Camus. The philosopher Alain Finkielkraut, a mainstream figure in French intellectual life who has been one of Camus' most consistent supporters, agrees with Camus that the great replacement is "not a conspiracy theory" but laments that the radicality of his friend's positions makes him "totally inaudible" in the French debate over immigration and identity.[19] Indeed, Camus' perceived outrageousness lies not so much in his ideas, which are increasingly mainstream in France in the third decade of the third millennium,[20] as in his rhetoric. Succinct and provocative

19. Quoted in James McCauley, "How Gay Icon Renaud Camus Became the Ideologue of White Supremacy," *The Nation*, 17 June 2019, https://thenation.com/article/archive/renaud-camus-great-replacement-brenton/tarrant/.

20. For various indicators of the prevalence of belief in the Great Replacement (either in its Camusian or conspiratorial form) in France, see Thomas Liabot, "Les Gilet Jaunes sont plus susceptibles aux theories du complot," *Le Journal du Dimanche*, 11 February 2019, https://www.lejdd.fr/Societe/sondage-les-gilets-jaunes-sont-plus-sensibles-aux-theories-du-complot-3855563; *Baromètre des intentions de vote à l'élection présidentielle de 2022, vague 18*, Harris Interactive, week of October 20, 2021, pp. 42-43, http://harris-interactive.fr/wp-content/uploads/sites/6/2021/10/Rapport-Harris-Vague-18-Intentions-de-vote-Presidentielle-2022-Challenges.pdf; "Immigration, 'grand remplacement': Macron reprend en privé des formules d'Éric Zemmour et Renaud Camus," *Valeurs Actuelles*, 24 November 2020, https://www.valeursactuelles.com/politique/video-immigration-grand-remplacement-macron-reprend-en-prive-des-formules-deric-zemmour-et-renaud-camus. It is notable that Éric Zemmour, who was a leading candidate in the French presidential race before the Russian invasion of Ukraine in February 2022, freely uses the term "great replacement" to describe the French demographic situation vis-à-vis non-European immigration. He is cited, for example, on the back cover of Nouvelle Librairie's 2021 edition of *Le Grand Remplacement*: "The Great Replacement is neither imaginary nor a conspiracy: it is the historical drama of our time."

terminology such as *the great replacement* – not to mention such incendiary language as *genocide by substitution*[21] to describe perceptible European demographic shifts in recent decades – are easily appropriated by ideological bad actors who, while likely having little or no familiarity with the substance of Camus' thought, are able to decontextualize his terminology for use as a racist cudgel in interactions with detractors. Indeed, one of the purposes of this volume – perhaps its most pressing purpose – is to make such a cudgel unavailable by filling in this contextual vacuum. Even so, although Camus has denounced the use of curt terminology as "absolute weapons of language," specifically the *reductio ad Hitlerum* that seems to haunt all difficult discussions of national identity, it is another irony of Camus' work that his own terminology, however clever it is in a writerly sense, has made a different set of absolute weapons of language available to determined, violent racists and white supremacists whose violence Camus abhors.

The Great Replacement, based on a speech Camus gave in the southern French city of Lunel in 2010, was published by David Reinharc in 2011 in a volume that included several other essays on political subjects.[22] The next year, Fayard and P.O.L., Camus' most prestigious Parisian publishers, dropped Camus after he rallied to Marine Le Pen in that year's presidential election. Then in 2014, Camus was brought to court and convicted of "inciting racial hatred" for a speech in which he appeared to liken suburban Muslim youth to soldiers in a war of conquest against France.[23] This professional collapse, from which Camus only recovered in 2021 when *La Nouvelle Librairie* published a vastly expanded edition of *The Great Replacement*,[24] was not the first scandal to mar Camus' career. In 2001, *L'Affaire Camus* erupted after Camus was accused of anti-Semitism for certain passages of his 1994 journal, *La Campagne de France*,[25] which P.O.L. had finally published in 2000. Despite the succor of two highly placed friends, Alain Finkielkraut and

---

21. This term is not actually of Camus' coining; he borrows it from Aimé Césaire, a writer, poet, and politician from French Martinique who died in 2008.
22. Renaud Camus, *Le Grand Replacement* (Paris, David Reinharc, 2011).
23. See the essay "Nocence, Instrument of the Great Replacement" in this volume.
24. See note 16 for reference.
25. Renaud Camus, *La Campagne de France: Journal 1994* (Paris, P.O.L., 2000).

Emmanuel Carrère,[26] Camus' reputation was permanently damaged by the scandal, a professional diminution Camus described in detail in his 2000 journal, *Corbeau*.[27] Like the scandal surrounding *The Great Replacement*, *L'Affaire Camus* spoke to an intractable difficulty in negotiating the often tense relationship in Camus' writing between perceived provocation, on the one hand, and, on the other hand, a relentless if not obsessive need to say everything, especially that which is, at least officially, unsayable. *L'Affaire* is thus worth investigating in some detail.

L'Affaire Camus

Camus' journal is perhaps primarily an exercise in unremitting self-inspection. Camus recounts in exhaustive detail his walks in the countryside, his interest in this or that potential lover, his health anxieties, his interactions with idiosyncratic neighbors in Plieux, where he has lived in the village's government-subsidized castle since the early 1990s. His moral introspection is unyielding, often leading Camus into dangerous territory when he enquires into his biases and prejudices, even his potential bigotry. It is essential to keep in mind that Camus' observations occur in the context of a personal journal in the literary form; a line of thinking he explores on one page is often reversed on the next, a conclusion entertained in the morning dismissed in the evening. The ever-looming possibility of reversal in the journal requires dedication to long and careful reading, a commitment by the reader to the *contingent* nature of the personal journal, which must, if it is to be an honest self-accounting, reflect the inevitably shifting and unstable nature of the human soul. Absent such a commitment, Camus is left dangerously exposed to readers who do not grasp the nature of his project, and who might therefore read a passing observation as a statement of indelible conviction.

Be that as it may, Camus' journal is not an incoherent postmodern mishmash from which no truth about its author can be drawn.

---

26. See Renaud Camus, *Étrangèreté: Entretiens avec Emmanuel Carrère and Alain Finkielkraut* (Geneva, Tricorne, 2003).
27. Renaud Camus, *Corbeau* (Brussels, *Impressions Nouvelles*, 2000).

Indeed, perhaps the principal theme of all of Camus' work is *obsession with the origin*, that is, the question of what constitutes the identity of things – or of people, even *peoples* – apart from convention or mere bureaucratic decree (that one can become French, for example, or any other nationality, simply by an administrative decision). If identity is not located in an *essence*, that is, in an identity of name and thing, of signifier and signified, is it therefore condemned to the presentism of convention, which, moreover, would tend to dismiss competing understandings of identity as instances of dangerous essentialism? Camus' answer is to propose a third way: identity, the origin of which is always beyond or beneath it and thus eternally out of reach, nonetheless has a history, a story, even a national story that cannot be wished away by administrative fiat. Can a person with French nationality, for example, partake of the "story of France" without having participated in it in the historical sense? Inversely, can a person with French nationality participate in this same sense (through family history, for instance) in the "story of France" without partaking of it presently?[28] Camus' response is that it depends – on commitment, on love, hate, or indifference toward France, on the strength of competing identities, etc. – but that there nonetheless exists a national story that serves as a basis of French identity, a kind of spiral of common meanings and references, built up over time, that billows up endlessly even as it adds and incorporates new chapters of the story at its periphery. Names, in the Confucian sense, are neither rectified nor invented out of whole cloth.[29] They must attend to their previous instances in the spiral of meaning if they are to have any meaning at all.

Camus' crime, as it were, in *La Campagne de France* was to have asked these questions in the context of Jewish identity and specifically

---

28. In the original French, "participer à" and "participer de" correspond to "participate in" and "partake of," respectively.
29. I am here referring to the doctrine of the rectification of names in Confucian philosophy. Names, in this tradition, should always coincide with the thing to which they refer; only a person with the qualities of a leader should be called a leader, for example, or the with the qualities of a prince be called a prince. When word and thing fail to coincide, especially at the top of the social hierarchy, disorder begins to infect the entire society from the top down.

the historically fraught relationship of Jewish identity to French national identity. And not only to have asked them, but to have answered that the former identity mattered in relation to the latter, to the point that an overrepresentation of Jewish voices in discussions about national identity, for example, might be, or might be susceptible to being, unbalanced. Camus' target in this criticism was the radio show *Le Panorama*, a literary program broadcast by the public radio station *France Culture*. Camus wrote, in *La Campagne de France*,

> The program is run by Michel Bydlowski. His fellow debaters are Antoine Spire, Roger Dadoun, Isabelle Rabineau, and a certain J.P. Grunsfeld, whom I do not know. Five participants, and what proportion of non-Jews, among them? Tiny, if not non-existent. Now, I find this not exactly scandalous, perhaps, but overstated, uncalled for, improper. And no, I am not anti-Semitic. And yes, I think that the Jewish race has brought humanity one of the highest spiritual, intellectual, and artistic contributions that has ever been. And yes, I think that the Nazi's anti-Semitic crimes probably constitute the most extreme point of abomination that humanity has ever attained. But no, no, and no, I do not think it is suitable that a discussion that has been prepared and planned – that is official, in other words – about "integration" in our country, on a public radio station, during a program of a general character, should take place exclusively among five Jews or persons of Jewish origin.[30]

Just as troubling to his critics was that Camus had, elsewhere in the 1994 journal, used the terms "collaborators" and "monopoly" to describe the debate's participants, terms that evoked at least connotatively the complicity of certain Jews in the deportation and murder of their co-religionists as well as the specter of a Jewish conspiracy of control reminiscent of the *Protocols of the Elders of Zion*. The incriminating

---

30. Cited in Ivan Jaffrin, "D'un scandale l'autre: l'affaire Renaud Camus et la faillite de la critique intellectuelle," *COnTEXTES* [online] 10 (2012), p. 6, put on line 17 April 2012, consulted 19 October 2021. http://journals.openedition.org /contextes/4975. See also Renaud Camus, *Du Sens* (Paris, P.O.L., 2002), p. 499.

passages of *La Campagne de France* thus appeared to summon a blood-and-soil understanding of French identity, one rooted neither in administrative decree nor history but in an immutable essence in which outsiders – Jews, in this case – were forbidden to participate.

The ensuing scandal broke on April 18th, 2001, when the journalist Marc Weitzmann, writing for *Les Inrockuptibles*, published an article entitled "On In-nocence" [*De L'In-nocence*] condemning Camus' reflections in the 1994 journal. Weitzmann declared:

> Well, one will be happy to learn where exactly the line of thinking and the commentary lie when Camus – in a fit of temper, he writes, out of his "passionate love for the French experience" – is saddened to see "this experience have as its main spokespersons" representatives of the "Jewish race;" when he explains that the latter, often French for only one or two generations, the poor things, "do not directly participate in this experience."[31]

A few days later, on April 21st, *Le Monde* published a press release by Jean-Marie Cavada, the president of Radio France at the time, calling for Camus to be sued, along with comments by Catherine Tasca, then France's Minister of Culture, who declared Camus' sentiments to be "deeply worrying."[32] Fayard, the publisher of *La Campagne de France*, withdrew the volume from bookstores that same day, only returning it to shelves a few weeks later in a new edition from which the offending passages had been removed. On May 18th, *Le Monde* ran a defense of Camus written by some of Camus' most prominent readers including Emmanuel Carrère and Frédéric Mitterrand.[33] A week later, another article appeared, still in *Le Monde*, condemning this defense (which, it should be noted, did not attempt to justify Camus' remarks but only expressed indignation that a book had been censored); among its signatories were Jacques Derrida, Philippe Sollers, and Michel Deguy.[34] Not missing the chance to make his own public declaration, Bernard-Henri

---

31. Jaffrin, "D'un scandale l'autre," p. 7.
32. *Ibid.*, p. 7.
33. *Ibid.*
34. *Ibid.*

Lévy also chimed in, writing in *L'Événement du jeudi* that Camus' statements were "absolutely pestilential" and urgently needed to be denounced.[35]

But what had Camus really written? The Parisian journalistic apparatus had condemned him on the basis of excerpts from the journal that were circulated and re-circulated just as *La Campagne de France* was being removed from bookstores and its incriminating passages expurgated. The initial flare-up thus gave way to attempts at more careful readings of the journal, which were able to supply the context – not to mention an appreciation of Camus' journal as a literary rather than polemical project –that had lacked at the height of the affair. The literary critic Philippe Lançon, for instance, wrote, "At the beginning, like those who had never read him, I had been content to condemn him on the basis of the wretched sentences I was reading in the press [. . .] Then I read him. Attentively. I discovered that he wrote elsewhere sentences that denounced the previous ones; and I felt I understood the meaning of the whole."[36] The historian Pierre-André Taguieff for his part declared that Camus' alleged anti-Semitism was "difficult to demonstrate" on the basis of Camus' statements alone.[37] Emmanuel Carrère, writing the next June in *Le Figaro* (the affair picked up again in the summer of 2002, presumably after the interruption of 9/11), condemned the denunciatory haste of Camus's detractors, who, he maintained, had "signed a petition on the basis of a montage of despicably doctored citations [. . .] His ever more numerous enemies were not content to refuse to read him, they boasted of not having read him."[38] Finally, Alain Finkielkraut, in *L'Imparfait du présent*, decried "that penitent and journalistic France" that was "not less worrying than the France pilloried in the person of Renaud Camus."[39] Influential detractors remained, including Jacques Kéchichian (Camus' writings were the symptom of an "old illness, [which was] never really treated");[40]

---

35. *Ibid.*
36. *Ibid.*, pp. 7-8.
37. *Ibid.*, p. 8.
38. *Ibid.*, pp. 7-8.
39. Alain Finkielkraut, *L'Imparfait du présent* (Paris, Flammarion, 2002), pp. 55-56.
40. Jaffrin, "D'un scandale l'autre," p. 9.

Élisabeth Roudinesco (Camus was a product of "ordinary anti-Semitism" and "old-fashioned French xenophobia");[41] and, of course, Bernard-Henri Lévy ("One can be a good writer and obsessively anti-Semitic").[42] Nonetheless, there had emerged what Ivan Jaffrin has called an "irreversible intellectual division" between the two sides in the affair:[43] either Camus was guilty, according to his enemies, of inciting racial or religious hatred in *La Campagne de France* and thus liable to prosecution; or those same enemies were guilty, "in the thoughtlessness and recklessness" of their denunciation, of the "the worst of crimes in the Republic of Letters."[44] The outcome was, and remains today, a stalemate.

Below, then, is a fuller version of the incriminating passage cited above, which Camus includes in his 2002 book, *Du Sens*, and which he presents in that same text as the product of an inquiry into his potential prejudices (anti-Semitism being from his perspective the most shocking and inexcusable prejudice in men of his generation).[45] Portions between brackets and in italics indicate those passages that were removed in the expurgated version of *La Campagne de France*:

> If I said what I really think, in any society today, I would immediately be lynched. And the societies that would not lynch me would only not do so as the result of a misunderstanding, and it would be with them, probably, that my deep disagreement would be the most real . . .
>
> [*France Culture's Le "Panorama" is being broadcast live from Marseille, today. It is essentially about immigration and its problems, about integration and its failures, about the difficult relations among the diverse communities of foreign origin—the oldest arrivals, Italians and Armenians, essentially, tending to reject the most recent arrivals, who are predominantly North African.*

---

41. *Ibid.*, pp. 9-10.
42. *Ibid.*, p. 9.
43. *Ibid.*, p. 8.
44. *Ibid.*, p. 10.
45. Camus, *Du Sens*, p. 381.

The program is run by Michel Bydlowski. His fellow debaters are Antoine Spire, Roger Dadoun, Isabelle Rabineau, and a certain J.P. Grunsfeld whom I do not know. Five participants, and what proportion of non-Jews, among them? Tiny, if not non-existent. Now, I find this not exactly scandalous, perhaps, but overstated, uncalled for, improper. And no, I am not anti-Semitic. And yes, I think that the Jewish race has brought humanity one of the highest spiritual, intellectual, and artistic contributions that has ever been. And yes, I think that the Nazi's anti-Semitic crimes probably constitute the most extreme point of abomination that humanity has ever attained. But no, no, and no, I do not think it is suitable that a discussion that has been prepared and planned—that is official, in other words—about "integration" in our country, on a public radio station, during a program of a general character, should take place exclusively among five Jews or persons of Jewish origin. They have opinions that are as precious and legitimate as any others, of course—more precious and more legitimate, perhaps, being more directly nurtured, probably, by sensible or familial experience. But they should not be the only ones to speak, on a general-interest channel, which is the property of no one, if not of the Republic.

May we be left in peace by the terrorism that does not permit us to open our mouths about these kinds of questions! This program and many others are profoundly biased by an excessively tendentious composition of the panel of participants. And I believe I have the right to say so. And if I do not have it, then I am taking it.

I am taking it in the name of that old culture and that native French civilization that are my own, whose accomplishments across the centuries are more than honorable, and that I regret hardly hearing anymore, in the country that was their own. If their voice is lost, it is not only, far from it, because it is covered up by that of "successive waves of immigration."] It is because their transmission is no longer guaranteed, because the educational system no longer teaches the new generations either their values or their means of expression; and because the elites, who

had been the most involved in this culture and in this civilization, have been decimated as elites by income tax, inheritance
tax, by obligatory public schooling, and by television, which has
long been the same for everyone."[46]

Camus admits that such sentiments are "disagreeable" and even "distasteful" but insists that the purpose of his journal is "to be true."[47]
"There are base sentiments there, there are stupid sentiments there,"
he explains in *Du sens*, "but if it happens that I have felt them, I would
have distorted the picture, I would have broken the 'reading contract'
[. . .] if I had kept them for myself."[48] To the charge, furthermore, that
he had accused *Le Panorama* of featuring "too many Jews," Camus re-
sponds that he "never thought, or wrote, that there were *too many Jews*.
I felt, on that day, and based on the subject addressed by the program,
that there were *not enough others*."[49] The issue raised, in Camus' telling, is not so much about identity as about representation. Surely being
Jewish matters in a discussion of a topic as broad as French national
identity, just as being Catholic, Muslim, or a Portuguese immigrant to
France matters to it as well. And yet, whether due to his rhetoric, his
vocabulary, his mode of assertion, or simply the unfiltered nature of
journal writing, Camus managed in the passages cited above to give
offense, and not just to those who had read him poorly or not at all.

Lawrence Schehr, for example, addressing a conference at Yale
University on Camus in the immediate wake of the affair,[50] objects to
Camus' vocabulary and what he sees as its inescapably connotative
character. Speaking voluntarily as a Jew, Schehr states, "But I do not
see this neutrality, for the words 'collaborator' and 'monopoly' are so
imbued with inseparable connotations that evoke stereotypes and history [. . .] Instead of wondering why all points of view are not represented [. . .] there is talk of Jewish collaborators and their monopoly."[51]

46. *Ibid.*, pp. 499-500.
47. *Ibid.*, p. 488.
48. *Ibid.*
49. *Ibid.*, p. 502.
50. The temporal proximity of the outbreak of the Camus affair to the Yale conference was coincidental.
51. Lawrence Schehr, "P.D.: Paroles Déplacées (L'Affaire Camus)," in *Renaud Camus,*

Camus' comments are troubling in Schehr's view because they evoke an age-old anti-Semitic trope: that Jews as "Israelites" are interlopers who out of indifference if not hostility to the traditional cultures of their host nations cannot be trusted to represent them. Rather, they may even seek to undermine them. Jews cannot really be French (or German, American, etc.), and to the extent they do become French at least officially, their loyalties remain suspect. Camus does not say any of this, of course. He even declaims at length in *Du sens* against the prejudice, if not the instinct, toward connotative reading that he sees in a reaction such as Schehr's (and which, he grants, is an understandable product of recent history).[52] That he appeals to the personal nature of the journal may seem, nonetheless, an evasion. Camus is aware that his journal is not truly personal, at least not ultimately, but is instead destined for publication by a major press. He may not deserve the connotative reading Schehr subjects him to, but this has not spared Camus the accusation of playing at a sort of kitsch that would knowingly if not cheekily obscure the boundary between responsible polemic, on the one hand, and knowing provocation, on the other.[53]

Camus' sentiments also offend against deeply-ingrained Republican notions of what constitutes the nature of citizenship and national identity. Sjef Houppermans, writing in *Renaud Camus, Érographe*, speaks to what outsiders to the French understanding of national identity might see, in fact, as the eminently *reasonable* nature of Camus' complaint against France Culture:

> What appears completely "legal" would be [. . .] the right to pose such a question, which one might generalize in this way: is it desirable that there should be an overrepresentation of any component of the population whatsoever in the discussion of "culture" such as a public channel offers it? A precise reading of context

Écrivain, eds. Jan Baetens and Charles A. Porter (Leuven, Peeters Vrin, 2001), pp. 119-130.

52. Camus, *Du Sens*, pp. 358-365.

53. See McCauley, "How Gay Icon Renaud Camus Became the Ideologue of White Supremacy," *The Nation*, 17 June 2019, for a similar observation. https://www.thenation.com/article/archive/renaud-camus-great-replacement-brenton-tarrant/.

therefore in no way permits incriminating Camus for reactionary sympathies or worse. He expresses, at most, the desire that other approaches to the works treated be possible through a more balanced composition of discussion panels.[54]

Houppermans' observation suggests something of the French rather than Jewish character of the hostile reaction to *La Campagne de France*. Unlike the United States, for example, the French Republic does not keep demographic data on the race and ethnicity of its citizens and residents. The "one and indivisible" Republic is to be matched, ideally, by a public identity that is equally one and indivisible. Communitarian identities, be they Jewish, Muslim, Christian, or other should accordingly be shed in the public square (indeed, the word "communauté" carries a negative connotation in French). Aside from the Jewish question, then, part of the scandal of the Camus affair would be its suggestion that the French understanding of national identity, a product of France's Enlightenment and revolutionary heritage, is exceedingly formalistic and thus inadequate. Unlike Republican citizenship, real identities are not abstractions, and to say that the latter do not weigh in the question of national identity amounts to a prejudice against reality. Being a French Jew, a French Catholic, or a French Muslim does not mean everything; but it surely means something. If a public discussion in the United States on national identity were to be composed of only one ethnic or religious group, the limitations of that discussion, if not its offensive nature, would be obvious. In this respect, *L'Affaire Camus* is a very French affair.

Nonetheless, the fact of Camus' having made these comments in a personal journal, even one destined for publication, makes rendering a final judgment of them difficult if not impossible. One can read the passages from *La Campagne de France* connotatively and take offense on the part of Jews and Jewishness, or one can stick to denotation and either defend the French understanding of national identity or bemoan its perceived inadequacies. One can do both, or one can do neither: there is always the possibility that everything one has concluded from

---

54. Sjef Houppermans, *Renaud Camus, Érographe* (Amsterdam, Rodopi, 2004), p. 23.

a reading of one page will be swept away by what comes on the next.[55] As Emmanuel Carrère puts it succinctly in reference to *La Campagne de France*, "One cannot say: Renaud Camus thinks this."[56] What is true of Camus' journal, however, is not true of the author's political writings, for very quickly after *L'Affaire*, Camus begins to formalize a cultural and political critique that will culminate in 2011 in *The Great Replacement*. Nor does the journal bear no relation to this later and more politically consequential work. In both can be found, on the one hand, the same tendency to splice pertinent cultural and political criticism with provocative language, and, on the other hand, Camus' perennial obsession with origins.

From Little to Great Replacement

Camus insists that the Great Replacement can only occur following a general process of deculturation or decivilization.[57] Demographic replacement in Europe is the culmination of a long movement of cultural decline, which has its roots not in mass immigration or an elite conspiracy but, rather, in the progressive erasure of bourgeois civilization. The bourgeoisie, which had preserved the aristocratic sensibilities of the Old Regime, saw itself gradually displaced over the course of the twentieth century by the preferences of the petty bourgeoisie, which rejected those sensibilities for their elitism. Camus calls this phenomenon the "Little Replacement." Dominated by petty bourgeois thinking, European nations felt obliged, especially in the wake of the Second World War, to attempt to expunge bourgeois cultural sensibilities from their societies, principally through changes in public education. The bourgeoisie had taken natural inequality in talent and intellect for granted, along with hierarchy in artistic and intellectual accomplishment; for this reason, it had to be banished for the sake of

55. On this point, see Alexandre Albert-Galtier, "Renaud Camus politique," in *Renaud Camus, Écrivain*, eds. Jan Baetens and Charles A. Porter (Leuven, Peeters Vrin, 2001), pp. 88-89; and Charles A. Porter, "Renaud Camus à Yale," in *Renaud Camus, Écrivain*, eds. Jan Baetens and Charles A. Porter (Leuven, Peeters Vrin, 2001), p. 5.
56. Camus, Étrangèreté, p. 33.
57. See Renaud Camus, *Décivilisation* (Paris, Fayard, 2011).

cultural egalitarianism, and with it the teaching of the history that had sustained it. This "teaching of forgetting" has had perverse results: since culture could not be reduced to mere access to culture, culture itself had to be defined down, leveled off to include anything and everything that a people or peoples did or valued. The very things that had nourished the identity of European peoples as peoples – a sense of high culture, respect for form, formality and social hierarchy, familiarity with a canon of classics, etc. – were brought to the level of any sort of ordinary personal or collective preference. One was no longer allowed to distinguish opera from pop, Mozart from Metallica, Montaigne from Mickey Mouse. To point out the inevitably unequal nature of talent and cultural accomplishment, even while supporting equal access to this inequality, now earned a person the accusation of contempt if not crypto-fascism.

A people who knows its classics does not let itself be replaced, Camus has insistently claimed. The deculturating process, on the other hand, leaves a people fatally exposed not just to internal decay but, more importantly, to other peoples, other cultures, and other civilizations that do not share the same egalitarian or "hyperdemocratic" scruples and therefore have no qualms about imposing their civilizational preferences on their European hosts. The effects of this Little Replacement, which had only concerned European peoples and their class quarrels, are then compounded by historical guilt stemming from the West's colonial misadventures and, more fundamentality, from the trauma of the world wars, especially the Second World War and the Third Reich's crimes against the Christian West's primordial Other, the Jews. Europe, which had been awash in militant nationalism, ethnic chauvinism, and anti-Semitism before the outbreak of war in 1914, is now so frightened of repeating its recent past that the merest suggestion of defending "traditional national identity" is met in the quarters of official France with accusations of reaction, racism, if not outright Hitlerism (and also fantasy – one of the main tactics of the media-political complex, Camus insists, being to claim that such a thing as traditional national identity never existed). Camus calls this inversion the "Second Career of Adolf Hitler," which he describes thus:

This posthumous career of the Führer is [. . .] no less monstrous than his career while alive, but its historical and geopolitical consequences are almost as vast, if not more so. Indeed, everything happens as if Europe, and of course France, having suffered from the Hitlerian cancer, had been and continued to be operated on over and over again by surgeons so fiercely resolved to eradicate the evil that they did not refrain from removing vital organs indispensable to the patient's survival, as soon as they were suspected of contamination. It is in this way that France, paying an exorbitant medical bill for a relatively brief period of her history, has been driven more or less consciously to will her own undoing, through the successive withdrawal of all the functions that are necessary for a nation to persevere in its being [. . .][58]

One of the most perverse consequences of Hitler's second career, Camus insists, is that it has rendered the teaching of the Holocaust – the very raison d'être of moral obligation toward the Other – impossible among the peoples toward whom this obligation is now most felt: postcolonial Muslim immigrants to France and their descendants.[59] France is foolish, moreover, to expect extra-European immigrants and their children to rally to a cultural identity about which the host culture entertains at best a sense of ambiguity and at worst feelings of shame. Little Replacism, out of hyperdemocratic concern for the European other – the proletarian, the peasant, etc. – teaches the culture to forget its classics, which are bound to and thus implicated in unacceptable class hierarchies. This teaching of forgetting having been accomplished, whatever remains of the original culture is then denounced by its curators due to shame at how that culture treated its external others (Jews, Arabs, black Africans, etc.). In this way, the course from Little Replacement to Great Replacement, from deculturation and decivilization to a new culture and a new civilization, is charted.

---

58. Camus, *Le Grand remplacement: Introduction au remplacisme global* (La Nouvelle Librairie), p. 331.
59. See, for example, Alain Finkielkraut, *L'Identité malheureuse* (Paris, Flammarion, 2013), pp. 113-115.

More is at play, however, in the Great Replacement than historical guilt and the machinations of the petty bourgeoisie. Replacism does not just denote demographic trends: it is the watchword of the epoch of global capitalism, in which everything – not only human beings but every element of reality, from products of human fabrication, such as automobiles and cities, to nature itself – is replaceable by its double and simulacrum. Both the countryside and the city are replaced by the "universal suburb;"[60] laboring men and women are replaced by machines; body parts are replaced by prostheses; mothers are replaced by surrogates; soldiers are replaced by drones; national cultures are replaced by global consumer culture; distinct human communities and their histories are replaced by "undifferentiated human matter." Far from a conspiracy theory, replacism in Camus' telling is the most obvious characteristic of our era, an observation of the planned obsolescence of everything up to and including human beings. Camus traces the beginnings of replacism to Henry Ford and Frederick Winslow Taylor, if not to the industrial revolution, and just as he laments the leveling of culture brought on by petty-bourgeoisification, he also bemoans neoliberal capitalism's tendency to transform diverse human cultures into an amorphous "human park,"[61] which globalism has liberated from traditional habits and attachments and converted to a worldview of generalized consumerism. The Great Replacement, as a demographic phenomenon, is a consequence of the broader logic of human replaceability: it imagines people and peoples as interchangeable units of nebulous universal humanity that are to be molded for the sake of the global market into a pliant, obedient, undifferentiated consuming blob.

---

60. Suburbs ("les banlieues"), especially inner ring suburbs, in large French cities such as Paris are roughly equivalent to inner city ghettos in the United States in terms of ethno-racial (and, in the French case, ethno-religious) segregation, poverty, and material blight. By "universal suburb" Camus therefore means "universal ghetto."
61. The expression is borrowed from German "posthumanist" philosopher Peter Sloterdijk, whose *Regeln für den Menschenpark* (*Rules for the Human Park*; Suhrkamp Verlag, 2001) generated much controversy by calling for the regulation of human "bio-cultural" reproduction.

The trouble for replacism is that facts on the ground have tended to hinder this universalizing ambition. The various immigrant cohorts that began flocking to France at the behest of big business owners in the 1960s, for example, have not been converted into homogeneous neoliberal goo: quite to the contrary. France is a nation increasingly threatened by communitarianism, ethnic and religious division, Islamism, and the potential for violent nativist reaction, and while it may be an exaggeration to say that immigration has been a disaster for the country, no one in the third decade of the twenty-first century can seriously claim that it has been an unmitigated blessing. An irony of ironies, the extension of western colonialism by neoliberal means seems to have led France, and much of Europe, to its present brink: having sublimated its erstwhile, crusading Christian universalism into open-to-all global humanitarianism, the West, in its universalist presumption, has forgotten that the rest of the world may not share its vision.[62] What prevails now in France is the result of this miscalculation, which manifests, Camus argues, in a toxic alliance of dogmatic antiracist ideology and capitalist expediency. In the first decades of the post-war period, the market demanded foreign labor, and nascent antiracism, responding to the Nazis' horrors, demanded that the cultural differences that foreign labor imported be respected, if not honored or even worshipped, out of penance. In the name of the very thing it wished to avoid, this increasingly maladaptive arrangement now threatens an entire continent.

The nature of this maladaptation lies, moreover, at the heart of Camus' complaint about meaning in *Du Sens*. The Cratylian conception of meaning – that is, meaning attached to an origin, to an essence, if not to a transcendent source – cannot be ignored in favor of a uniquely Hermogenian conception, which would limit meaning to pure convention and, in the case of notions such as citizenship and

---

62. For an examination of this phenomenon, see Chantal Delsol, *Le Crépuscule de l'universel* (Paris, Cerf, 2020). Along similar lines, see also Mark Lilla, *The Stillborn God* (New York, Knopf, 2007). For a discussion of Western universalism vis-à-vis non-European immigration, see Douglas Murray, *The Strange Death of Europe* (New York, Bloomsbury Continuum, 2018).

national identity, to administrative fiat.[63] The French people, as Camus writes in *The Great Replacement*, did not emerge "fully armed from Jupiter's thigh,"[64] but neither was it a bureaucratic invention of the Directorate, the Napoleonic Code, or the Third Republic. The inhabitants of what the Romans once called Gaul have, since the fall of the Western Empire and the rise of the Merovingians, if not going all the way back to Vercingetorix, experienced a history that, while not hermetically sealed to the outside world, nonetheless constitutes a national story distinct from that of other peoples and other lands. Only something with the force of an ideology – and replacism is an ideology *par excellence* – could blind people to this anthropological common sense: that human populations are not interchangeable, and to mix culturally disparate groups of people together in the same territory is a recipe for strife, as much for the newcomers as for the native population.

The disasters of the world wars and especially the Hitlerian abomination rightfully urged openness on a traumatized Europe searching for atonement. But this adaptation to greater openness embraced a radically Hermogenian understanding of meaning that, in a paradoxical nod to Cratylus, maladaptively assumed that all the peoples of the world were assimilable to the West's post-war, post-Hitlerian self-conception: secular, humanistic, humanitarian, liberal and implicitly universalist. Whether one is more sympathetic to progressive or populist views on European immigration, the shortsightedness of this assumption must seem apparent. Camus' views, put in these terms, come across as remarkably ordinary. That Camus remains, nonetheless, a toxic figure therefore says something not just about his rhetoric and lexical choices, jarring as they may be to some, but also about the increasingly fragile "open society" moral consensus of post-war Europe.

---

63. The reference here is to Plato's dialogue *Cratylus*, in which two characters, Hermogenes and Cratylus, debate whether words have natural or merely conventional meanings; that is, whether the meaning of a word is arbitrary or, rather, intrinsically related to what it signifies. Hermogenes defends the former position and Cratylus the latter. Camus expounds at great length on this question in *Du Sens*; the reader will find a précis of this discussion in the essay *The Great Replacement* (pp. 107-108 in this volume).

64. Camus, *The Great Replacement*, p. 118 in this volume.

Camus' Responsibility and The Shelf-life of Worldviews

In his book *Return of the Strong Gods*, R.R. Reno writes apropos of Karl Popper, perhaps the foremost éminence grise of the post-war moral settlement:[65]

> The imperative is bracingly simple: *Never again*. Never again shall we allow totalitarian governments to emerge [. . .] Never again shall the furnaces of Auschwitz consume their victims. This imperative – *never again* – places stringent demands upon us. It requires Western civilization to attain self-critical maturity with courage and determination [. . .] We must banish the strong gods of the closed society and create a truly open one.[66]

Reno contends that a "return of the strong gods," that is, resurgent assertions of collective and national identity in both the West and elsewhere, will be an inevitable feature of the twenty-first century. The process of identitarian neutering that the West, and especially Western Europe, underwent in the second half of the twentieth century is, as far as human societies go, unusual and unsustainable, and it cannot be expected to endure beyond the shock of the Second World War's horrors. Accordingly, in place of flimsy notions of openness and inclusion, which, far from being neutral, have acted as an acid on strong forms of identity vital to maintaining the lives of peoples and nations, the West must draw from the wisdom and traditions of its past in order to rediscover and reassert the strong gods that once sustained it against its civilizational competitors. Reno does not say just what those strong gods might be, but their return, he believes, is unavoidable, and the West, faced with a variety of renascent nationalisms, must work to ensure the return of the best possible gods.

In the meantime, the weak god of the open society – if it really is a weak god – remains remarkably tenacious for reasons that, while perhaps not always compelling, are at the very least intelligible. No guarantee

---

65. Reno is specifically concerned with Popper's book *The Open Society and its Enemies* (London, Routledge, 1945).
66. R.R. Reno, *Return of the Strong Gods* (Washington, Regnery Gateway, 2019), p. 4.

exists, after all, that contemporary Europe or any other multicultural society in the West or elsewhere will not descend into ethnic conflict in response to some trigger.[67] Diverse societies are fragile experiments, all the more so when their components, as is the case in France, are marked by long histories of violent conflict, such as the perennial antagonism between the West and the Islamic world. Even a fierce critic of Camus can grant that the situation in France concerning non-European immigration is hardly ideal. Éric Dupin, for example, writes,

> The "great replacement" is the panicked, hostile, and exaggerated expression of a reality that cannot however be silenced. The changing of the ethnic composition of the French population is, in principle, only catastrophic for enthusiasts of a racist vision of the world. The problems it poses are nonetheless real, in particular due to the geographic and social particularities of populations of extra-European origin.[68]

An instinctive reaction to the threat of a dumpster fire is to avoid mentioning the dumpster, in the hope that carnage-seeking miscreants will not throw a spark on it. Such is the attitude that Camus understandably inspires in a certain kind of right-thinking person: "Yes, the problems you address are real, but you cannot go around using terms like 'great replacement' or 'genocide by substitution.' Do you want to start a civil war? A solution will eventually present itself. In the meantime, please keep your ideas to yourself!" This kind of sentiment is motivated not only by fear of violence – though certainly such fear must be at play – but also by an earnest and eminently comprehensible moral commitment. If one believes, in a generally Nietzschean sort of way,

---

67. Some contemporary French writers have imagined this very thing. Laurent Obertone (nom de plume), for example, imagines in his *Guerilla* trilogy France's descent into civil war after police kill nominally Muslim, ethnically Arab teenage drug dealers during a botched arrest in a bad neighborhood. See Laurent Obertone, *Guerilla, Le Jour où tout s'embrasa* (Paris, Ring, 2016); *Guerilla, Le Temps des barbares* (Paris, Magnus, 2022); and *Guerilla, Le Dernier combat* (Paris, Magnus, 2022).
68. Éric Dupin, *La France Identitaire: Enquête sur la réaction qui vient* (Paris, La Découverte. 2017), p. 85. For additional French academic criticism of Camus, see Jean-Yves Camus [no relation to Renaud] and Nicolas Lebourg, *Les Droites extrêmes en Europe* (Paris, Seuil, 2015), pp. 243-244.

that human history is most accurately described as an endless conflict between oppressor and oppressed, between haves and have-nots, then the "fight against discriminations" – that is, the possibility of correcting something so chronically nasty in human nature as group selfishness – can take on the trappings of an all-consuming moral worldview. In this context, a person like Camus becomes a worldview threat, a *Weltanschauung* enemy. It is perhaps for this reason more than any other that he has inspired an attitude of such virulent repudiation.

The trouble, however, from the Camusian perspective is that even the best of intentions vis-à-vis openness, multiculturalism and the like can have tragic consequences. No guarantee exists that fair treatment of a minority will have the desired effect of assimilating it into the host culture; vast dissimilarities in religion, family structure, attitudes toward nepotism, and any number of other cultural particularities can overwhelm even the most well-intentioned champions of multicultural tolerance. One can formulate the question this way: although it may be desirable and even morally satisfying that people of different cultural cohorts should set aside their quarrels and get along in public, how wise is it, not as a matter of moral aspiration but of anthropological prudence, to invite often wildly disparate groups of people to dwell in close proximity to each other?

That it is not very wise at all seems, at least in the French case, to be an increasingly common answer. To return again to Finkielkraut, who in *L'Identité malheureuse* describes what might be called a French version of "white flight" from France's inner suburbs:

> The native French have lost the status of cultural reference point that was theirs during preceding periods of immigration. They no longer influence anything. When the cybercafé is called "Bled.com" and either the fast-food restaurant or the butcher shop or both are halal, the longstanding inhabitants experience a disconcerting sense of exile. When they see conversions to Islam multiply, they wonder where they are living. They haven't budged, but the world around them has changed. Do they fear foreigners? Are their hearts closed to the Other? No – they feel like strangers in their own homes. They used to embody the

norm, but now they are on the margins. They used to be the majority in a familiar environment; but now they are the minority
in a place they no longer control. This is the situation they are
reacting to when they go live elsewhere. It is because they no
longer want to feel exposed that they are hostile to the building
of new housing projects in the communities in which they've
chosen to take up residence. The more immigration increases,
the more the territory splinters.[69]

Finkielkraut's assertions find support in recent studies by Christophe
Guilluy and Bernard Rougier, who have documented, respectively, the
ethnic splintering of the suburbs in the wake of mass migration and
the rise of Islamic communitarianism in certain immigrant-heavy
neighborhoods.[70] Journalistic accounts such as *La Communauté* by
Raphaëlle Bacqué and Ariane Chemin, or Geraldine Smith's *Rue Jean-
Pierre Timbaud*, tell the story of a France sobering up to the reality that
its urban peripheries, and even parts of its urban cores, are increasingly
under the sway of Islamists, who form alliances of convenience with
drug dealers for the de facto control of neighborhoods.[71] Prosperous
city centers, which are shielded from ethnic and cultural recomposi-
tion, can enjoy a palatable dose of multiculturalism in the form of
exotic restaurants, cheap child care, and other perks of cosmopolitan privilege. Meanwhile, the suburban native population, for whom
multiculturalism is simply another difficulty to be endured along with
crime, unemployment, and creeping Islamization, flee to exurban
zones where their economic situation often ends up being worse.[72] The
phenomenon is as troubling as it is seemingly inexorable: a France split

69. Finkielkraut, *L'Identité malheureuse*, pp. 118-119.
70. See Christophe Guilluy, *Fractures françaises* (Paris, François Bourin, 2010) and
    La France Périphérique (Paris, Flammarion, 2014); and Bernard Rougier, *Les
    Territoires conquis de l'islamisme* (Paris, Presses Universitaires de France, 2021).
71. Raphaëlle Bacqué and Ariane Chemin, *La Communauté* (Paris, Albin Michel,
    2018); Geraldine Smith, *Rue Jean-Pierre Timbaud* (Paris, Stock, 2016).
72. Such was the fate, for example, of many of those involved in the "Yellow Vest"
    protests at the beginning of Emmanuel Macron's first term. Having moved from
    suburban to exurban zones, many of these inhabitants of "peripheral France"
    could not afford added commuting expenses that would have been imposed by an
    increase in fuel taxes.

in two by the unintended consequences of mass and especially Islamic immigration, in which the ugly specter of armed civil conflict does not just lurk in the minds of far-right provocateurs and internet trolls, but also colors the imaginations of government ministers.[73]

Where do Camus' ideas sit in this civilizational muddle? Is he a teller of inconvenient truths whom the media wrongly vilify and distort into an ideological bad actor? Or a conduit, as some have suggested, between the respectable right and the ethnonationalist right?[74] Or rather simply a good old-fashioned French racist, a prickly *boomer* from a bygone xenophobic age? These questions will find as many responses as the number of those to whom they are posed; in the end, careful readers will have to rely on their own judgment. One portion of responsibility that it does seem reasonable to attribute to Camus, however, is the very thing that makes his writing so compelling: his peerless ability to name, pithily and provocatively, social phenomena that, if they are to be addressed in the sphere of politics, ought to be designated by less arousing terminology. The term "great replacement" has certainly aggrandized Camus, but at the expense of yielding, in our age of digital virality, this bit of lexical cleverness to racist ne'er-do-wells. Camus has deplored throughout his writing the use of "absolute weapons of language" (*reductio ad Hitlerum* being the most common not to mention lethal example) to paralyze critics of multiculturalism, mass migration, and other sacred cows of replacist ideology. It is, as I suggested above, a central irony of his work that his own terminology has come to serve the same function in the hands of racist conspiracy theorists and their minions.

Yet one could just as well object, in defense of free expression, that an author should ever be condemned for the ignorant and unlettered

73. See, for example, Gérald Darmanin, "Il faut stopper l'ensauvagement d'une partie de la société," Interview by Arthur Berdah, Jean Chichizola, Christophe Cornevin, and Albert Zennou, *Le Figaro*, 24 July 2020, https://www.lefigaro.fr /politique/gerald-darmanin-il-faut-stopper-l-ensauvagement-d-une-partie-de-la -societe-20200724.
74. See Thomas Chatterton Williams, "The French Origins of 'You Will Not Replace Us,'" *New Yorker* 27 November 2017. https://www.newyorker.com/magazine/2017 /12/04/the-french-origins-of-you-will-not-replace-us. Williams is reporting a comment by Mark Lilla.

distortion of what dim and murderous people deem to be his ideas. Indeed, in Camus' case, there is no evidence, and much reason to doubt, that the most violent partisans of "great replacement theory" – Brenton Tarrant in Christchurch, New Zealand, and Patrick Wood Crusius in El Paso, Texas, to cite the most shocking examples – had read Camus at all.[75] And even if one should insist that Camus' terminology is needlessly and recklessly provocative, it remains the case, given the evolution of the meaning of words, that "great replacement" might one day come to signify something very different from the conspiratorial meaning so often attributed it. A British survey conducted in 2021 revealed that the share of white Britons living in London had decreased from 86.2 percent in 1971 to 36.8 percent in 2021.[76] It is difficult to see how the term "great replacement," should it be shorn of its racist connotations, would not be a strong candidate to describe this revolutionary demographic shift. Future generations, of whatever mix of backgrounds, could very well use it for just that purpose.

A final matter: I wrote above that a purpose of this volume – its most pressing, I suggested – is to provide the sort of explication and contextualization of Camus' ideas that is necessary to wrest them from the hands of racists of all stripes.[77] "Great Replacement" and its attendant vocabulary have already made the rounds, as it were, on the internet

---

75. See Renaud Camus, *La Dépossession* (Paris, La Nouvelle Librairie, 2022), pp. 246-255, esp. p. 254.

76. Andrew Sullivan discusses this development in a Substack post from December, 2022: https://andrewsullivan.substack.com/p/england-his-england?utm_source =profile&utm_medium=reader2.

77. Lest one be tempted to believe that racist conspiracy theorizing is the unique province of white nationalists, the President of Tunisia, Kais Saied, told his National Security Council on February 21st, 2023, "there is a criminal arrangement that has been prepared since the beginning of this century to change the demographic composition of Tunisia . . . there are parties that received huge sums of money after 2011 in order to settle irregular migrants from sub-Saharan Africa in Tunisia." His comments, which were made public, were greeted with outrage in the press. See, for example, Erin Claire Brown, "Tunisia's President Embraces the 'Great Replacement Theory,'" *News Line Magazine*, 27 February 2023, https:// newlinesmag.com/spotlight/tunisias-president-embraces-the-great-replacement -theory/#:~:text=After%20a%20fortnight%20of%20political%20arrests%20 and%20detentions%2C,across%20the%20country%20where%20many%20 migrant%20workers%20olive.

and thus around the world, and had it struck us at all that a translation of Camus' political writings into English would benefit those who have adopted and adapted his terminology to evil ends, we would not have undertaken it. Persons whom it will benefit, on the other hand (if "benefit" is the right word), are all those who, having been unable or unwilling to read Camus, have nonetheless denounced him in the press and elsewhere by associating his name and his ideas with the most unspeakable crimes (committed by people who have not read him either). It is one thing to (rightly or wrongly) accuse an author of racism when one has read him; it is something else altogether when one has not. While such shooting from the hip, so to speak, involving matters of the greatest reputational risk is something that polemical journalists and activist intellectuals may permit themselves, it is understandably intolerable to serious scholarship. It is, in plain terms, intellectually dishonest. Far from seeking to set the record straight, then, in the matter of Renaud Camus (white supremacists notwithstanding), I am content that there simply be a record, one which attentive readers of whatever political, ideological, or moral persuasion may assess at their leisure, and from which they may draw their own conclusions.

Louis Betty

Madison, WI, July 2023

The Communism of the
Twenty-First Century [2007][1]

One of the few good things to come out of the tiresome "Finkielkraut affair"[i] of late 2005 was a felicitous expression of Finkielkraut's, according to which antiracism could be considered – will be, doubtless *already is* – "the communism of the twenty-first century." For my part, I find this polemical metaphor extremely enlightening and fecund, and I am very grateful to its author for it, as I am for his many other good deeds.

But let us not take comparison to mean two things are alike . . . One of my friends claims to be the only speaker of the French language to still know what the verb *to compare* [nb. *comparer*] means, and he takes exception every time he hears someone say, "*this* cannot be compared to *that*." In his opinion, anything can be compared to anything else since *to compare* in no way means to *liken*, much less conflate. I highly doubt that Finkielkraut meant that antiracism is for us today exactly the same thing that communism was in the last century. Rather, his idea, if I may be so presumptuous as to say, is that antiracism holds the same position in relation to our twenty-first century that communism held in relation to the twentieth; that it plays the same role; that its historical function is similar; that its influence, ability to inspire action, and salience in public discourse and in the depths of conscience are of the same order of magnitude.

---

1. "Le Communisme du XXIᵉ siècle," in *Le Communisme du XXIᵉ siècle* (Vevey, Éditions Xenia, 2007), pp. 27-62.

A first difference, however, and it is significant, is that antiracism has no gulag, as far as we know. And while one may in my view speak with some legitimacy of the species of *terror* that it has imposed, it must be acknowledged that this terror rarely imprisons (and is not always wrong to do so when it does), that it does not to my knowledge torture, and, with the exception of a few just wars, that it has not killed very many people so far. Like its counterpart, however, it does destroy lives, wreck careers, sweep entire existences under the carpet – individual existences, of course, and in great quantity, but the existences of peoples, too.

Another difference is that communism, at least during an initial period – a very long initial period, which continues to this day in Asia – made the states and societies where it was put into practice more powerful (unless this was by conquest, of course, as in Eastern Europe): it made Russia stronger, China more respected, Vietnam more formidable. Antiracism, by contrast, undermines the nations and civilizations that it submits to its rule; it deprives them of all means of defense, making them so many open cities. It is certainly a formidable power, but it is a *pure* power, a power for the sake of power, coinciding with itself, and from which the states that claim to adhere to it have nothing to hope for and everything to fear – except those, of course, and there are many of them, that, even as they nominally place themselves under its iron rule like all the rest, only make external and diplomatic use of it, and do not for a moment dream, no more so than do their populations, of taking its dictates seriously within their own borders.

We touch here on an ambiguity relating to the meaning of the term *power* and the notion of *being in power*. One might say that communism was in power, that it was the name of certain regimes, that it was the political system of several states; and that this is not the case with antiracism. But one might just as well say the contrary and with as much, if not more, pertinence. Admittedly, I do not know of any regimes that, for purely social reasons, declare themselves to be antiracist in their very name. But the overwhelming majority of existing regimes nevertheless present themselves as such, as *antiracist*, even if, as we have just seen, this is not always the case – after all, communist regimes were themselves often communist in name only. And all institutions of global reach loudly proclaim their antiracism, inscribing it in black and white above the entrances to their temples and in their basic texts, so that it more or less directly dictates the law under which we all live and all nations of the Earth are in theory subject to it, with the result that even Switzerland can be rebuked in its name, as we have lately seen.[ii] Communism, thankfully, was never able to impose itself on such a scale. That the service records of the two parties to our comparison are not exactly of the same nature there is no doubt, but in point of their influence and effects they come quite close.

For, in the weighted tally that I am attempting here, all is a matter of scale. All depends on the level at which we place ourselves. If we choose to position ourselves at the level of France, for example, we see that communism never governed this country, whereas antiracism, to the contrary, has been in power here for several decades. Indeed, it is a kind of state religion, the most sacred established dogma and virtually the only one – the last – the ultimate objective of public schooling, the one to which we above all cling when most of the others were lost along the way long ago.

It is true that, even in our country, which it never governed alone, communism was a very powerful system able to take in hand the lives of hundreds of thousands of individuals from cradle to grave. But this was only true in particular municipalities and in the broad swathes of territory that these often-adjoining districts comprised. Antiracism, for its part, has the Republic itself very officially in hand at every level of decision-making, and the latter loudly boasts on every occasion of its subservience. It is a formidable machine for doling out positions, seats, pensions, honors and sinecures, chairmanships and "odd jobs." On the one hand, it alone is permitted to speed along careers and distribute perquisites, emoluments, professorships, appointments, subsidies, director's fees, exhibitions, publications, and "eligible" candidacies – much more so, indeed, than was ever the case under communism, which lacked the ability to exert leverage at this scale and whose efforts at control in retrospect seem those of a comparative dilettante. On the other hand, antiracism has ample opportunity – and God knows it does not waste it – to exclude, ostracize, proclaim the social death of individuals, rightly or wrongly shatter careers and lives, dole out threats and sanctions, sideline suspects, authorize and incite pile-ons, bless executions.

Communism had one or two newspapers, a few influential but narrowly distributed journals, two or three never particularly robust publishing houses; antiracism, for its part, reigns over the whole of journalism without a single honorable exception, over the entire media, over all mainstream publishing.

Crucially, the courts are all devoted to it, something they never were in the case of communism, and render their decisions entirely in keeping with its precepts, if not indeed its instructions.

An essential common feature of these two ideologies – at least *diachronically* – is that, at least at the dawn of their respective eras of greatest extension, both presented themselves as eminently *well-meaning*, to such a degree that they passed more for *moral codes* than for ideologies. Indeed, both — but antiracism to a much greater extent and much more persuasively than communism – have been able to pass for the exclusive holders of moral authority, with which they came to be genuinely conflated, their discourse and positions seen as rigorously coinciding with it.

In one case as in the other, this is a crucial aspect: for it allows them to have, not *adversaries* with whom one may calmly debate, but only irreconcilable enemies whom one can only hope to destroy. One unexpected consequence of this is to confer upon them – but once again upon antiracism much more so than upon defunct communism – a sort of monopoly on hatred, an exclusive right to vomitory execration, a joyous duty to abominate; passions that, as a matter of internal tradition, they incessantly denounce in their opponents (or in those whom they consider such), but that, with time, wreak havoc upon them much more so than they do upon the latter. It is those who talk most of hatred who feel it most intensely. They reproach you for yours with a face and language ravaged by theirs.

"Every anticommunist is a dog,"[iii] as the famous saying goes. Every anti-antiracist is a pit-bull, a worse-than-dog, a less-than-dog, a hyena, a worm, the proverbial Foul Beast.

The anticommunist was a monster because he blithely accepted the people's immiseration and profited from their exploitation. He had no intention of lifting a finger to put an end to social injustice, on which the power of his class or his own pleasure depended, if not both. What's more (or less), he fought to perpetuate this injustice. Clearly, he could only be driven by a thirst for evil, pure wickedness, a desire to harm, vile delight in the misfortune and humiliation of others – at best a criminal blindness, a loathsome insensibility fatal to others and that one could only hope would one day prove just as fatal to him.

In the case of the anti-antiracist, things are even simpler, even clearer, even more contemptible. It must first be said that he is obviously not an *anti*-antiracist. To call him such would be to give him far too much credit; he is just a *racist*. And of course, with a few rare exceptions (lost souls who no longer have anything to lose), no one wants to be a *racist*, with the result that antiracism has as it were no enemies who dare accept the label as their own. Antiracism is therefore accustomed, as was communism in times past, especially when it was in power (and particularly in the people's democracies), to see all those who do not sufficiently express or otherwise evince enthusiastic agreement with its views and precepts as its enemies, if only by default (for it has a great need of enemies, as they are its very sustenance). The trouble is that one must endlessly increase the dosage, whence this impression that our chattering classes are merely talking in their sleep, a source of so much amusement abroad to all but our friends, who are grieved by it. One would think that all the spirit of rote learning, long a mainstay of our primary school system but now dead and gone, has taken refuge here, in these pre-fabricated pop songs, these novels written with an eye to the prizes they might win, these academic keynote addresses, these ministerial declarations of intent, these long-winded speeches given to inaugurate priority education zones,[iv] these morsels of talk-show bravura, this patter of salesmen and public entertainers, which are so many listless reiterations of good doctrine, with bonus points and canned applause forthcoming every time their recipients manage to slip in the biggest magic words (*mix-raced, cultural pluralism, social cohesion, equal opportunity, nice neighborhood, blending, diversity, multiculturalism, Toledo, we're all immigrants, Wolof ancestors*, etc.).

But it is necessary to linger for a moment on this terminological sleight-of-hand, which automatically and entirely against their will and convictions makes racists of anti-antiracists, of opponents of anti-racism, indeed of anyone who might in some way object to its ideological and material domination. This sleight-of-hand is one of the secrets of antiracist power. Thanks to this stealthy maneuver, which greatly facilitates things, anyone who opposes it is either a thoroughly wretched being or immediately becomes one by virtue of his opposition.

And indeed, it is possible that they really are. It is possible that this is the price of their freedom, a sort of byproduct of their ignominy. Thus, the only true opponents of sexual repression when it was at the height of its power were "morally lost" individuals, as one used to say – if they dared defy it, it was uniquely because, having renounced all morality along with all dignity, they ran no risk of falling even lower than they already had. It was unknown whether they were sexually free because they were thieves, liars, traitors, informers, and murderers or if they were all these things because they were homosexuals, adulterers, perverts, pedophiles, aficionados of group sex, and Stakhanovites of pleasure.[v] Having granted themselves the freedom to lead their sexual lives as they so wished, they believed they had in this way broken through the moral wall separating good from evil, confusing the exercise of this freedom they had won, entirely by their own weakness, with their other depravities. Too often and in a similar way, the only people who openly oppose antiracism are racists, as antiracism itself claims. As long as this remains the case, antiracism has nothing to fear.

For, as long as there are only racists to challenge it, the power of antiracism is absolutely unshakeable. It is a little as if, in the case of sexual repression, only child rapists were to rebel against its reign, principle, and injustices. And indeed, antiracism is perfectly aware of this fact, and this is why it has nothing more pressing to do than describe as racist anyone who raises the least objection to it or asks it embarrassing or displeasing questions.

Racist opposition to the antiracist ascendancy over all of society, that of the real racists – the genuine anti-Semites (of right and left), the neo-Nazis and Holocaust deniers, the pimply-faced champions of white supremacy – only reinforces it, for it underscores the need for it and offers a solid pretext and even legitimate grounds for its endless consolidation.

I trust I will be forgiven, but I see no other way out of this tete-a-tete between racism and antiracism than what I have elsewhere called, following Barthes, bathmology, the (Barthesian) "science of levels of language," which allows us to pass from a second to a third level and makes it clear that not every expression of opposition to antiracism or the abuses of its power is to be put in the same bag. While racism and anti-antiracism may very well occupy the same structural position vis-à-vis antiracism at times, they do not do so at the same level of the spiral of meaning and should in no way be conflated. The distance between one (racism) and the other (antiracism's double) is even greater than that separating each of them from antiracism. And the road that separates them can only be traveled (but to what end?) by way of antiracism. Yet putting everything in the same bag is precisely where antiracism most excels. And it would not at all be surprising if only a language-centered, semantic, semiotic approach should be capable of untangling what is above all a confusion of language, skillfully maintained if not deliberately created.

In this domain, the meaning of words is so twisted, so vague, and in general so improper that there is nothing easier than to make them mean what we want them to mean and to make them serve every tyranny, even if that of course means disguising them – but this is child's play – as counter-tyrannies.

Extremely reprehensible on moral grounds well before being so on ideological and political ones, *racism* was originally the defect that led one to conflate individuals with the group to which they belonged by birth, reduce them to this belonging, and commit violence or injustice against them should one believe there was something for which to reproach the group in question. Racism is a violent action, a violent opinion, and in both cases a kind of assault. And so long as racism is only that, this defect or misdeed, antiracism is absolutely beyond criticism; there is nothing to reproach it for, for it is above reproach.

But that's just it: since the unquestionable ignominy of racism establishes the invulnerability and, dare one say, *uncriticizability* of antiracism, the latter became an ideology, a dogma, a power, a tool of power, and almost an industry (it is one of the biggest employers in France, lest it be forgotten) as soon as it was no longer just active moral and political indignation. As such, it is in its interest to indefinitely extend the range of things to be admitted under the designation of *racism*. And God knows it has not refrained from doing so. From that moment on, nearly everything became racism – everything that displeases, inconveniences, or merely irritates antiracism. Instead of antiracism defining itself in relation to something stable and preexisting, something morally and intellectually well-circumscribed, for which it would be the "anti-entity," as it were, it is racism that is defined by and in relation to antiracism – that which antiracism has decided is racist is *racist*, starting with anything that dares challenge its power of course.

It must be said that the ambiguity regarding racism, the ability conferred upon this word to mean anything and everything, is only a second-line ambiguity, a second-layer amphibology, the second defensive wall of antiracism. The first, more forward layer of ambiguity concerns the word *race*, which, in contrast to the word *racism* – as we have just seen, an object of indefinite and unlimited semantic extension – has suffered a vertiginous contraction of the enormous spectrum of meaning that it had in Classical French. So as to better curse it at its leisure, antiracism very curiously pretends to only hear in it the meaning that true racists have given it, an absurd, pseudo-scientific meaning that never represented more than a tenth – the most stupid and sinister tenth – of everything that these four very useful letters have meant across the ages; coerced and compelled, we have thus learned to mourn it like so many other things.

With these ambiguities regarding *racism* and *race*, antiracism has executed a pincer movement, allowing it to banish from speech, conversation, newspapers, all media, political discourse, and, above all and most seriously, from one's very ability to perceive the world everything that has to do, not just with *races*, in both the broad and absurdly narrow senses of this word, but also with ethnic groups, peoples, cultures, religions as groups or masses of individuals, civilizations as hereditary collectivities, origins, and even nationalities to the degree that these nationalities would claim to be anything other than matters of pure administrative belonging, a convention, a continuous creation. Antiracist man stands naked before his fate, he comes from nowhere, no past protects him. He begins with himself, with himself *now*. On a planet ideally without borders, without distinctions of any kind, and without nuances, he is a traveler without baggage, a poor devil. In a sort of senility of perpetual beginnings, of established infantilism, of (star)-academic[vi] puerility, he invents himself as best he can from one moment to the next. As soon as it is not a matter of pure convention (the much-vaunted "documents"), belonging is only perceived and presented as a burden, a defect, a dead weight, a cumbersome load to be gotten rid of as quickly as possible, a cursed inheritance.

Entire swathes of knowledge, of culture, of the accumulated understanding of the species are thereby rejected, brought low, buried. Even more seriously, it will be agreed, as a matter of convention and subject to the most severe punishments, that entire swathes of experience, of current events of course, but more immediately of everyday lived experience, of moving about, of inhabiting the Earth and inhabiting the city, of sensing what happens when one goes down to the street, when one takes the bus or the subway, to say nothing of the now-sinister trains, that entire swathes of time, entire swathes of facial expression, entire swathes of embodied existence do not exist, that one does not feel them, that one does not see them even when they are staring you in the face (sometimes almost literally) – that it is all *in your head*, in your stubborn, recalcitrant head.

It is doubtless no coincidence that one of today's most tiresome refrains, just as oppressive as the self-destructive but indefatigable *it is true that*,[vii] is the undying and comical *it will be said* . . . It will be said *indeed*, as they say in English! We live under the sign of *it will be said*. *It will be said* that standards are rising, *it will be said* that France is one of the countries where immigration is lowest, *it will be said* that the proportion of foreigners has not budged in half a century (although it should be noted that it has actually decreased somewhat in recent years!). *It will be said* that rates of delinquency are not disproportionately high among "immigrant-origin youth," *it will be said* that, contrary to what people believe, detailed studies show that birth rates among the "new French" are in no way higher than those of the others, *it will be said* that *we gotta stop* saying all the time that there's more violence than there was fifty years ago. *It will be said* that France has *always* been a country of immigration, that French art was above all created by foreigners, that our country is above all an idea, a universal idea – that's whatcha gotta understand.[viii] And whatcha mean by *foreigner* anyway? Like Petain's posters but this time showing some poor wretch just escaped from the Roissy detention center,[ix] antiracism dares you to answer *yes* to the question:

"Are you more French than he is?"

Ooh la la . . . Take care how you answer!

It will be said that you are not. No one is more French than anyone else.

And just as with *it is true that*, sensitive ears will hear a siren just beginning to sound in the distance, a warning that, in these parts, truth is in serious danger of being trounced or is perhaps already walking on crutches, one leg in a caste and one arm in a sling, *it will be said* discreetly heralding the gigantic and ever-growing accumulation of *it-will-not-be-saids*. It is perhaps in this way that the antiracist regime most resembles former communist regimes. I speak of *regimes* here because, with the possible exception of the Red Belt (which has now become a *Green Belt*, albeit not in the ecological sense of the term),[x] communism was never a *regime* in the French case, which is thus not equal to the comparison; instead, one must look to the Soviet Union and its former "Eastern Bloc" satellites. Of course, here in France, the *Humanité* of the Mr. Waldeck Rochet or Mr. Roland Leroy[xi] eras made a laughing stock of itself with the fantastically effective filter it applied to current events prior to allowing them into its pages, as well as by the enormous mass of "counter-truth," to speak like Georges Marchais,[xii] with which it burdened reality. But if one were to live under the bewildering shadow of that mass, one had to place oneself there voluntarily, if only by buying the newspaper or following party directives. Today's last remaining communists may very well claim they *did not know* about many things, but in order to not know they would really have had to go to a great deal of trouble (albeit trouble they inflicted upon themselves with a passionately militant heart), for there was a large anti-communist press in France at that time. Today, with the sorry exception of three or four racist rags, there is no non-antiracist press, and even less an anti-antiracist one. It is for this reason that we must instead seek our paragons in the old Soviet Bloc. If, as I believe with Alain Finkielkraut, antiracism really is *the communism of the 21*st *century*, it is communism in power that it most resembles, the communism on the other side of the Iron Curtain, not the laughable little communism that preceded it in its most powerful fortresses and principal zones of practical implementation.

I am even inclined to think that, in what concerns "information," as it is ironically called, antiracism *à la française* clearly beats out Soviet communism in point of its overall mastery of the situation, its art of blocking every exit, its omnipresence, and its ability to engage in uninterrupted euphemism, obliterating everything in its path. After all, neither Stalin's Russians nor even those of Brezhnev or Andropov had our ubiquitous television sets. Television is the principal tool of antiracist power, through which it can broadcast its dogmas and transmit its insistent *Weltanshauung* to every Frenchman and woman for three and a half hours a day on average. It would be a mistake for this power to only make use of this incomparable tool during the nightly news, even if that is when the perpetual indoctrination sessions are most intense. Not for an instant does it loosen its grip on the medium and thus the population. Gameshows, entertainment, news reports, variety shows, talk shows: not for a second is the spectator permitted to forget reality – not reality such as it really is, no doubt, but the reality of his subjugation, reality as it should be and soon will be, in a better world, one in which the spectator himself will be better, even more antiracist, even more enamored of multicultural mixing, even more impatient for universal fusion – a new man.

It is the wretched made-for-television movies that are doubtless burdened with the most onerous requirements. Indeed, one no longer even has the heart to make fun of them. In one's distress, one cannot help but admire the poor directors, still capable of pretending to tell some semblance of a story, even though, with every scene, every shot, every line, one gets the distinct impression that they are required to do what must be done, to say and to make others say what must be said, so that holy antiracist doctrine may be more firmly fixed in people's minds, reflexes, worries, and hearts. In such conditions, it would be truly out of place to complain of a lack of creativity. It is already a miracle that there is still the appearance of a "work" at all.

Antiracism is not content to show us images and comment on them for us – images and commentaries that are so many methodical obfuscations of the real – it makes images out of us and films us at all times and in all places. Neither communism at the height of its reign nor the worst, most Orwellian nightmares and predictions had imagined that everyone might be observed at every hour of the day and night in the least of his movements, in stores, in banks, on the sidewalk, on train platforms, in trains, in buses, in classrooms, on freeways, everywhere. It will be said that it is not antiracism in itself that has gradually but ever more rapidly subjected the world to this systematic police surveillance. No, it is not antiracism as such: it is a power of which antiracism is the chief dogma and which is induced to adopt such measures by the type of society that antiracism has created, a society without social compact, without Hobbesian *covenant*, without convention of innocence,[xiii] without any sort of brotherly love, one in which violence is thus ready to well up at any moment.

This power very skillfully finds a pretext to consolidate its own ascendancy, to reinforce itself as power, in the objections that are made against it, the grievances that are submitted to it, the evils for which it is responsible.

"You're afraid," it says, "you think you're not safe? You say that there are now attacks in trains, that there are attacks in the corridors of the metro, that you no longer dare go home or leave, that your stairwell isn't safe, that there are more and more neighborhoods where you dare not go, glances you dare not return, hours during which you dare not live, sidewalks you must step off while lowering your eyes? I hear you, I understand you, you can trust me. We're going to give you more police, we're going to put police officers on the trains, we're going to put many more police officers on the metro, we're going to put police officers in the train stations, in the airports, on the streets, in theaters, in stores, wherever it's dangerous because there's a crowd, wherever it's dangerous because there's no one, at the entrances of middle schools and high schools, in middle school and high school courtyards, along their hallways, in classrooms if necessary, in amphitheaters, in laboratories, in post offices, everywhere, everywhere, everywhere, everywhere they're needed, don't you worry. I don't think it's normal that French people should be afraid. I'm here to reassure you. We'll put police officers everywhere and cameras at every street corner, at every corner of the countryside, at every corner of the stairwell. Don't be afraid, vote for us, we won't abandon you: if necessary, half the population will keep watch over the other half, and vice versa."

Without a doubt, without a doubt, that is all well and good, but you do not really understand the purpose of this lovely little police force about which you are told, what order it supports and what power it reinforces. Not yours, in any case, neither your well-being nor your sense of safety or justice: for every time that you turned to it in those times when you still somewhat believed it was there to protect you, it in essence told you exactly the same thing as your television, as your radio, as your newspapers, and as your politicians: namely, that you were dreaming, that you had been dreaming, that you were tired and were exaggerating, that you had to get some distance, put things in perspective, that one hoped you were capable (come on now!) of seeing things from something other than your narrow point of view, that the law was the law and there was nothing to be done about it, that maybe if you had witnesses who were willing to testify, that of course you can file a complaint if you absolutely must and if that might relieve you somewhat, but you must know that it could cause you a lot of trouble, well yeah, obviously, and it costs a lot and takes a long time, and when all is said and done are you really sure you want to rush into this just to make yourself feel good for two minutes? And anyway, I don't think it'll be possible, it's too early, it's too late, you didn't go and speak to who you should have, you didn't follow the right procedure, and are you really sure I mean one hundred percent sure that you didn't

provoke those kids a little bit you've gotta understand that with unemployment and racism and police profiling no support systems and
all that?

In any case, this was never your ideal for society, police and ever
more police, cameras and ever more cameras. This is not at all what
you were asking for. You have been misunderstood. No, what you
would have liked is . . . (the way things were before, I guess).

But I'm aware and so are you that it would be better for you, in your
interest, to not go into too much detail about what you would have
liked – you're going to put yourself in the wrong. This vast security apparatus whose promising deployment we just told you about? It is upon
you that it will first come down if you keep going on about how things
were before (and anyway, *before what*?). Antiracism has better things
to do than listen to you; it is there not to hear you for your own good.
At best, if it is having a good day, it will try to explain to you what
you *really* mean and are incapable of understanding because you are
too close to the theater of operations. That's what prevents you from
seeing things calmly and objectively. It will explain you to yourself.
Perhaps it will even assign one of its journalists to you for just this purpose or even, if your case warrants it, one of its beloved sociologists.
Sociologists are the regime's golden boys. They will explain what happened to you. With neat charts and unanswerable statistics, they are
capable of translating everything into anything and its opposite; these
will allow you to understand at your leisure the ways in which you
were wrong and why what must be done at the scale of the city, of the
Polity, of the whole country, is more of the same but better, with more
resources this time and the political will to truly see things through.

Sociology is to antiracism what Lysenkoist biology was in its time
to Stalinism. But as this comparison makes clear, the antiracist regime
is something quite distinct from the claustrophobic Soviet regime: it is
a true worldview, global, totalizing, non-negotiable, capable of governing all aspects of your existence and of knowing them better than you
ever could. Biology is well and good, but in the end it rarely makes an
appearance outside of scholarly discussions and amphitheaters and
only indirectly influences one's existence. Sociology is something else

entirely. Not only can it describe for its masters the world they want to exist (a rather dark one because of malicious people, but amenable to reform with the right resources and the political will to truly see things through), but it can also see to all the secretarial work: drafting legislation, canvassing the terrain, putting life's non-professionals in their place. You merely have to ask it for reports – and, as far as reports go, it is even better than the police and not necessarily more expensive.

If sociology is the triumphant science of the regime, it is in part because she is the queen of the "human sciences," so named as if humanity were a material rather than a species, a specimen rather than a virtue, and the humanities nothing more than a giant compilation of statistics, but also because everything that was once rightly or wrongly called culture has collapsed around it.

It is the egg of Columbus.[xiv] And I certainly could not say whether the collapse of culture was caused by antiracism (what we have here agreed to call *antiracism*, the ethnic hybridity-worshipping society we live in, and which, it must be said, has no more to do with the etymology of its name than does pedophilia with its) or the contrary, that it was the collapse of culture that led to the triumph of antiracism. One can defend each thesis as easily as the other and with equally good arguments. All that one can note with certainty – and it cannot be overemphasized – is the chronological coincidence of these two phenomena.

I do not for my part believe in a conspiracy. I do not believe, for example, that certain people, for the sole purpose of establishing an antiracist society or allowing one to be established, consciously willed the death of culture and deliberately planned its demise – by, for example, destroying the educational system and abandoning to television the task, so aptly named, of in-forming brains, divvied up into pie charts and market shares. No, I do not believe that. I do not believe in anything so carefully decreed. Alas, no, what I believe is that there are obscure movements in the depths of the species, subject to the very laws of tragedy, starting with the first of them, which has it that the wishes of men and of civilizations whose disappearance is foreordained shall be granted. That education became egalitarian was one such wish:

that wish has now come true, no one learns anything anymore, the re-savaging of the species is underway.

What I do know, by contrast, and this time with certainty, is that a living culture, in the full sense of the term, would never have tolerated the triumph of antiracism in the form and meaning it has taken among us. A people who knows itself – let us say "who knows its classics," to keep it brief – such a people does not accept death because that is what is asked of it, does not consent to its disappearance so as to be reborn emptied of itself, does not resign itself to being melted down without resistance into a violent but officially undifferentiated mass, which retains nothing more than its name and that – yet one more humiliation – only for a time. A people who knows its language, who knows its literature, who remembers its civilization, and who preserves in its midst a cultivated class, *elites* (though certainly not in the pathetic sense the new masters have given this word), such a people does not let itself be led to the scaffold without a fight, nor for that matter meekly let itself be told that it is not a people, that it never was one ("And *what* is 'a people' for you, anyway? Can you tell us exactly what you mean by that?" Oh dear oh dear oh dear . . .).

The organization of ignorance, the teaching of forgetting, the re-savaging of education, and cathode-ray decerebration were absolutely necessary, sine qua non conditions for the establishment of antiracist society in the form in which it is sadly prospering before our eyes. But, once again, I am in no way claiming that the pioneers and champions of antiracism consciously desired this forgetting and deculturation, nor that they methodically implemented this daft re-savaging. They doubtless took advantage of a happy historical coincidence, that's all. Indeed, one would be quite wrong to judge them by the sorry automatons that one now sees flailing about in their name, moving like puppets on a string when one pushes the right button at the right time, reciting their catechism in answer to every question they are asked in their poor, arthritic language, all sore ankles and rusty joints, like the perforated cards of an earlier era of data processing or the metallic rolls of player pianos. No, nothing like them: like the pioneers of communism, the pioneers of antiracism were often men and women of great intelligence, driven by the loftiest moral intentions. Indeed, were we not ourselves, I would add with a note of melancholy vanity, among their number?

Nor do I believe the converse, that the advent of antiracist society was the sole or even principal cause of the cultural collapse of our country or even of the first manifestation of that collapse, the implosion of the educational system. In my opinion, its advent can at most be seen as a belated cause, an opportunity for delivering the coup de grâce. National culture and antiracist society were, it is true, radically incompatible. This is sufficiently underscored at the symbolic level, I think, by the thorough-going inversion of meaning that a word like *discrimination* has undergone – a word which, in the language of culture, refers to the greatest of virtues, the very exercise of intelligence, the quality par excellence of thought, whereas, in antiracism, it refers to the queen of all mortal sins (making a very bathmological, farcical return under the pleonasm, "positive discrimination").[xv] No composite population would long accept that the particular culture (or language) of one of its components be imposed as the collective culture (or language) of the whole, particularly when that particular culture is the least loved among them, the least testosteronically prestigious, the most rapidly shrinking as a proportion of the whole, the most laden with every evil, with every crime, with every negative responsibility. Indeed, it is unlikely that composite populations are amenable to any common culture, since culture is first and foremost (at least chronologically) the voice of the dead, their creative presence, and such a society has no dead, except those generated on a daily basis by its internal confrontations, brand-new dead of no cultural import. Since it seems that it must have one, it thus has no option but to call anything and (above all) everything *culture* – the entertainment that seeps from its television, for example – just as, from a lazy habit of language, it continues to speak of *education* when referring to the boorish ignorance instilled in places dedicated to that purpose.

We here touch upon, and it is on this that we shall conclude, a famous difference between communism and antiracism – a difference indeed so great that it partly invalidates the comparison or rather inverts it: for, if it seemed an exaggeration to compare antiracism to communism, going so far as to call it, in a spirit of provocation, "the communism of the 21st century," in another sense, from a different perspective, it appears to be very far from saying too much and in fact says too little. Even in the countries where it was practiced the longest, communism coincided neither with a collapse of the educational system – far from it – nor with a repudiation of cultural heritage. That such a coincidence may indisputably be observed in what concerns the antiracist regime suggests that there is no conceivable end to its ascendancy, and that there is no reason to expect, contrary to what happened in the case of communism, that any walls will come down – to the contrary, one might almost wish they *go up*.

The Second Career
of Adolf Hitler [2007][1]

In the wake of the bombings of Berlin and the capitulation of Nazi Germany in 1945, there were some people who did not want to believe that Hitler was truly dead. Terrified for the most part, though hopeful in certain cases, they had convinced themselves that the Führer had been able to escape by some secret passage in his bunker and would someday return.

He has not returned, thank God. But as time passed, as Nazi crimes became better known, as the horror of the concentration camps came to occupy a larger place in collective memory, and the bewildered silence that had followed the discovery of the death camps lifted, Hitler nonetheless made a kind of return: a kind of return in *intaglio*, as an inverted figure, a counterproof, a negative pole *par excellence*, and therefore an obsession. This role as the absolute embodiment of Evil was certainly not ill-deserved; no one was better qualified to play it than he. The trouble was that, having once again become very present in this perverse way – as *idée fixe* for an entire continent – he would acquire the means to show that, dead though he was (dead but not buried), he had not said his last word and could still do harm. Not as much as the first time, surely, nor as directly or criminally, but in a more insidious, specious way as befits a phantom, deeper, more lasting, and, in

---

1. "La Deuxième Carrière d'Adolf Hitler," in *Le Communisme du XXIᵉ siècle* (Vevey, Éditions Xenia, 2007), pp. 11-26.

the end, of yet greater historical and geopolitical consequence. This is what I mean by his "second career."

It was as the backstop of all utterances and every negative statement, the supreme horizon of every prospect of condemnation, and the ultimate counter-argument in every bitter debate that his spectral presence manifested itself. This is what, following Leo Strauss, others before me have very rightly called *reductio ad Hitlerum*. And I believe I am quite well placed to judge of the aptness of this designation and its power as a tool of polemic since I myself have been described, without the least hint of humor, as *worse than Hitler* by Madame Laure Adler (or perhaps it was MRAP).[i]

When used in this way as an absolute weapon of language, as its supreme fulmination, the atomic bomb of maledictions, Hitler served to once and for all condemn or silence anything a person might say, or *believed* he might say, or thought he might at least *insinuate* should it have any connection, however slight, to Hitler, to anything he did, anything he wrote, anything he thought. In this domain, however, accusation equals condemnation. Suspicion equals guilt. And, for the potential target, risk equals ruin. What we had here, in other words, was a formidable weapon best kept out of the hands of the general public (or so one would have thought). And yet there it was, available over-the-counter, no prescription needed. Nay, it was freely distributed on every street corner to journalists and schoolchildren alike, to talk-show "regulars" and brothers-in-law bloated from their Sunday meal, together with a detailed instruction manual (easy, no?) and a brochure encouraging its moral use at the least prompting or no prompting at all.

Hitler having become roughly synonymous with *racism* (to say nothing of anti-Semitism), it was enough for anyone desirous of peace of mind, power, or worldly success to don the mantle of *antiracism* and thereby kill on sight – intellectually and conceptually but also socially and, of course, politically – any opponent, squash any challenge. Indeed, there would have been hardly any drawback to this had antiracism kept to what its name seemed to promise: the moral condemnation of racism and the campaign to oppose it politically, to oppose, that is, any effort to reduce individuals to their origin or subject them to violence or humiliation because of it. But the obsessive presence of Hitler at the tail-end of every accusation, negative thought, and argument conferred so much exhilarating firepower upon those who invoked it that, drunk with power or for reasons of pleasure or ambition, they were tempted to resort to it on every occasion. To do so, they significantly, indeed almost indefinitely, enlarged the range of application of this incredibly powerful weapon. It was in this way that antiracism, overcome with joy at the irresistible force, the quasi-infallibility and invulnerability conferred upon it by the real or merely suggested evocation of the hideous phantom *Adolf Hitler*, set about enlarging its doctrinal corpus and domain of intervention beyond all measure. Far from targeting true racism as had been the case in its early days – a sufficiently weighty task in its own right, one might have thought – it henceforth got involved in prohibiting, not only all reference to races, it goes without saying, but also to one degree or another all reference to *ethnicities, peoples, civilizations,* diverse *cultures, origins* in general, and *nations* in their temporal aspect, that is, their heritage, transmission, and survival.

As a result, because of Hitler, because of the crimes that Hitler and his followers committed, the incomparable atrocities for which they were responsible, entire sections of knowledge, history, experience, judgment, indeed reason itself collapsed, disappeared, became impossible to even mention, were tacitly (and not always so tacitly) forbidden. Yet, what these collapsed sections of knowledge and thought were knowledge *of,* the history from which they were made, the everyday or thousand-year-old experience upon which they were built, what reason and judgment, moral and political, had sought to define and order or, more modestly, observe and note in them – this something nevertheless continued to exist under the prohibition, nevertheless still endured in the depths of time and geographical space and often at their very surface, along their borders, in their various neighborhoods, their housing projects, and their suburbs [nb. banlieues].[ii] In short, it no less pursued its historical labor, sometimes hidden, sometimes violent – at first hidden and then violent.

It is all well and good to say, from a horror of history and to curse the memory one of its most nefarious figures, Hitler, and one of its most tragic moments, the Third Reich, that there are no more peoples (except as an effect of purely administrative decisions – voluntarist, "Hermogenian," and profane). But if one only succeeds in convincing one's own people of this and not the others, one has merely condemned it to death.

It is all well and good to say – in order to humiliate one's elders and out of resentment towards them – that there are no more countries. If your compatriots are the only ones who believe you (and you arrange things so that they hardly have any choice), you have merely condemned them body and soul to conquest and slavery.

Having taken the form of a term-by-term and purely mechanical inversion of perspectives, the second career of Adolf Hitler consisted in declaring before the world but above all before the West and first and foremost Europe (which to its misfortune had much better seats than the other continents to the first criminal exploits of this diabolical ghost) that the ethnic distinctions and hereditary dimensions of civilization did not count, that origins were nothing, that native forms of belonging had no importance and that even if, by some mischance, these things had real existence and actual influence on the affairs of men and those of states, one must act as if this were not the case, ignore them in speech and action, deny them any relevance and forbid that reference be made to them. Peoples were taught, not only that they did not exist, but that they had never existed. Any sort of *we* with the least claim to historical consistency was angrily prohibited.

Thus was born, under Hitler's inverted crook and in dread of him (a dread that proved a tremendously effective mode of presence for this consummate dictator), a totally imaginary world, a world that was sentimental and sanctimonious, unctuous and unforgiving, tyrannical and impotent (tyrannical towards its own, impotent in what concerned others), and that took it upon itself to paper over the guilty real world, which was suspected of virtual, potential, or possible Hitlerism. This imaginary world then went about severely scolding the real world every time the latter humbly sought to remind it of its reality, be it only by raising a finger to ask a little question or by simply revealing its suffering. And then it was told, with statistics to hand and the threat of prosecution for good measure, that it was in every way mistaken about itself, that it did not know what it was saying, did not see what it was seeing, and was not really suffering from what it thought it was suffering from. In short, that it was all in its head, entirely in its poor little head, a mere *feeling* of this or that: *insecurity, deculturation, change of people*, or *conquest*. And if it had the bad taste to insist, this insistence was declared criminal.

Of course, the effort to paper over reality out of virtue or simple ideological conformity did not meet with the same success everywhere in the world. Haunted by Hitler, this ultra-antiracist, post-Hitlerian society insisted, for example, that there were no races, but, at the same time, that races should not be meddled with given their sensitive nature nor were they to be subject to the least criticism, a rule that held just as much for any *ethnicities*, peoples, *communities*, religions, cultures, or civilizations that might in one way or another be seen to vaguely resemble or coincide with these races from the point of view of the individuals concerned. This post-Hitlerian, inversely Hitlerian society was thus only able to thoroughly impose itself in lands (mainly Europe but to a lesser degree North America) that the first Hitler, the real one, he of the *first career*, had so infamously stamped with his seal. Elsewhere, the ghost was much less active. It can even be said that there are vast regions of the planet, heavily populated and very restless, particularly to the south and southeast of Europe, where he frightened no one. One might almost add: *to the contrary.* This is because in these places, the *ghost* of Hitler had yet to arrive (an *inverted* ghost, as in the West, reigning *a contrario*, shaping territories and minds in *high relief* through his totalitarian memory). Indeed, despite long effort, the *first* Hitler, he of the first career, had barely just arrived. These places had not moved *beyond* him, much less *obsessively* beyond him, as is our case, but were still *short* of him, even if sometimes *just* short of him, it must be acknowledged, as evinced by the unflagging success of *Mein Kampf* in the bookshops, souks, and "department stores" of the Middle

East or the recent speech given by the President of the Iranian Republic calling for the outright destruction of Israel.[iii]

In short, the situation was, still is, still is more than ever similar, *mutatis mutandis*, to that described by François Mitterrand in a famous speech: all the pacifists on one side, all the missiles on the other. On one side, all the ultra-antiracist experts in *reductio ad Hitlerum*, together with their dependents, disciples, interns, you, us, me; on the other, all the peoples, ethnicities, "communities," religions, cultures, and civilizations that, having had no direct dealings with the first Hitler, are not particularly obsessed with him, and, not feeling compelled to judge the world and its vicissitudes in terms of him, in reaction or relation to him, are highly indifferent in what concerns him, when not positively enthusiastic, and, on the whole, do not for a moment consider abandoning their perennial ways of seeing things simply because in certain parts of the world people might accuse these ways of seeing things of having some overlap with those of Hitler. What I mean is that, on this side of the fence between pacifists and missiles, between ultra-antiracists and native allegiances, no one dreams of displaying his pacifism or thinking that ethnicity is meaningless, that communities of religion or civilization have no importance, or that origins are entirely devoid of relevance or ought to be. In these parts, I am afraid there are even individuals who recoil neither before the word *race* nor before the thing itself, if only to coarsely invite our race, yours, or that of your mother to endure, if I have understood correctly, certain rather abrupt sexual intimacies.[iv]

Let us not even speak about the *thing*. But the *word*, it must be reiterated, the word is looked upon with absolute horror (albeit with the best reasons in the world) by all the horrified dependents of Hitler's ghost. This is of course true of *race* but also of all its derivatives and distant cousins as well, even those one might have thought a bit more presentable. For that matter, it is rather curious that both racists and antiracists should have come to an agreement, as it were and in this way underscoring the strange commonalities entailed by their all-too-perfect symmetry, that this rich and complex term, so deeply ingrained in the French language and French literature, is only to be understood in an extraordinarily narrow, if admittedly corrosive, scientific – or, rather, *pseudo*-scientific – sense, which at most occupies a tenth and doubtless even less of its true semantic range. The word *race* had been good enough and noble enough for Malherbe, Racine, and Bernanos, useful enough and honorable enough for de Gaulle and Georges Pompidou, a fact that, in passing, tends to confirm that the second career of Adolf Hitler did not fully begin until twenty or thirty years after the first had ended. Between the two, there was a period of latency during which the Führer was perhaps really dead and had yet to return. The idea that races did not exist had yet to be invented, to the nearly exclusive benefit of France and, moreover, the French language. This of course became easy once the term was exclusively understood in the only one of its meanings that was completely untenable: that to which the racists had yoked it to the exclusion of all others. It thus came as little surprise that never had human beings seemed so narrowly conditioned by their race than once there no longer was such a thing. Never had race seemed to so determine public opinion than once it had ceased to exist; never had one been able to so accurately predict everyone's position on the most important questions; never had the distribution of opposing armies in the clash of civilizations that awaits us been so rigorously commanded. Never have individuals so happily sung in their branches than once they were taught the tree was imaginary. One would swear that this boorish twenty-first century will be not so much religious as racial.

It is the appearance of the race taboo between the third and fourth quarter of the last century that was, I am convinced, the decisive moment in launching the second career and producing its first effects. The unprecedented prohibition on all references to race, even if only in the vaguest and most approximative sense of this term, which also happens to be the soundest and most profound, the least scientific and the most literary, the least biological and the most political, the least dogmatic and the most poetic, threw open the gates behind which civilization, forms of independence, countries, national myths, and the true diversity of the world had always taken shelter. With it, with this precisely metonymic curse hurled upon memory, global interchangeability – the essence of replacism and necessary condition of the Great Replacement – became possible. It is therefore to this and, indirectly, to Hitler, who is its fulcrum, that we to a large degree owe the situation in which we find ourselves, one in which we are left totally defenseless vis-à-vis the change of people and thus civilization, and which is surrendering Europe to invasion, her hands and feet bound by a web of laws and, above all, ideological constraints. More precisely, it is the same semantic sleight-of-hand mentioned above that, on the very legitimate pretext of banishing the race of a Vacher de Lapouge, a Chamberlain, or a Rosenberg,[v] has in its purifying frenzy also banished that of Charles de Gaulle and his famous, oft-quoted remark ("We are above all a country of the white race, of Christian civilization, etc."), together with that of Georges Pompidou, doubtless the last President of the Republic to have very naturally and innocently spoken of *our race* ("a deep reaction of our race," "in the very character of our race . . ."), at the Paris Institute of Political Studies on December 8th, 1972. It must be noted by the way that to speak of *race* in connection with the French suffices to establish that one is not a "racist" . . .

Incidentally, the late date of President Pompidou's speech is enough to show that *antiracism as power* and nearly absolute power, the power that Alain Finkielkraut has aptly called *the communism of the twenty-first century*, was not directly or immediately born of the death camps, contrary to *antiracism as a moral code* and its simple, oh-so justified injunction: *never again!* As I have already stressed, the second career of Adolf Hitler is independent of the first. Admittedly, it owes everything to the latter but it does not follow in its immediate wake. There was no passing of the torch between the two. This lacuna between the earthquake and its inverted aftershock suggests that the latter case has external, tertiary causes. And indeed, in order for the latter to take place, around the time of the "second oil crisis," it was necessary for there to be a felicitous (or rather fateful, depending on one's point of view) meeting between moral antiracism, which was the very legitimate son of the Holocaust, and the great financial interests that had emerged from the Industrial Revolution in its late, Taylorist, Fordist,[vi] and even, so to speak, *post-industrial* phase: something, not just rootless, but immaterialized, disincarnated. These two forces, once the inevitable moment of distrust had passed, quite rapidly became aware that they shared enormous interests in common. From their quickly consummated marriage of convenience, *replacism* was born, that monstrous charlatan bedecked in the gold of antiracism, its Frankenstein's monster, which generally bears its prestigious last name, *antiracism*, and would ultimately strangle it. In this connection, one need only think of the increasing impossibility of discussing the Holocaust in the context of a lesson that is nonetheless based upon it,[vii] or the stubborn defense on the part of officially certified antiracists of the most retrograde and, more often than not, most *racist* forms of behaviors and dress[viii] so long as such actions and outfits proceed from the most *victimary* individuals and most essentially victimized "communities", to whom – and not without a whiff of paradox, for this strongly resembles racial privilege – everything is consequently permitted. Replacism is antiracism biting its tail.

No matter: Under Hitler phase two, under Hitler inverted term-for-term, under Hitler *terminus ad quem* of every argument, anything having to do with "ethnicity" is to be loathed, especially if it is exacerbated by the slightest pretense to interpretation. It has been decided that origins and allegiances, even when they seem to weigh heavily on the course of events, are not, in fact, able to explain anything. With the possible exception of cooking, textiles, and music, in a pinch – and even then you have to be careful . . . – official opinion declares that "ethnicity" must never be understood as a cause or invoked as an active motivation. You may say *social* (*by all means*, as they say in English); you may say *economic*; you may say *psychological*, if you must, or even *generational* (a young person, young people . . .) – but please say no more than that.

It is this post- and, of course, fiercely anti-Hitlerian way of thinking (how could it or we ourselves not be?), which, alone at the helm for the past thirty or forty years, ever since Hitler began his second career – a subterranean and inverted one, dazzlingly obscure, oxymoronic, and devastating – it is this way of thinking, I was saying, and I hope one will be grateful I do not call it *negationist*, though I am rather tempted to call it *de-negationist*,[2] it is this Arabo-white-washed, sentimental United-Colors-of Benetton, repressive hands-off-my-token-Arab[ix] way of thinking that has forged the world in which we live, the Europe that we are trying to build and that it impedes, the country we once believed was ours and that we are day after day told is actually open to whomever so wishes – that is, to no one, but to us a little less than the others. At a moment when this world appears ready to explode and this country go up in flames together with thousands of automobiles,[3] with its daycares, police stations, and fire trucks, it is very tempting to place the blame on this way of thinking and its obvious blindness, its carelessness and improvidence, which we might even dare call *criminal* if only to imitate its own way of expressing itself (after all, we are its children).

It has not yet reached its moment of crisis, however, and still less of introspection. Ethnicity? *Ethnicity?* What could *ethnicity* possibly have to do with anything? Neither the word nor the concept are part of the repertory of current doctrine and you would do well to steer clear of them. Why not instead say and try to convince yourself to believe that what is happening is of a *social and economic* nature? This does not commit you to anything and opens many doors. And above all do not go and claim that, far from being the *cause* of "events" (as was said fifty years ago[4] and as will be said again, I sense [after all, from an historical point of view, the protagonists are more or less the same]), genuinely "economic and social" phenomena – the dilapidated state of neighborhoods and lives, and the despair it entails – are merely a *consequence* of the ethnic situation, as the facts demonstrate. If you were to insinuate that, it is not your automobile that will burn; it is you. And the two camps might be able to mend fences for a moment around this lovely bonfire.

---

2. And now *psychiatric*: the appearance of the famous *mentally unstable person* [*déséquilibré*], one of the era's capital human types, a major figure of the history of ideological self-delusion.

3. The original version of this text was written in the fall of 2005 and is contemporary with the serious upheavals then taking place in the suburbs.

4. Cf. the *Algerian events . . .*

And yet, and yet . . .

The social and economic state of the suburbs, we are told, has nothing in common with that of the city centers, and the condition of the children and grandchildren of immigrants, the living conditions that are their lot, are miles away from those enjoyed by the presumed descendants of the Gauls (and the Iberians, Lusitanians, Volsci, Samaritans, Sorbs, and even Lusatians). Without a doubt, without a doubt . . . It is true that the social conditions of today's Europeans greatly surpass those enjoyed by native stock Frenchmen and women in times past, these latter indeed having much more in common with those to be observed in the countries of origin of today's immigrants, who one might say naturally enough duplicate or nearly duplicate them in the new territories to which they spread.

We have stopped welcoming individuals and blundered into welcoming peoples and have done so all the more blithely as we no longer really know what *people* might mean, as inverted Hitler dictates. Our guests, by contrast, remember perfectly well. And now that they are among us, they continue, with that innocent obstinacy typical of all peoples (which is sometimes a little *nocent*, all the same), to resemble who they are, much more faithfully in any case than they resemble what we were. And, indeed, they appear to have no particular regrets about either of these things. They have not read Adolf Hitler, even backwards. They have not seen the old newsreel footage or read the reports detailing his infamies. Their children, as I remarked, even appear to be reluctant to learn of the worst of his crimes. This is not our history, they say. This only concerns you. And it is thus that, meaning having executed a complete about-face, antiracist society, born of the Holocaust, will soon no longer be able to teach the Holocaust (for reasons of antiracism).

Europe is like a patient who has suffered from a terrible cancer – Hitlerism – and who is endlessly operated on and reoperated on by terrifically thorough, if perhaps not always very professional, surgeons. Having decided to leave not even the least hint of disease, not a single area exposed to danger even if it is totally healthy, no lingering concerns, however minute, once they have been imagined, the surgeons attend to the most hidden recesses. The trouble is that, in following this regimen, these over-zealous practitioners have left the patient more than three-quarters dead, for in their glee to extract they have removed all vital functions, instinct for survival, and desire for life. The patient is officially alive, no doubt, but he has no more heart of his own, no lungs, no brain, no entrails, no loins, no arms or hands that might take hold of his destiny nor legs that might carry him if only to flee from the horror of his condition. Everything in him has been replaced by cold, artificial machinery, which the doctors regularly assure themselves can contract no disease and feels nothing. Even the most alarming news does not reach this closely watched patient and one would wait in vain for it to affect him in any way.

More than any other factor – more than the global, post-industrial tendency toward the replaceability of everything by everything (and first of all man by man), more than cultural and spiritual collapse, more than the ever-growing demand for equality (all of these agents being intimately linked to one another, moreover) – it is the entirely legitimate and well-founded loathing we feel for the denizen of Berchtesgaden and Wannsee, this loathing and its consequences, its influence, that have opened the doors of our country and our continent to immigrants, at least in their present proportions. Indeed, absent this sentiment of horror compounded by shame, which has ordered all our thoughts and feelings, what nation, what civilization would have suddenly accepted what it had throughout its entire history refused with all its being and strength at the cost of often appalling sacrifices: to share its soil with one or several other peoples? What would the *poilus* of the Great War say if they saw today's France and its capital, suburbs, and neighborhoods, which are so cruelly named "working class," no doubt because the working-class people from whom the immense majority of combatants at the battles of the Marne and Verdun were drawn have been driven out of them? And their German counterparts, what would they say about their country? It is true that, of all the countries of Europe, Germany is no doubt the one in which, rather logically, the second career has been the most effective – that is, the most devastating. There, Hitler the ghost has had an even greater effect

than did Hitler the Führer, and this destruction of European civilization, beginning with Germany, which racism nearly brought about in
1945, appears within a hair's breadth of being accomplished seventy
years later by Madame Merkel, powerfully assisted, it is true, by the
European Union and Monsieur Juncker.

Yet while the newcomers, be they Turkish, Algerian, Moroccan,
Senegalese, Pakistani or other, all of whom to such a great extent owe
their presence here to the historical abomination of Nazism, while they
may be willing, more often than not, to reluctantly and as if in passing
say that they feel the same way as we do about it (and even more willingly since they know everything they owe it and the dialectical utility
it still offers them), they hardly intend to push its historical recollec-
tion to the extremes to which it has led us. As I have already remarked,
they know all too well what it means to be a people; and many of them
are very particular about questions of territory, as the horrible death
of Jean-Claude Ivroas,[5] the unfortunate photographer of streetlamps,
abundantly testifies. Yet it is towards a classic territorial conflict that
we seem headed, *nolens* in one case, *volens* in the other.

And now it seems that the flames consuming France are a problem
of architecture and urban planning. Economic and social factors no
longer suffice to explain everything, apparently. And so once again it
is the turn of urban policy, as they say. It would appear that we have
not done a good enough job accommodating our guests or new fellow
citizens: this is the root of the problem. Yet our *former* fellow citizens
had in their time seemed happy enough with similar and indeed often
more rudimentary facilities, which they carefully tended, as one would
a very valuable possession. Were one to build in Clichy-sous-Bois as
one builds on the avenue Paul-Doumer,[x] I am not for my part sure that,
after four or five years, the Boumediene-Bouteflika[xi] aspect would not
gain the upper hand or that the elevators, social or otherwise, would
work as hoped. Inverted Hitler may say what he likes: when it comes

5. While photographing a streetlamp on October 27th, 2005, Jean-Claude Ivroas, an
    employee at an urban lighting company, was killed following a brawl with two
    black men and an Arab who were of the opinion that he had no business being
    there.

to living, working, loving, reproducing, managing how we look at each other or run the street corner (to say nothing of apartment building stairwells), peoples have very solid habits fomented by long effort on themselves or by equally long periods of slackening. Our people no longer needs to travel to closely observe the habits of others. Alas, its eyes are now only good for crying. Will it arm itself with its tears?

The Great Deculturation [2008]¹

With Carla, it's the real deal.
The Head of State

The presidential campaign, the election of Nicolas Sarkozy, the early days of his new administration, the social unrest that followed the return from summer holidays, the new disturbances that shook immigrant suburbs that fall . . . All of that had largely erased from people's minds, under the entry for 2007, the memory and last echoes of those controversies of a cultural type that had, for once, caused something of a stir at the very beginning of that year.

The most important of these related to the Louvre: on the one hand, our great national museum was said to be loaning, for a fee, a part of its collection to the city of Atlanta, Georgia; on the other, some of its masterpieces were to be entrusted to Abu Dhabi's new museum. Oddly, in order to get the public (which was otherwise largely indifferent to the issue and rightly so) to accept these transactions, which at first glance were hardly in keeping with the cultural traditions of our country or indeed those of any other, the following explanations were offered: First, that these initiatives were essentially *cultural* in nature and not in the least commercial. They were intended to reinforce France's prestige in various parts of the world and to establish or strengthen bonds of friendship and mutual curiosity with the inhabitants of these regions. Second – but also *at once, at the same time* – it was argued that the Louvre stood to profit handsomely from these initiatives, which would allow it to fit out new exhibition rooms and perhaps even – though I am only speculating here – open to the public rooms it had

---

1. "La Grande Déculturation," in *Le Petit Remplacement* (Paris, La Nouvelle Librairie, 2021), pp. 175-269.

grown quite accustomed to finding closed. In short, it was a win-win proposition: the supposed commercialization of culture obviously had no bearing whatsoever on the relationships established with Atlanta and Abu Dhabi; and the Louvre would derive significant financial benefits from these relationships.

However enticing these explanations may have been, the sound of tinkling bells in the distance nevertheless prevented one from entirely subscribing to them. For the very people who offered them drew our attention to the necessity, *in the twenty-first century*, of maximally profiting from the prestigious *Louvre brand*, which in their view had been far from adequately monetized.

We never listen to language as closely as we should. Yet it is always very eloquent. It teaches us much more, in general, about what its users say, what they want, what they think, and the family of thought to which they belong than they care to tell us – indeed, quite often more than they themselves know. All book lovers who use the internet, for example, have had the rather traumatizing experience, early on, of being asked by some giant online bookseller – one of those that can legitimately boast of resources vaster than anything ever dreamed of by Compagnie, La Hune, Ombres Blanches, Le Furet du Nord, and Kléber[i] combined – and this while they merely wished to order Kant, Catherine Pozzi, or Saltykov-Chtchédrine – of being asked, I say, how they would like their *product* to be delivered or what gave them the idea to purchase this *product* and whether they knew that people interested in this *product* are also very often interested in some other *product*. Sometimes it is not the *product* that is in question but the *item*. In any case, be it *item* or *product*, the word is enough to make it clear to lovers of books or literature that they are not in friendly territory. And as soon as we have been told of all the profit to be made from the *Louvre brand* – profit that it would be absurd not to make, that we must urgently and imperatively make – we know that we have exited the domain of culture.

Or might it not, to the contrary, be the domain of *culture* after all? As I often remark and others have remarked before me, the word *culture* does not make for a good line of defense, whether it be for the thing itself or for those who fight on behalf of what it (poorly) denotes. We have certainly made this word, this name, our own and given it our greatest consideration. We have lavished it with our respect and declared – continue to declare – a love of sorts for it. But perhaps we should have been suspicious of the somewhat too-recent origin of the flattering meaning we typically attribute to it – one or two centuries, no more. Perhaps we should not have forgotten that *culture* appeared, if not on the ruins of, then at least as a proxy, almost a replacement, for art, knowledge, literature and *belles lettres*, the humanities, for *reading* in the sense one meant when, in the classical era, it was said that a man was *well-read* – but in order to show that he was thoroughly well-rounded and fully corresponded to the ideal of the *honnête homme*, the same individual also had to have taste, savoir-faire, politeness, and the social graces, all qualities which made him eligible, if he so wished, for entry to polite society, and which allowed him to speak for civilization and to participate in it just as he partook *of* it. Yet we are not going to get into the old debate between *culture* and *civilization* here, entwined as it is with its excessively ritualistic variations, depending on whether one is speaking of France or Germany, for example. It should be enough to recall that culture is to self-fulfillment, such as it was understood during the reign of Louis XIV or the Enlightenment, what *aesthetics*, the advent of which Hegel noted and reluctantly hastened, is to art: a kind of second degree, mourning the naïveté of its origins, but also, perhaps, that of a society mourning its lost power to believe and create.

While recently completing work on a short book about contemporary art exhibits in Toulouse's subway stations, I noted my amusement one morning while listening to the radio at hearing a woman who was very active on the *cultural* scene admit, at the conclusion of a large European symposium just held in Paris, that she was having more and more difficulty taking the word *culture* seriously or even tolerating it. Having been mixed into every sauce and asked to mean everything and its opposite, I suppose the word had ceased to mean anything at all to her. Of course, what so amused me that morning was that this woman, Catherine Clément[ii] – someone who, to my knowledge, has all of the correct thoughts and who, through her books and *cultural* activity, precisely, has even contributed in no small measure to establishing what a decent person may and may not believe and above all what such a person may and may not say – had come within a hair's breadth of sounding like Baldur von Schirach. Or was it Goebbels or Goring or that character from a Nazi play, the one who drew his revolver or his Luger or who flipped off the safety lever on his Browning whenever he heard the word *culture*?

Madame Clément of course said nothing about *revolvers* or *safety levers* and one may be sure that the reasons for her exasperation are as far removed as possible from those of Nazi dignitaries or playwrights. The fact remains that in both cases the word *culture* exasperates, as does culture itself. It exasperates, perhaps, for what it is but much more so for what it is not, for what it is no longer. A full turn of the semantic spiral having taken place, the words that caused such justifiable indignation when they issued from the mouth of a henchman or minstrel of the Reich can, seventy years later, turn up in almost identical form, "fresh and cheerful as on the morning of battle," in that of an intellectual of unassailable reputation, at least on this particular point. I believe I know what Catherine Clément meant, and I am not far from thinking the same thing, a fact that does not put me in a situation in which it is easy to lament culture and its unenviable fate, as I am nevertheless doing here. Let it be said that one of the evils that has befallen culture and that threatens to kill it once and for all is the fact that various emanations, impostures, and ectoplasms travel about under its name and identity, successfully performing the world over. The noise they generate and the pace they set give the public the illusion that culture has never been in better shape. And yet we are watching it die before our very eyes.

A misnomer from the outset, culture was born of one abuse of language and is now dying of another. These terminological approximations, which as it happens are entirely in keeping with the usual erring ways of speech and thought (especially when, in their thirst for adventure, risk, and new experience, our protagonists search for one another the world over and through a thousand dangers, under a thousand borrowed identities, with all the misunderstandings that follow from and give substance to this epic farce), can be perfectly explained by reference to history, sociology, and economics – these three modes of exegesis being very closely intertwined, of course. It would moreover be erroneous to conclude that, since we are here confronted with a question of *vocabulary*, only words are involved. Even in the ambiguities from which they are built, words merely reflect (rather faithfully, if involuntarily) the evolution of what one is tempted to call the "balance of power," a term no less relevant, in my view, for the whiff of "retro" that hangs about it. The difficulty obviously consists in simultaneously keeping an eye on semantic shifts and social transformations without ever confusing them or entirely separating them one from the other, without believing that one is directly dependent on the other and without imagining that their respective trajectories are totally independent, without hoping that one will tell us everything about the other and without fooling ourselves into believing that nothing is to be learned from either concerning the movements of the other. One must make do, even if only for an instant, with partial truths, with propositions that, without being correct on every point, nevertheless contain a strong or significant truth content, with predicates that are more true than false, shortcuts that temporarily neglect certain well-founded objections of detail but that alone lead to the only truly enlightening point of view.

With the possible exception of strictly scientific disciplines and then only in the *hard* sciences, the demand that all truth be *pure* is one of the greatest sources of blindness, of the enslavement of speech, and of the subjugation of thought. If one wishes to silence and ridicule a man, one need only require that every proposition uttered by him and the least word from his mouth be strictly correct on every point. If one wishes to stifle an idea, prevent something from being revealed, or obsessively focus on small matters of detail in the disclosure of some situation (and the most glaringly obvious are the easiest to obfuscate when language is turned against them), it suffices to reject the least shortcut or approximation in the manner in which they are expressed.

All censors know that truth is not pure. It is multi-layered, jumbled, contradictory, full of enclaves and of enclaves within enclaves. And these enclaves within truth are themselves falsities, vague approximations, exceptions, counter-truths in the way one speaks of counter-currents, second-tier truths, which contradict truth but which are no less true for all that and no less part of truth's empire. When loss and waste, misunderstanding and improper appropriation of meaning by each party are forbidden in the transmission of messages, there will be no more messages.

Let us suppose, for example – and this is not scrupulously exact, though clearly more true than false – that the reign of culture coincides with that of the bourgeoisie. In the intellectual and "artistic" sense that interests us here, the word *culture* appeared even as the pressures of the Enlightenment, the industrial revolution, and fledgling liberalism were eroding the rhetorical and linguistic arsenal that once served to ideally define the intellectual, moral, social, and formal relationship of the *noble* man, the gentleman, and their avatar the *honnête homme* to thought and knowledge. He disappeared or rather was erased by his very ubiquity, became ridiculous by his omnipresence, emptied himself of all meaning by centrifugal disintegration and the exponential dissemination of his instantiations at the very moment that, upon the ruins of the bourgeois conception of one's rapport with the world, what I have called the "the dictatorship of the petty bourgeoisie"[2] was established, a globalizing (if not totalitarian) mélange of hyperdemocracy and resentment, of proletarianism and the spirit of terminological conquest, of all-out mediatization and a visceral horror of mediation.

That the word *culture* triumphed at the same time as the bourgeoisie, for as long as the latter did and no longer, in no way means that the word only had a bourgeois meaning. For the bourgeoisie itself, the word *culture* was universal and timeless: it referred to the entire "cultural" heritage, everything that had formerly been encompassed by the words *art, knowledge, reading, education, research,* and *humanities.* Among the bourgeoisie's adversaries, on the other hand, or among social groups and individuals who simply found themselves outside of it

---

2. *La Dictature de la petite bourgeoisie*, interview with Marc de Saune, Éditions Privat (2005), and The Author (2016).

(if only in a temporal sense), two conceptions entered into conflict with one another, a conflict that continues to this day to some degree.

The first of these extra-bourgeois conceptions did not challenge the bourgeois definition of culture, that is, its universal and timeless character. On the contrary, it took this conception at its word, asking only (if such can be said) that this culture, the nature and content of which it did not contest (the latter, of course, being always in a state of evolution but enriching itself over time by a process of accumulation), be universalized and made timeless in its very reception. It asked, in other words, that this conception of culture be de-gentrified, democratized, disconnected from the bourgeoisie and its period of hegemony. In short, that it be open and available to all. This was the conception to which architects of school reform originally subscribed, as was also the case of such figures as Malraux, Jeanne Laurent, and Jean Vilar, the institutional and artistic champions of sweeping cultural policies (most of whom were also bourgeois but that is not the question here . . .). In their minds, there was no ambiguity as to what constituted culture; the problem was how to make it available to all. The task was to *decentralize*, both socially and geographically, to fan out from the centers (Paris, the educated classes), whose primacy and supremacy was unquestioned, so as to irrigate all regions and social classes.

Conversely, according to the second definition – this one extra-bourgeois, or anti-bourgeois, or post-bourgeois – the bourgeois definition of culture was by no means universal and timeless: to the contrary, it was purely bourgeois all the way down, from its nature to the contents that that nature entailed. In a word, it was false. Culture was not at all or not only what the bourgeoisie had said and believed it was. It was, at the very least, infinitely *more*. Here, a new subdivision opened up between those who wanted to maintain, in the heart of the culture, if only in a vestigial or testamentary way, what the bourgeoisie had said and believed culture to be, that is, a heritage and inheritance and corpus, and more radical types who held and still hold that this very corpus is a bourgeois invention, that its subject matter is suspect and void of relevance, if not inherently toxic, and that it has no place in . . . in . . . in what, to a certain degree, continues (alas) to be called *culture* (it is here that appears the terminological complexity that so severely complicates this debate). While this latter way of thinking still doubtless has some way to go before it achieves dominance, it is constantly gaining ground. Were one to yield to it, one would discover, not only that it in no way coincides with culture as that term was understood in the bourgeois regime; it excludes this understanding of the word, does not encompass it, does not want it to be part of its content. Here I am alluding to those who, ever more audibly, consider, not just that Corneille or Racine, for example, have nothing interesting or valuable to communicate to today's middle school students, but that they are tools for dominating, oppressing, intimidating, and even *deculturating* them, tools that must be combatted and rejected as such, Corneille and Racine along with them. There is no need to clarify that the *deculturation* at issue here – deculturation via culture, whether it be the deculturation of the uncultured via culture as that word was formerly understood or rather the deculturation of other cultures by classical French culture – is not the subject of this short essay . . .

I say *bourgeois*, *bourgeois* culture, *bourgeois* values and I employ this term because of the links between the word *culture* – the word here concerns us as much as the thing – and the bourgeois class's period of political, semantic, and social domination. But here one must be clear that *bourgeois* and *bourgeoisie* are in this instance to be taken in a sort of *generic* sense in order to signify, in the post-bourgeois linguistic arsenal, domination *in general*, a bygone domination that must nevertheless still be combatted, a revolting and unacceptable domination. And of course, the domination in question is ethnic – one would be tempted to write *racial* were that allowed – at least as much as it is of class. It is a domination of origin, of origins, at least as much as it is economic domination. It is a domination of skin, of color, of skin color, complexion, the configuration of capillaries, name, and neighborhood at least as much as it is one of money, income, or employment rate.

It must be noted that, in France's diverse and diversifying society (a process of generalized mixing that is very far from complete and may never be), the French with the most ancient claim to being French, to having been on the scene the longest, the "native French" [nb: les

Français de souche], as we no longer say and cannot say, it seems (it apparently depends on who is speaking . . .), the "natives" [nb: les souchiens], the *sous-chiens*,[iii] as some people might insinuate, in the same way one spoke of *Untermenschen* – these indigenous people, these autochthones, *are seen as* a bourgeoisie, "function" (quite unwillingly) as a bourgeoisie, are in a bourgeois position (a compromised situation that, whatever its few, residual advantages, entails and will continue to entail serious threats). This situation is only compounded by the fact that, in Newspeak, the word *working class* [nb. populaire][iv] has today been perverted to almost exclusively mean *immigrant, populated with or consisting of immigrants or their descendants*, if not *extra-European*, as if it has once and for all been agreed that the only people remaining in France are the neo-French. Thus: *working-class neighborhoods*, a *working-class uprising*, "a candidate who should be helped by his Arab-sounding lasting name in a district with a heavily working-class electorate."

Given the hugely preponderant role it has played in the great deculturation now underway, one can never insist too much on the coincidence, inevitable if perhaps accidental (or rather obeying mechanisms whose determinisms and concatenations are too close for us to observe with certainty), between the *democratic* crisis of French culture, linked to its status, real or supposed (in part real and in part supposed), as a class culture (bourgeois), and what one might call its *ethnic* crisis, linked to its indisputable status as a national culture, that is, its status until recently as the hereditary culture of a given ethnic group, what one called *the French people*, in the now narrow and archaic (and forbidden) sense of this expression. The *ethnic* crisis of culture, in which the national community as a whole (or all inhabitants of the national territory) refuses to accept as its own the culture of just one of its parts (that of the so-called "native French"), has been superimposed upon but also tremendously exacerbated the *democratic* crisis of culture, in which the social body as a whole has in just the same way refused to accept as its own the culture of just one of its parts (that of the bourgeois class).

The expression *refuses to accept as its own* is a little over-hasty and not entirely accurate for it takes as resolved the debate to which

I alluded above, that of attempting to determine and decide whether the set of references, values, and works that in France have until recent decades been understood to constitute culture – by which I principally mean *inherited or patrimonial* culture, since this is how culture used to be understood – was only of interest and value to a given class, for which it became a privilege, or whether it should instead be considered precious by *all* classes of society and *all* citizens. Whether it only had validity and purpose for French people of French ancestry or whether it should instead be seen as something worth acquiring for all citizens and residents of our country. It of course goes without saying that these two layers of problems do not precisely overlap. Yet they largely coincide and the manner in which questions arise and evolve at one level or the other may be described as homothetic. Structurally, they present the greatest similarities and each domain has much to learn from attempts to answer or reformulate these questions in the other.

The first promoters of the great movement to democratize culture – the *pioneers*, as one would put it today – did not for their part have the least doubt. There is, moreover, a certain way of formulating the equation or syllogism that confronted them. Had they accepted its logic, they would immediately have had in full the answer to the question they were not asking and thereby learned what was going to happen and has, in my view, indeed happened:

   a) Culture is a class privilege;
   b) This privilege must be abolished;
   c) In doing so, culture is abolished (since it *is* the privilege).

Of course, the founding fathers of this movement did not understand it in this way at all. In order to deceive themselves, in my opinion, they took advantage of the ambiguous way in which Proposition *b* was formulated. In fact, what they meant, understood, and wanted to convey by "this privilege must be abolished" was: this privilege must be abolished *insofar as it is a privilege*. It must be stripped of its privileged status but retained as culture, its content preserved and shared without in any way changing its substance or what gave it form and value.

As will be clear by now, my hypothesis, indeed my conviction, is that, despite its apparent absurdity, the mathematical and syllogistic rigor of the argument says more and contains more truth, more closely coheres with what has taken place, than the sensible, decent, and reasonable accommodations that one was naturally tempted to make on its behalf without further thought.

For my part, it is the first proposition that I would be inclined to correct, explicate, "qualify." It is not that I question whether culture is a privilege; it is that I am not entirely convinced that it is a class privilege (despite everything that supports this opinion from an historical point of view). It seems to me that culture can just as well be an individual privilege at the same time. But as soon as one sees it as a privilege *in any case* – that being a privilege is part of its essence, that possessing it, if that is the right word, or being its custodian, is *inevitably* a privilege – one cannot, if one sets great store by culture, desire the abolition of this privilege. The entire syllogism thus collapses as soon as it is articulated and does so well before reaching the regrettable conclusion entailed by any too rigorous reading.

That it is a privilege to enjoy alone or nearly alone (as at the Villa Medici) the silence and solitude of a magnificent park in the middle of a great city is undeniable. One may, as a matter of democratic conviction, abolish this privilege by opening the park to the public at all hours. There would be no more privilege in effect. But there would also be no more silence, no more solitude, no more contemplation in surroundings of absolute beauty. Yet it was these very things that were the privilege, much more so than the park itself. For there are many other public parks in the city almost as beautiful or just as beautiful as this one.

I long ago adopted as a fixed metaphor for this familiar structure the story of the Judgment of Solomon in the first of its iterations. Two mothers lay claim to the same child, with apparently equal rights over him, it being equally likely that either is what they say they are, that is, the *true* mother. At the risk of committing an injustice, the king can only give the child to one of them. He can also – and this is the option he pretends to adopt – have the child cut into two equal parts and give each of the supposed mothers one half of the corpse. Justice is respected, as is "democracy" (or rather equality). There is no privilege but there is also no longer a (living) child.

Around the same time that the first champions of the social democratization of culture were promoting measures that, in their minds and that of the public, should make it possible to achieve or at least make significant progress towards achieving their stated objective, the first champions of its ethnic democratization, while perhaps somewhat less explicit about their intentions, were no less resolute. It was not uncommon, moreover, for these to be the same people. They held that French culture, the validity and value of which they did not at this stage think to challenge (all the less so since this culture, its validity, and its value, in their eyes passed for *universal* because it was *universalist . . .*), was in some sense by definition, by some sort of unwritten historical law, the privilege, if not of an ethnic group, then at least that of a community: that of several-times hereditary Frenchmen, those whom we never know what to call. And it was necessary to strip them, not of this culture, certainly, but of this privilege, of this privilege *insofar as it was a privilege* and as such unacceptable in a good antiracist democracy. Newcomers had to be brought to this culture or rather *it* had to be brought to *them*. It was necessary to ensure that they meet, marry, comingle.

In both cases, it gradually became clear that the content of a culture – and one could doubtless say the same of *Culture* as well – is in no case independent either of the number of those who share it or of their social, economic, ethnic and . . . cultural characteristics (since the fundamental ambiguity of this word and its derivatives is destined to pursue us till the end). There is not, on one hand, a culture – French culture, for example, with a capital C – that exists as a stable entity, its content forever determined in advance (even as it continually expands to incorporate new artifacts), and, on the other, the larger or smaller quantity of people who receive, share, and participate in it. The latter varies automatically with the former. The content of a culture changes with the number and the nature of those who share it or are supposed to share it. And the same goes for the content of an education, of the subject matter that an educational system is tasked with transmitting, of the programs that this system provides or can provide.

Those who claim to harmonize culture and equality, education and equality, and to introduce equality (even if just *some*) into culture and education are deceiving themselves, or deceiving others, or both, for there is a radical, fundamental, insurmountable incompatibility between these domains, these fields, and these values. Equality is as absent from culture as it is from nature. The most beautiful proclamations can merely recognize, or impose, or claim to impose *legal* equality or equality *of rights*. And this is a heroic and a magnificent act of defiance directed against everything observed in nature and among men. Equality is not natural and it is certainly no criticism – quite the contrary – to point this out. Neither are *in-nocence*, civic peace, and the rule of law. Equality is a constraint that certain civilizations impose on themselves with great difficulty, in general against their oldest traditions and instincts. Nor is it cultural, except in one of the modern senses of this adjective, according to which equality, by dint of long practice and an overall conformity of disposition, is said to have been incorporated into certain cultures more so than others. At the risk of being immediately contradicted, for example, it might be said that American culture *is deeply egalitarian*. But culture or Culture, in the sense of the "Ministry of Culture,"ᵛ is on no more familiar terms with equality than is nature, where equality is at best an accident, a coincidence, an occasional approximation. Equal access to culture can and no doubt must be imposed by the law, albeit as an ideal that can never be fully realized. But this is equal access to inequality.

As modern ecological thinking is abundantly aware, equality among men (or among peoples, nations, ethnicities, civilizations) destroys nature as soon as it becomes de facto rather than merely de jure – that is, as soon as it becomes economic equality. The only exception – but no one seriously desires this, except perhaps the most intrepid champions of degrowth – is the case in which equality is achieved from the *bottom up* or at least via an alignment of the lifestyle of all the planet's inhabitants with the lifestyle and consumption habits of the bottom half or even bottom quintile of the distribution. For the Earth would not survive any general realignment of levels of consumption with those of the richest countries. Oddly enough, the same holds true for culture.

Culture could never survive – indeed, *is not surviving*, as is doubt-lessly already clear – were the cultural level of all humanity or simply the totality of a people to be brought into line with that of the most cul-tivated individuals or classes. Such an alignment could only take place at the price of radically deculturating those culturally privileged classes and individuals, irreparably impoverishing culture throughout the world. One might find this observation surprising, for the natural ten-dency is to believe that, unlike most commodities (water, gas, oil, petro-leum . . .), science, knowledge, and even *taste* (though in this term one already senses the sting of the paddle) are quantities that can be indefi-nitely extended through transmission, proliferation, contact, exchange, and advantageous cross-fertilization. For while they are a privilege, as we have seen, this quality adds nothing to them; it is a simple charac-teristic, not a value, and they would not suffer from its loss. Indeed, the knowledge possessed by one group is not diminished, except perhaps professionally or as a matter of market value, by that possessed by an-other. The culture with which one person is endowed deprives no one (although it may provoke much irritation, jealousy, or even hatred) and is in no way diminished by the increasing culture of others around him – quite the contrary, it has everything to gain from a more favor-able environment. Neither the metaphor of Solomon, the two mothers, and the single child nor that of the garden, closed or open to the public, thus appears relevant here. Culture does not die for being shared; it could be split in two, divided by a thousand or sixty million, and would be no less alive for all that. The joy it provides is too intimate, too inter-nal to what one is (or should be) to be in any way reduced by broader dissemination within the population. Knowledge is not a raw material. To spread, extend, broaden, or disseminate it among the public should have no effect on its volume or consistency nor on the quantity of ac-cumulated reserves. And yet it unfortunately appears that culture is a raw material after all, for some poorly understood law of social physics would seem to dictate that, while culture may be moderately increased, it may by no means be indefinitely expanded.

We are perhaps dealing here, in a still inexplicable way, with a cu-rious variant of the principle more or less improperly attributed to

Pareto, which in its (very) vulgarized version holds that in every society eighty percent of the wealth is always held, whatever else is the case, by twenty percent of the population. While there may be upheavals, the scale always returns to these proportions. It would be puzzling if, in the domain that interests us here, the same numbers should obtain. In what concerns culture, however, it seems likely that they are even more striking and that ninety-eight percent of culture or more is in the hands or minds of one or two percent of the population. In each of these cases, an effort can obviously be made to change this. In the domain of economics, it is far from being out of the question (if also not quite certain) that, beyond a certain threshold, any such expansion of prosperity would be detrimental to global wealth. In the cultural domain, by contrast, it does seem – and this is terribly unfortunate – that, beyond a certain degree, the dissemination of knowledge is damaging to its sum and harmful to cultural literacy.

The explanation for this bizarre and, at first glance, far from scientific phenomenon is doubtless to be had by carefully distinguishing between the synchronic and the diachronic. The *spread of knowledge* and the *expansion of culture* must not only be seen in the static terms of a distribution table, the snapshot of the state of a given society at a given moment. One must also and perhaps above all grasp the active process to which these expressions refer, the quantity of *time* they entail. Time, as usual, is the key to the mystery. That its quantity is for its part also not inexhaustible and that it is, as we shall discuss below, the most precious resource, is precisely what culture teaches, here rather oddly agreeing with the language of business and commerce. However, time is not so much *money*, as one says in English – that is, a unit of exchange – as it is the substance of being itself. And yet the time, money, and effort – though above all the time – that a society devotes to developing knowledge in one area is not allotted to increasing it in another. A cultured man does not become so by an act of God, a pure revelation without beginning or end. His culture is the result of work, exercise, and the slow convergence of favorable circumstances, of a long exertion of will within himself and by countless others, those who willed and built schools, raised libraries, and organized their shelves, wrote books, made art, and spent many hours conceiving, preparing, and delivering their lessons. Because it is so dependent on time and is perpetually besieged by competing desires, hostile interests, active negligence, and pedagogical error, such labor is no more inexhaustible than is water, natural gas, or petroleum – and neither, in this sense, is culture.

The case of the baccalaureate degree,[vi] grotesque to the point of caricature, offers the most convincing example here. At various times in the past, the baccalaureate was a diploma obtained by no more than two, five, or ten percent of an age cohort. We are all familiar with the ideal, so proudly embraced by several successive governments, of seeing to it that eighty percent of the school-age population obtain it. Alas, we know that this ideal has nearly been realized. We also know that, in the transition leading from one state-of-affairs to the other, the baccalaureate was radically transformed. It would certainly be difficult to give precise figures here but it does not appear exaggerated to assume that, between the baccalaureate obtained by ten percent of the population and that which is conferred upon eighty percent of another age cohort (or the same age cohort in another era), the proportional relationship as concerns the true meaning of the diploma, the degree of maturity achieved by its recipients, their knowledge of language, syntax, and spelling and their capacity for argument and logical reasoning, for stringing ideas together, for rigor and demonstrative coherence, is about ten to one – to take no chances, perhaps we should just say *five* to one. The overall degree of educational achievement required for the diploma is roughly a fifth of what it was in the middle of the last century, when most of today's baccalaureate holders would never have made it to their senior year or perhaps even their *sophomore* year.

Between the culture of a cultivated class and mass culture, the difference is the same and is of the same kind. The only problem is that in neither case can this difference be observed synchronically. For, just as there cannot be a baccalaureate for ten percent of the school-aged population in an era when the baccalaureate is awarded to eighty percent of that population (when it is not called a *licence* or even a *maîtrise*, to say nothing of those barbarous names – *D.E.U.G., D.E.S.S.,*

D.U.T.[vii] – that so clearly evince deculturation, no less than the frequent boorishness of their holders), there can be no culture of the cultivated class nor indeed a cultivated class at all in a time of mass culture. One precludes the other, especially in a democratic regime. In a democratic regime, mass culture cannot tolerate the culture of a cultivated class, a culture that is not necessarily *anti*-democratic – it has even done much for democracy – but, inevitably and by definition, *non*-democratic.

More precisely, it is culture itself that is essentially non-democratic. Or, to be even more precise: the concept of democracy has no relevance here. In fact, the fields of human activity and reflection in which democracy is not relevant are very numerous – love, for instance. Democracy is a *political* system, admirably defined by Winston Churchill, the principal merit of which is that it in theory generates (or should generate) the fewest malcontents. Decisions having been made (again, in theory) with the direct or most often indirect – and in general *very* indirect – consent of a majority of citizens, the latter can only blame themselves for the potentially poor outcome of what they are assumed to have desired and chosen. Elsewhere, I have used the term *hyperdemocracy* to refer to this transposition of the democratic system of the political field to various other fields (if not *all* fields) where, in my view, it has no business. And yet this system functions rather well or at least less poorly than most of the others (Churchill again) for the purpose of governing states. And all the better, perhaps, since the will of the majority is more efficiently filtered, interpreted, and reinterpreted through it by intermediate institutions and bodies – a process of filtering and reinterpretation that television, nonstop opinion polling, and the general mediatization of the world (an unfortunate misnomer, for what this process actually establishes is *immediateness*, a lack of mediation) makes much more difficult. But this system does not work at all and even has, in my view, a totally devastating effect in domains such as the family, education, and culture (all of which are indeed closely linked to one another).

Here, it is important to clearly distinguish between two things that public debate contrives to conflate in the interest of better muddling everything: on the one hand, family, education, and culture within a democratic society, which necessarily confers upon them a certain number of particular characteristics (though this is not what is at issue at the moment); and, on the other hand, family, education, and culture *as democracies themselves, as democratic systems.* That is to say, the transposition of a political and, secondarily, social system – democracy – upon fields for which it was not designed, which reject it with all their might for reasons of radical incompatibility, and which, if they do not manage to reject it and are forced to submit to it, perish under its weight.

The tendency to conflate democracy with its central value, equality, only exacerbates the devastating effect produced when democracy intervenes in these incompatible domains. Neither family, nor education, nor culture is capable of accommodating equality. The first two and above all the second, education, still only require its provisional and conventional suspension: as a matter of convention, the child is the equal of neither his parents nor his teachers over the course of his upbringing, a fact that in no way infringes on the fundamental equality of rights among individuals and between generations (as each reaches maturity, that is). But on this point culture is more radical and stricter in its demands and in what it excludes. Equality is not suspended for a moment, during childhood, an hour of class, or a year of study; it is stamped with a fundamental and permanent lack of relevance. It bears repeating: the only suitable relationship between equality and culture – and it is very indirect and totally external to culture itself – is the difficult, very difficult, nearly impossible, though certainly desirable provision of equal access to the radical inequality, the labyrinth of primordial inequalities that is culture.

To become cultivated is to become unequal to oneself. It is also – though it is much more difficult to win acknowledgement of this point in a hyperdemocratic society (and it is worth repeating that such a society is by no means the supreme achievement, consecration, or epitome of political democracy but rather its imperialistic transplantation into domains that are foreign to it), and, while it may be incontestable, it is not of paramount importance here – it is also to become unequal to others, to those who are less cultivated. Unequal to them not from a legal point of view, of course, but from a cultural one; not in law but in spirit. It is not insignificant that people used to speak – and it is telling that the term has fallen into disuse, perhaps because of its distasteful association with animal husbandry [nb. élevage = rearing/breeding] – of *raising* [nb. élever] children and of children and other people as being more or less well-*raised*.[viii] I prefer to retain the term's suggested connotation of *elevation, of altitude*. To become cultivated is to *raise one's self up*, to become *elevated*, to learn to see things and the world from a higher vantage point.

The problem, perhaps the whole problem (and this no doubt goes to the heart of the issue, debate, subject, the thoughts it inspires, and the resistance it provokes), is that raising oneself *culturally* or through education is also to raise oneself *socially* to one degree or another. It goes without saying that these two movements in no sense overlap. They in no way amount to *a single movement*. But it is not infrequent that their trajectories and rhythms in part coincide and this peculiarity has greatly harmed culture, which is more or less explicitly accused of being the hallmark or even the substance of social inegalitarianism, which is necessarily frowned upon, considered reprehensible, reprehended. And yet culture finds itself in the most difficult of positions when it comes to defending itself against this criticism as it is, in a general sense, far from unfounded.

In hyperdemocracy, nothing is allowed to be superior to anything else if that superiority might be suspected of having the least social character, if only by implication, connotation, or Pavlovian association. In this way, it becomes impossible to defend artistic genres long considered to be *superior*, for the adversary usually finds it easy to highlight the real or supposed ties between these arts, which are now only *allegedly* superior, and social classes whose "superiority" is no longer acceptable and could only be defined as so-called superiority, to the point that one can only mention it between scare quotes: what "superiority"? A characteristic slogan of this ideological and (consequently) aesthetic situation is that the minor arts do not or no longer exist. One effect of this, paradoxically, is that arts formerly considered minor but that have obvious historic ties to the privileged classes (to not say "upper" or superior) – think metalsmithing or cabinetmaking – have benefited from this declassification. The major beneficiaries of this move to abolish the hierarchies between genres, however, consist, on the one hand, of art forms that were once taken to be less elevated variants of the major arts, as the crime novel, science fiction, and comic books were seen in relation to literature and painting, and, on the other, arts formerly considered to be of a popular character, starting with what were once called "variétés" [nb. pop music, show tunes] but are now described as *music* without any further qualifier, having first annexed the vocabulary of traditional *music* (*concert, recital, composer*) before expelling the latter from its own traditional terminology, forcing it to find new qualifiers for itself – *classical* music, "great music," educated music – even if this means that *contemporary* educated music, at the receiving end of this war of words, sinks into total unintelligibility. In *Cran d'arrêt du beau temps*, Gérard Pesson[ix] marvelously describes the curious social status of the contemporary composer who, beyond the narrow circle of his colleagues and a handful of admirers, has the utmost trouble explaining what he does for a living. And the near-totality of the public today cannot for a second imagine that educated music, what it still calls in more reflective moments "classical music," can be more modern, more innovative, and more "avant-garde," as people used to say, than Kyo or the Scissor Sisters.[x] All appearances to the contrary notwithstanding, the mere fact of forward movement, be it social (art for everyone) or generational (art for "young people"), is celebrated as aesthetic progress.

Another paradox, incidentally, is that the adversaries of hierarchy in the arts – and thus of culture in the traditional sense, since the latter is all hierarchy – wield hierarchy itself as a weapon (and this is a great tribute) to advance their cause. To fight distinction (between genres), they appeal to distinction (between artists, styles, trends, levels of quality). In opposing the idea, repugnant to them, that educated music might in some fundamental way be superior to *variétés*, or literature superior to comic books, or, for that matter, painting to graffiti, they claim that *variétés, popular music, comic books, graffiti*, and so on are meaningless categories and that everything and its opposite can be stationed under these words, the best and the worst (which is not false), that one must distinguish over and over again, a proposition to which we can only wholeheartedly agree. It is useless to point out in response (not that it generally comes to this, the argument having been swung against its victim like a knock-out blow from a cudgel) that the undeniable existence of hierarchies within each of these categories, or genres, in no way entails an absence of hierarchy *among* genres. That even if a good composer of variétés may indeed be a better musician than a bad composer of educated music, a great composer, in the classical sense of the term, remains a greater artist, his art more elevated, the range of emotions he summons broader, the means at his disposal more complex, and his humanity deeper than the best pop singers or his peers. And, having said this, it will be taken as tainted by class prejudice, indeed by prejudice pure and simple.

What we might call the *social barrier* – that is, the impossibility against which one collides in affirming, transmitting, or defending any values whatsoever (and, above all, cultural values) as soon as they can be accused (and they always can be) of being class values and in this case the values of classes that have been seen, if only by themselves, as "superior" – this barrier, taboo, impossibility has greatly contributed to the paralysis that has gradually spread throughout the French educational system. In its first republican iteration, which more or less died on the barricades of May 1968, this system did not shy away from more or less openly and even officially embracing its twin cultural *and* social roles, that is to say its mission to preserve the cultural privilege of the culturally favored classes (the bourgeois education of children of the bourgeoisie) while secondarily ensuring that these classes be replenished by new recruits through the small-scale redistribution of this privilege to individuals from other classes who had demonstrated the talent and avidity to learn, the wherewithal and desire to attain to general culture, which at the time, as a matter of class privilege, was none other than bourgeois culture.

The aim was twofold: to pass on the cultural heritage of the cultivated classes (understood as the cultural heritage of the nation) to the next generation; and to extend this cultural heritage to a few deserving

children from other classes, whether they be the petty bourgeoisie, the
peasantry, or the proletariat. It is here that one encounters the concern
for democratic and republican values in its first instantiation. Not all
members of the bourgeoisie were cultivated, of course, but all truly cultivated individuals (in contrast to those who were merely *educated* . . .)
were *ipso facto* bourgeois (at least in the eyes of the bourgeoisie). We
must not be deceived, for this was something on which everyone, re-
gardless of their class position, more or less tacitly agreed: the role of
the educational system was to turn a few young petty bourgeois, a few
little peasants, and the occasional offspring of the working class into
bourgeois. Not necessarily political or ideological bourgeois (at least
at first) but economic bourgeois, vestimentary and residential bourgeois, bourgeois by deportment, above all cultural bourgeois, first and
foremost by virtue of their speech. Language (vocabulary, syntax, pronunciation) was the gateway to the bourgeoisie, in the same way that
we today understand it to be the great marker signifying that the bourgeoisie has exited the scene, that it is no longer the bourgeoisie that is
speaking and expressing itself (and this marker operates in complete
independence of the so-called "socio-cultural level" of profession or
income).[xi]

The old process providing for small-scale assimilation to the cultured class by dint of study, merit, intelligence, and willpower had
some total success stories but the pain with which it was often associated among those who were subjected to it should not be forgotten. On
this point, literature offers abundant testimony, as it also does to the
confusion felt by the sons of peasants, skilled tradesmen, and workers
who acquired new cultural and social status by way of their diplomas
and labors. On the one hand, this new status was often poorly and
reluctantly acknowledged by the older, hereditary beneficiaries of the
same status. On the other, it also often opened a breach, the source of
malaise, between the new bourgeois, insecure in his bourgeois status,
and his class of origin, starting with his family – his parents, siblings,
friends, and childhood comrades.

Of course, except in the case of potentially delusional repudiation
(wherein an individual, newly promoted within the field of culture and
the cultured class, deceitfully maintains that his social and cultural

origins are not external to it), this breach, being difficult to avoid, is denied, repudiated, and, as far as possible, rendered less perceptible and acute. It is typical, for example, for the newly promoted person to deny any discontinuity between his point of departure and his point of arrival, repeatedly asserting that he has stayed "true to his origins," and, in evidence of this claim, only adopting, whether voluntarily or otherwise, a limited number of the practices and attitudes normally associated with his new cultural status. Despite the education he has received, for example, he retains the accent of his place of origin (an accent that, in France, all discretely agree to discuss only under its *regional* aspect, even though it is or was no less of a *social* characteristic – and, in this respect more than the other, potentially an object of discrimination since in the cultivated classes one has "no accent" [this absence of accent obviously being perceived by members of other classes as an accent like any other]) or votes like his parents, like a winegrape grower from Hérault, or a schoolteacher from Allier, or a milling machine operator from Aubervilliers, even if he lives on Avenue du Saxe, the Île Saint-Louis, or Rue de Longchamp.

But the more this break with one's origins is denied in speech and practice (out of a sincere concern to align speech with practice, perhaps), the less it is truly consummated and the less the passage from one cultural level to the other is realized from the point of view of culture in its traditional sense and that of the old "cultivated class." From the perspective of culture in the old and, perhaps, eminently *social* sense of the term – its way of seeing and of hearing – an individual who is well-educated and who can therefore legitimately lay claim, if only in his heart of hearts, to the status of a cultivated man, will in this way not be recognized as such if he retains the accent of his working-class and regional origins. As this form of social exclusion and denial of recognition is seen as ridiculous, an obvious injustice and without justification given its reliance on *social* rather than cultural considerations, however, those who submit to the officially or tacitly recognized ideological corpus of democratic and, especially, hyperdemocratic society will say that these considerations are totally without relevance, nay shocking, revolting, unacceptable. The question of accents has been settled: the cultural and, especially, the intellectual level of a given utterance shall be judged without the least regard to the accent in which it is uttered. To this end, it will be established as a principle that accent, elocution, and intonation have no normative bearing in what concerns culture.

And this is as it should be. The trouble is that, for reasons of the same type – social reasons but also, soon enough, political, ideological, and even *moral* ones (in hyperdemocracy, ideology wastes no time in passing itself off as a moral code) – the number of formerly normative elements in culture that are stripped of this quality, declared irrelevant or a-relevant, is constantly increasing. Accents will no longer be taken into account, for to take them into account might have social implications, which are by definition unacceptable: a cultivated man or woman can henceforth (and this *henceforth* is already half a century old by now) have a strong working-class accent, that is to say, an uncultivated one by the lights of the old, repudiated criteria. In the same way and for the same reasons, one will no longer take *elocution* into account, which by the same token will have been relieved of any culturally normative connotation. *Pronunciation* will no longer be taken into consideration, it being similarly exempted from any qualitative implications as these might pass for marks of discrimination (which they indeed are, if not necessarily in the sense meant here). Soon, vocabulary itself will be excluded from the field of cultural relevance as will syntax, why not, out of hyperdemocratic concern to exclusively concentrate on the message – that is, the meaning – stripped of all superfluous regalia (it will be said). As matters of taste or, worse yet, *good* taste, these are naturally subject to class variations, whose echoes must necessarily be banished from the field of culture. Thus, at the very moment that the field of culture shows a tendency to indefinitely broaden ("cultural activities," the "culture industry," and the famous "everything is cultural," a wan variation and reflection of the even more illustrious "everything is political"), at another level it undergoes draconian reduction – an aporetic concordance that can obviously only be explained by the semantic instability of the terms, starting with that of *culture* and its adjectival derivatives, which are obliged, if only to survive, to mean everything and anything *at the same time*.

Considered here and with very good reason as a subdivision of culture, education is obviously the domain where these difficulties resulting from the relations (complex, imperfect, contradictory, fluctuating but nevertheless sufficiently strong to be compromising) between culture and social class (or the "sociocultural level," as one says nowadays) are the most crudely rampant. Simple "instruction," with its focus on meaning, on simple *meaning* (but we know that it is never so simple as it should be in this process), on data, facts, and content independent of connotative vibrations (a fantasy, of course, but one that has its place all the same) is still more or less conceivable. But *education* (a domain less expansive than culture, it is true, but infinitely broader than *instruction*) is thoroughly cluttered (one need only consider courtesy, politeness, codes of social conduct, and so-called *good manners*),[xii] entangled, and intertwined with social references – all of which, in a hyperdemocratic climate, are so many dishonest compromises.

To put the matter brutally, for brutal it is, and speak less than precisely – though more precisely than imprecisely – to educate is to educate in the manners, rites, and ways of speaking (which threaten to become ways of thinking and even of feeling) of the educated class, that is, *horresco referens*, of the "upper" class. There is no difficulty (at least in theory, but we will see that there nonetheless remain a few difficulties, some of them serious) when the individual to be educated is himself drawn from the educated class. It is a major problem, however, when this is not the case. Or, to describe this stumbling block otherwise – specifically, in the jargon of pseudo-sociology, which is by definition more suitable (this is what it was made for) – to educate the offspring of what are customarily called "culturally disadvantaged backgrounds" or attempt to do so is to propel them, if not into "culturally privileged circles," then at least, as a start, into culturally non-disadvantaged ones. In short, it is to change their milieu, by teaching them rules, codes, principles, tastes, values, language, and interests foreign to those of their origins.

This would not be a problem at all or at most a comparatively small one if to educate was not also to de-educate; if to learn was not also to unlearn; if to teach was not also to refute. It is not just a matter of providing something *in addition*. Alas, it is also – and this is where the suffering alluded to above comes in – a matter of modifying, criticizing, questioning, dismissing, nay eradicating that which cannot serve as a foundation, base, or support for this something *in addition*. And yet this foundation to be dismissed, this spurned source of support, is, to put it briefly – but only *here*, for in reality this substitution takes time and does not occur without difficulty for those who oversee it or reluctance and sorrow for those who are subjected to it – nothing less than the culture of the parents, above all their language, accent, and way of speaking. The process is very unpleasant and always has been. Its essence is nothing other than the necessarily painful effort of conveying to a child or person in general, possibly an adolescent or adult, and this without telling him explicitly, that his parents speak poorly, that they express themselves poorly, that they reason poorly, that they are interested in the wrong kinds of things, or at least that one should not imitate them in one's speech, self-expression, ways of thinking, and personal interests.

It will be said that things are more complicated than this. In saying so, one runs hardly any risk of being mistaken, in this regard or (almost) any other. Fortunately, it is always possible to dissimulate, tact will make itself heard (or hold its tongue), and instruction does not necessarily involve explicit repudiation of what preceded it. Instead, it may be said that what instruction supposes and offers is a *detour*, even a full circle, at the end of which what one temporarily had to abandon in order to see what was to be seen from the outside once again comes into view as precious, worthy of love, indeed irreplaceable. It nevertheless remains the case that, in the type of instruction demanded by any democracy worth the name that seeks to spread culture to the masses by way of education, there is always and necessarily a phase, which may last some time, during which what some apparently call the "learner," if he does not himself hail from a cultivated background or already happen to be educated, is more or less firmly called upon to *unlearn* what he owes to his place of origin, his family, his father and mother:

"No, that is not how you say it. You say . . ."

"But that's how people say it where I'm from!"

" . . ."

And yet the chances that this eminently delicate phase – delicate for the teacher, of course, but much more so for the student, torn as he is between two loyalties – would meet with success were fairly good when the student found himself alone or shared his predicament with only a handful of classmates, a small minority encouraged to integrate, if possible, into a large and robust cultivated class, sure of itself, its rights, its prestige, and its virtues and already represented in the classroom by the majority of students. For those subjected to it, the process was painful. It could be humiliating, hurtful, even psychologically unbearable. Yet it was not unusual that it succeeded: there are and have been tens of thousands of individual examples, all bearing witness to the former effectiveness of the Republican system of education. The same process becomes vastly more uncertain, however, in a context of mass education, where the proportions are inverted. *Number*, here, is a matter of crucial importance in evaluating the likelihood of success, as is always the case when discussing integration. The task now becomes to ensure that a large majority consisting of children from outside the cultivated class have access to a cultivated class that is rapidly shrinking, does not dare speak its name, and no longer dares present itself for what it is – for what, moreover, it is less and less, it being difficult for a thing to exist when it is not at liberty to acknowledge its existence.

We all know how important the existence of a sufficiently broad and robust middle class is to a country's economic development and prosperity. At the same time, I also believe – it is a subject on which I have already written and will not revisit at length here – I also believe that, for culture to survive, for it to be spread within a people, there must be a sufficiently large but not-too-numerous cultivated class, constantly replenished by new recruits. In other words, this cultivated class must be open and malleable but make no promise of hereditary permanence to its members. At its center, however – and this is the most difficult thing to have acknowledged in a democratic society and is almost impossible to even state in a hyperdemocratic one – it must nevertheless contain a hereditary core.

As this idea or observation or conviction is extremely unpleasant, it is generally agreed that it must be false. Hyperdemocracy and its correlate, dogmatic antiracism, which is to antiracism what the former is to democracy, have the same way of dealing with unpleasant ideas (*ideologically* unpleasant ones, for they have no problem adapting to bad news about the environment when it has no ideological connotation). They do so by establishing it as an axiom that such ideas are false, refuse to examine them, refuse to hear them, and declare that those who, despite it all, dare support these ideas or at least submit them for discussion are despicable, indeed criminal. One such idea: that, in a general way and notwithstanding any and all exceptions that one might raise (first and foremost, that of the genius), it takes two or three generations to produce an individual of thoroughly accomplished culture. Such was the serene conviction of nearly all earlier centuries and most civilizations; today, it is totally out of the question to entertain it. If it were shown that heredity and culture were closely linked, we would still prefer to sacrifice culture out of a horror of heredity, which is antidemocratic *par excellence* as soon as it takes on the trappings of privilege. Yet this is what has happened, for the link has indeed been demonstrated, as the metaphorical vocabulary associated with the word *culture* time and again shows: *heritage, patrimony, transmission,* etc. Culture is the culture of the dead, of parents, grandparents, elders, ancestors, the people, the nation, even of what we are no longer allowed to call – so great is the consensus that it does not exist – *race*. It is no accident that the latter is *persona non grata*. But with its fall and banishment, everything that concerns lineage, heritage, and patrimony is swept away; and culture is stricken as a result.

It goes without saying – but such is the situation of generalized suspicion, intimidation, nay ideological terror that what goes without saying must today be infinitely repeated, rehashed (the beloved children of the intellectual regime and the auxiliaries of its thought police being content, for their part, to neither say nor write anything else . . .) – it goes without saying, then, that culture has never been and never could be *purely heritage*. With each generation, it is partly renewed, broadened, enriched along its margins, as all cultured classes are, or should be, or were supposed to be when they existed. Having said that, it remains the case that heritage and culture, the language of the dead, the sediment of generations and time are absolutely central to culture and that, without these things, it withers and has no meaning or import.

Hyperdemocracy competes with democracy on its own terrain (for if it succeeds in toppling democracy, this is often by inordinately extending it, stretching it beyond all measure, and spreading it where it does not belong), abolishing the cultivated class by means of taxes, television, and the "one middle school"[xiii] system (in the broadest sense) on the grounds that it is also, in part, a socially privileged class, a fact which, though not false, is intolerable to the hyperdemocratic mind. But without a class to represent it, model it, and bring it to life by incarnating it, culture is helpless; it no longer has the authority or the strength and prestige needed to impose itself as something to *join*. What holds here – and this is neither the first nor the last time that we will encounter this parallel – holds for the nation as well: one can only join something that already exists, that has a visible appearance, a body, an image. And these incarnations, these embodied symbols, representations, and entities must be desirable, self-confident in their existence, bearing, and rights and must love themselves. Without a cultivated class, without heritage or heirs to inherit it, the latter discredited by the dual and even threefold nature of their heritage (cultural primarily, but also social and economic), there is nothing left to *join*, no longer any model, reference point, or corpus of *classics* to serve as standard and inspiration, if only in being more or less gently "revisited," challenged, or disputed. Any effort to at all costs preserve a refuge of inherited values, starting with the structure of this hierarchy, which was their essence, is faced with the libelous accusation of *contempt* – which, in hyperdemocracy, is the same as being found guilty.

"But aren't you being a bit *contemptuous* when you talk about comic books?" (Or popular films, pop singers, mass entertainment, the Prix Goncourt, reality television . . .).

There is nothing to say to this. The accusation of contempt is an absolute weapon of language, all the more so as cultural contempt, which is already difficult to tolerate in itself, is implicitly suspected of being coupled with social contempt, which is totally unacceptable, or worse yet ethnic contempt, an appalling, not to say actionable, offense.

After having for a time served as an impure inducement to culture ("Cultivate yourself, you will improve your social standing!"), the very imperfect, very approximate, very irregular link between social and cultural level, the existence of which cannot (unfortunately for culture) be entirely denied, became fatal to it ("Cultivate yourself, you will acquire the values of the dominant class – all the more foolish as they no longer dominate – in the context of education, this is what the famous classroom insult *buffoon* more or less conveys: *sycophant* and *traitor* in one.)

The phenomenon by which culture is compromised through conflation with its disavowed traditional supporters is obviously reduplicated and amplified by the situation created, particularly in high schools and middle schools, by mass immigration. Not only is culture more or less explicitly accused of being an instrument for subjugating the masses to a dominant class (which will be rendered even less dominant, as is desirable, the less effective this instrument becomes, the more this process is refused, the more impervious the people become to bourgeois values and especially the scale of those values); but French culture as well, in France, is more or less (but now rather *more* than *less*) explicitly accused of being an instrument for subjugating immigrants and the children and grandchildren of immigrants (most of whom have brought their own values and their own culture with them) to a dominant ethnicity (which will be rendered even less dominant, as is ideologically desirable, the less effective this instrument becomes, the more this process is refused, the more impervious that immigrants and the children of immigrants become to "French" values and especially the scale of those values). To the accusation of contempt, which serves to undermine any attempt to maintain the hierarchy that is central to the old conceptions of culture, is added that of the now well-known *lack of respect*, which serves among other things, very much among other things, to eat away at any effort to maintain the predominance of a properly "French" culture in France.

Antiracism comes to the rescue of hyperdemocracy by precluding or at least severely impeding, nearly ruling out, the transmission of values, codes, rites, and *works*, to begin with, that might rightly or wrongly incur the criticism of belonging to a formerly dominant caste, class, or ethnicity or to a caste, class, or ethnicity that might still claim to be dominant, it being a civic, democratic, and antiracist duty to oppose such claims (if only by not learning what it would teach us). Yet there is hardly anything in our culture and its classical canon that is not susceptible to such accusations, and so every self-affirmation of culture receives, as a reply, an aggressive summons to prove whatever is being advanced. This is to turn things on their head, for the primary aim of culture is not to sit in judgment of its own content. It is culture that, once in place, authorizes judgment, including judgment of itself, of course, retroactively. It is a heritage in the sense that it presents itself as something already judged, a body of jurisprudence. But hyperdemocracy and dogmatic antiracism refuse this jurisprudence with one voice, claiming that they took no part in its elaboration, which is almost entirely true. They seek to permanently rework everything. But culture is like the constitution of a state: it only has meaning when it is set down once and for all, even if it must be enriched and perfected over the course of time with the help of certain amendments and wise additions. If the legitimacy of their articles is challenged on a daily basis, there is no more constitution, no more culture. Indeed, it is they who judge us, officially, not we who judge them.

Hyperdemocracy does not want hierarchy but culture is nothing without hierarchy. Dogmatic antiracism wants to know nothing about origins yet culture is just a groping search for the origin, and it is only through this always-disappointed quest – necessarily disappointed for the origin is always higher, always further upstream – that it attains the universal. There is no culture possible under a hyperdemocratic and dogmatically antiracist regime, and we are in fact seeing it disappear before our eyes. That it is supposedly everywhere only deceives those who wish to be deceived: culture is everywhere because it is nowhere. This is the result of a semantic sleight-of-hand to which the specious origins of its name leaves culture particularly exposed. Everything that even remotely involves entertainment, leisure activity, or the management of free time, provided that it does not involve love or sports (and even these could be filed under the vast rubric of "cultural activities," for what could be more "cultural," after all?), is now adorned with the name *culture*, whether it be cave tours in Touraine, macramé workshops, electro-pop concerts, or one-man comedy shows – so many pretexts for *cultural activities*, all taken into account by the sociologists and statisticians of culture with a detached soul and indifferent heart. Even gastronomy has been annexed. Even the institution most contrary to culture, by which I mean television, is nominally classified under its banner, not on the grounds that it is sometimes cultural, which is not completely false (though less and less true), but on no grounds at all, unless it is because it participates in the culture industry, in the same way as popular cinema, Disneyland, and the mass production of popular music on records and DVDs. Like the "Louvre brand," this single oxymoronic term, "culture industry," in fact suffices to prove that we are indeed far removed from what culture used to be.

Ever since the social sciences made their great coming out in the media, those who maintain the contrary, the enthusiasts, the Friends of the Disaster, those who are under the spell of the times, have turned to figures, statistics, and the number of entries – those great tools of sociological deceit – to persuade the people and individuals that they did not experience what they experienced, did not see what they saw, that they have recklessly generalized from their impressions. It would seem, for instance, that there have never been so many people in museums nor such crowds at major exhibitions. And how true this is! A man such as Jack Lang[xiv] cites these facts, these figures, these crowds at every opportunity, rehearsing ad nauseum his old dream according to which culture has over the past thirty years won over countless new strata of the population, has progressed (albeit *unevenly*, too *unevenly*, he clarifies with a scrupulousness that does him honor) into every nook and cranny of the land, has spread like the cozy warmth from a fireplace into all the rooms of the French house, if not of château Europa. Alas, if culture has spread, it is like Perette's milk[xv] or rather like a precious holy oil that has escaped a ciborium dropped by careless or semi-apostate clerics, its dribbles now drying into a crust on the loosened flagstones of the sanctuary.

That there are more people than ever in the vicinity of works of art, that more "content" is constantly being downloaded, and that the number of new books keeps growing – these truths are as true and are of the same species of truth as that truest-of-all propositions according to which there have never been so many baccalaureate degrees. With the result that a high school graduate is incapable of writing a simple letter or indeed a vaguely polite email without a large number of spelling errors. And this is to say nothing of the college essay, even though the undergraduate degree is more or less officially the new high school diploma. At museums and major exhibitions, meanwhile, it is impossible to see a painting. Many visitors barely even think to do so, in fact: they come to see the museum or to have seen it and to have "been" at the "exhibition." But the handful of museums that do not indulge in large media campaigns to "attract a more diverse audience," "bring people together," or even "build relationships" are deserted (this is one of the rare bits of good news in our time). And the same paintings that the publicity-addled crowds mechanically jostle with each other to see at the Grand Palais spend the rest of the year peacefully reposing in their usual solitude in Valenciennes or Agen, if not across the street at the Petit Palais.[xvi]

Our era and society are thoroughly mediatized and dependent on their media masters and yet what one sees reigning everywhere is the *im*mediate, or the absence of mediation. The media themselves are unmediated, which just goes to show just how poorly they, too, are named. Our contemporaries dislike nothing more than mediation, detour, delay, syntax, manners, proprieties, form – in short, literature, art, culture, and all the protocols of positive alienation, which put the elsewhere in the here and now, the not-me in the me, and the other in oneself to the great horror of all the triumphant *oneself-isms*, though who can say whether they are the chief propagators of ignorance or its purest manifestation, its perpetrators or its product.

Nothing exists culturally except that which has a place in the media – but this place tends to substitute for the thing itself. Every writer who has had an article written about him in the press frequently encounters this, to him, stupefying sentence:

"I read your article."

"*My article*? But I did not write an article . . ."

"Yes, yes, you did, your article in *Le Monde* (or *Le Figaro, Le Nouvel Observateur, La Gazette de Dieppe*, no matter), last week . . ."

"But I did not write an article for *Le Monde* . . . Aaaaaaah, an article *about* me, an article about my book."

"Yes. It was pretty good, I thought."

This person does not at all appear to understand your astonishment and seems to take it for an affectation, vain nitpicking, a very literary form of retraction: an article by you, an article about you, what's the difference? Sometimes you do not even manage to put things so clearly for him, to get him to acknowledge that two different reading experiences are involved or give him a glimpse of the subtle difference between one and the other. All he sees is a quarter of a page in an evening newspaper, little matter the substance, still less who its author might be.

Indeed, the author is a concept very much linked to culture. It only existed in a confused state before and will no longer exist, so to speak, after – that is, in the era into which we are now rushing headlong or have already entered. *Cinéma d'auteur* is a very significant expression in this regard. In very broad strokes, it roughly lays out the contours of cinephilia. It is obviously true (and fortunately so) that a handful of great filmmakers still have their share of passionate admirers, those who go to see a film because it was made by this or that director. But that a film should be *by* someone was hardly understood before the advent of the great cinephilic era, which lasted thirty or forty years – a much shorter reign than that of culture and shorter yet now that the latter is done.

In this regard, one may wonder whether there is a simple coincidence or rather a mysterious organic link ("Although puzzling questions, [they] are not beyond *all* conjecture . . .")[xvii] between the advent of this *dis-origination*, or more precisely de-authorization (which has always figured in the arsenal of ignorance, it is true), both in the deculturated neo-culture (but in this case the phenomenon has been underway for thirty or forty years and has lost much of its salience) and in what once appeared to be the apex of learned culture, the structuralist-scripturalist milieu of "textual theory" (I fear it may here be once again necessary to call upon good old-fashioned bathmology to account for this simultaneous expulsion of the author from Cerisy-la-Salle and TF1).[xviii]

In general, the fact that another uses the same words or names that one has uttered oneself is a good gauge of the quality of communication – that he does not simply make do with hearing or agreeing with them but instead *pronounces* them. In fact, it is also a good gauge of love, or its end, or true interest in something or someone, true curiosity. You are interested in this composer or this site, you speak about it with your beloved, perhaps it is an occasion for a trip or a walk. The other person seems to be enjoying himself, or at least is taking it in good stride. But is it you whom he is interested in, you who at this moment do not displease him at all, or is he instead genuinely interested in what so pleases you? Words are what will allow you to determine the matter, the words themselves, their appearance or absence in mouth and memory. How often has it been observed, once love or companionship has faded, that interests thought shared between two parties were only shared circumstantially due to love, friendship, or desire and that one was in fact alone, always alone, as one will be at death?

Old age also is also characterized by this inability to internally repeat what it discovers, to record it, to make it one's own. It hears what it is told (with some exceptions), understands it, receives the information but never reflects on it, digests it, or adds it to its already overflowing catalogue of words, names, and facts with which it knows, judges, loves, and perceives.

The same holds for the question of the author in post-cultural society, above all in the realm of cinema. If you ask someone discussing a film *by whom* that film is made, that person will usually understand the question and will even answer you, even if that means first looking up the information in *Pariscope* or *Télérama*,[xix] But never, on his own initiative, will he tell you that a film was made by so and so. Since he has himself no use for it even if he finds it intelligible, such a notion is not part of his conception of cinema, perhaps not even of his conception of the world. The few words that circumscribe this notion, beginning with the small word *by*, indicating origin, do not come naturally to the tip of his tongue. When he talks about a film, he mentions the screenplay, the story, the *plot*, the genre, the category, the setting but above all the actors. And, indeed, it is not unusual and very much in keeping with the post- or para-cultural (as one speaks of *para-pharmacology* or *parapsychology*) idiolect that, when asked, "who is this film by?" he answers by naming the lead actor or actress. And if he does use the expression *a film by* on his own initiative, what follows this *by* is the name of the film's star. In point of ownership, initiative, and authority, he sees no more difference between an article written *about* someone and an article written *by* someone than he does between a film made by someone and a film in which someone is featured. If there is a difference, it is to the advantage of the actor: in his mind, the film belongs more to the actor than to the filmmaker, a role he neither understands nor, above all, attends to in any way.

It will be said that what I am depicting here is a non-cultural condition rather than a post-cultural one – a condition of ignorance, which has always existed, rather than the present condition of culture. But the new condition of culture is that it no longer has one, at least in the public sphere. Rather than being an implicit repertory of shared references, which can serve as a meeting place for a people or a nation, it is to the contrary a private affair, a hobby like any other, a little eccentric and even a little ridiculous, like tyrosemiophilia or sigillography. What is tacitly implied is not knowledge but ignorance: it is the latter and the latter alone that is being addressed. Even in the pages of the so-called prestige press, journalists are instructed to no longer speak of Gainsborough, Musset, or Nietzsche but of *the English painter Thomas Gainsborough (1727-1785)*, *the romantic poet Alfred de Musset (1810-1847)*, and *the German philosopher Friedrich Nietzsche (1844-1900)*. The possibility that the reader might have access to dictionaries, encyclopedias, or search engines and might see it as his job to briefly inquire into matters he finds it difficult to follow is not for a moment entertained. The problem with this approach is that, since ignorance has been established (alas, doubtless with good reason) as the single currency of public life, the only foundation upon which we can rely with absolute hyperdemocratic confidence, one must always return to it, always start over from the beginning, just as in the classroom one must teach to the level of the worst student, such that not only is no progress made, with knowledge always diminishing and the average level dropping from one week to the next, but culture indefinitely recedes further beyond reach. The sad result of thirty or forty years of mass education and intense cultural promotion *à la Jack Lang* is that newspapers no longer have readers. There are many reasons for this, it is true, but the simplest and most parsimonious is simply that our fellow-citizens *no longer know how to read*, that their attention span and capacity for concentration rarely exceeds one minute, and that they find it intolerable that a political article should have anything to say about *Boulangism*, since what do baguettes and croissants[xx] have to do with it after all.[3] However much editors-in-chief might beg their journalists (ever younger, ever more credentialed, ever less educated, ever less well paid) to write ever more simply, to use fewer and fewer words, to avoid employing subordinates as much as possible ("But I don't even have a secretary!"), the increasingly unimpressive result is nevertheless less and less understood. For readers convinced, unless they have a PhD, that a minister's portfolio refers to a government minister "from a diverse background,"[xxi] it is all too complex, all too pretentious. This is why literature majors end up working in business, their employers believing that they can at least count upon them to intelligibly respond to clients and suppliers.

As least as much as architecture and music (including "music" in the most recent sense of the term), cinema and cinephilia (and their divorce) are very clear examples of what I have just observed regarding the gradual elimination of the concept of the *author* from the public mind. But a word must doubtless be said here, even if for the last time, about *actors*, who, alongside famous athletes (themselves also *performers*), have unsurprisingly become media darlings and the new masters of the world—sometimes quite literally, as we saw with Ronald Reagan and, more recently, the ex-Terminator, Arnold Schwarzenegger. And the masters of the world who did not start out as actors, professionally speaking, surround themselves with actors, take pride in their friendship on equal terms with actors, model themselves after them,

---

3.   This is attested by Jean-François Kahn, in *Le Monde*, on Sunday, 6 January and Monday, 7 January.

claim to be starstruck by them, and indeed are starstruck by them, after the fashion of our current president (though in his case they are mainstream actors with "popular appeal" rather than great actors in the cultural sense, who are admired by their peers and by lovers of theater and good cinema). The only way to recognizably achieve greatness here is to "make good box office." And this is not just the case in the performing arts – unless one is to consider all art, in our media-saturated society, to be performing art. In Yasmina Reza's book about Nicolas Sarkozy,[xxii] since we happen to be speaking of him in passing, the President is heard saying that he wants to meet Marc Lévy, offering this explanation:

"I'm sorry, but a guy who sells millions of copies? Yeah, I'm interested . . ."

One could hardly do a better job underscoring the natural affinities of hyperdemocracy (or merely media-conditioned democracy, with its incessant public opinion polling) and para-culture. At least Marc Lévy, as far as we know, only owes his success to his books. Most of the other authors we see on the sets of so-called cultural programs are not famous because they have written books; they have written books because they are famous. It is thanks to their prior celebrity that publishers have published them and it is thanks to this celebrity that the reading public buys their books and they are invited on to literary talk shows. Instead of *literary* talk shows, one would do better to speak of *bookish*, or *bookstore*, or *bookistic* shows (shows "that concern books"). In general, literature only occupies a miniscule place among books and this already miniscule place is becoming trifling on television, as is also the case on the radio to a hardly lesser degree. Here as elsewhere and on the pretext of what Laure Adler used to call "deciphering the news" when she still called the shots at France Culture (and this was what she considered to be the essential mission of the station she managed and is her idea of culture *today*, in the post-heritage era) – here as elsewhere, on the radio, on television and in libraries, in newspapers and magazines, authors and properly *literary* works are suffocated by the pressure of the social sciences. But as they are still too cultural for audiences molded by thirty-plus years of mass education, the social sciences are in their turn driven from the field by politics, political debates, "political literature," books written by male and female politicians (or their ghost writers), in other words by the very actors of the news cycle, which no one even pretends to "decipher" anymore, drowning as it is in the squid ink of ideological dogmatism and the desire to "educate" the public. For thus is it now known, this perpetual and omnipresent, pseudo-antiracist, and hyperdemocratic indoctrination, a standing insult to all citizens and adults. Even politics ultimately finds itself driven from this essentially televisual public square by entertainment news and celebrity gossip. Indeed, it becomes indistinguishable from them since they remain the only form in which politics can still lay claim, if only for the sake of tolerance, to a legitimate place on air during primetime viewing hours.

A curious effect of the immense progress that has supposedly been made in spreading culture among the public, as Jack Lang and other fanatical sycophants of the disaster idyllically describe it, is that everything has as it were been taken down a notch, if not more. Just as, in the universities, instructors and students must permanently strive to make up for the work not done in high schools, in high school compensate as best they can for the negligence of middle school, in middle school plug the gaping holes left by elementary school curricula, in elementary school attempt to instill in pupils the few indispensable foundations that kindergarten did not put in place, and in kindergarten, I presume, vainly struggle to make up for the irremediable shortcomings of pedagogy (this time, in the true sense of the adjective) entailed by the currently dominant (hyperdemocratic) conceptions of the family and parental authority – so in the same way do the television stations and radio stations officially devoted to or designated as "cultural" (in the case of France, I am mainly thinking of Arte and France Culture)[xxiii] pride themselves on performing the role that the channels and general interest stations of public broadcasting fail, in spite of their mission statements, to perform.

Arte airs a few documentaries, some excellent, most incredibly botched, on various pressing issues of the day or on some country or other in the world. The rest of the time, excepting the occasional opera or play from the classical repertory, it presents dubbed – that is, adulterated and thus non-cultural and non-cinephilic – versions of a few masterpieces from the history of cinema. Much more often, it is nasty little Finnish, German, or Armenian films that only owe their cultural credentials to the fact that they were filmed on a shoestring budget, beneath a dangling lightbulb, the shaking camera almost perceptible. As culture is known for its impecuniousness, it is by this impecuniousness that, in a sort of Pavlovian reflex, one is asked to recognize culture. And if by any chance the theme chosen for the evening – for example, the Hanseatic League or High Middle Ages – does exhibit some true cultural ambition, this single instance of ambition allows Arte to sleep peacefully and rest on its laurels, with the feeling of a job well done, no matter that this subject, which promised to satisfy the last stalwarts of culture (in the true sense of the word), is given the "docu-fiction" treatment, with capes, swords, and scabbards, to say nothing of the synthetic images that, by their ugliness, stupidity, and lack of relevance to the stated subject, would cause even the producers of children's educational programming to blush. *Caroline Chérie* serving as the principal illustration of the French Revolution, *Mayerling* of Habsburg Vienna, *Maciste contre Troie* of Homeric literature, *French Cancan* of the history of impressionism, and so on.[xxiv]

While this happens, France Culture, fully occupied as it is with "deciphering the news," invites a hundred times more sociologists, trade unionists, politicians, judges, and human rights activists than it does writers, philosophers, artists, and scholars. And, by dint of programs about the working conditions of café servers, the tragedy of the salt marshes, or the life of female prison inmates (all programs that would perfectly suit France Inter if France Inter was not so busy following "music" news), France Culture almost never has an occasion to mention the Greek philosopher Plato (5th-4th century B.C.), the Italian architect Palladio (1508-1580), Maine de Biran, Cyprian Norwid, or either Manzoni. Under the alibi of "deciphering" (an alibi that fools no one), culture is everywhere banished by its diametrical opposite: *news* ("Alvaro Melian Lafinur, we've invited you to join us because you've had some very important news this week . . ."). That is, by the dictatorship of the present, the ever-closer adherence to the moment, the general coincidence of what is contemporary with what is happening, of oneself with the self.

There is no need, moreover, to place excessive blame on these poor institutions. They chase after their meager audience as best they can and their dereliction merely reflects the situation created by thirty-plus years of a collapsing educational system and the decimation, nay the unsystematically systematic eradication of the cultivated class. No doubt these channels would like nothing more than to broadcast *genuinely* cultural programming from dawn to dusk. But, if only by absenting themselves, their listeners and viewers have made it clear that this is not what they desire. After one or two generations of teaching ignorance, media stupefaction, and the social erasure of the traditional recipients of art and knowledge, who have not been replaced by others, there is no longer any audience for culture *strictu senso* – none of sufficient size, in any case – in the view of those who run television stations, whose eyes are glued to the ratings reports upon which their jobs depend. There is no more audience in the public square for anything other than straight entertainment; no more audience for anything other than immediate information about the immediate moment; no more audience for anything that does not faithfully hold up a mirror to *oneselfism*; and no more audience, *a fortiori*, for what must rather often be called *boredom*, the beautiful boredom of culture – that delay, that detour, that postponement of meaning and of understanding, of enjoyment and intellection, by which one may so often recognize great works, great ideas, and advanced learning, together with what they demand of their aspirants in terms of mediation, temporary alienation, self-detachment, and non-coincidence, demands that are, in many cases, the conditions of their brilliance.

There is little doubt that an improbable effort to restore cultural values, freeing them from the obligation, so contrary to their nature, to always grow the audience – and yet it would doubtless grow but very slowly and incrementally, without sacrificing anything of the hierarchical, selective, and classificatory essence of culture, art, and knowledge – that such an effort would adopt as one of the first

measures to be taken the creation of a *truly* cultural television channel and radio station since these essential roles are no longer fulfilled
elsewhere. Their programming would not cost much, for, once again,
it is not culture that requires significant expenditures but rather the
eternal and tedious amusement of ignorance, which must always start
again from zero. These undertakings need only draw upon the reser-
voir of excellence that still exists, though driven underground: that
of science, art, hermeneutics, erudition, and beauty. Theater, opera,
"films d'auteurs" from all eras, all countries, scholars, artists, connois-
seurs, art historians, writers, musicians, philosophers, and thinkers –
all would finally be allowed to speak without constant interruption or
being forced to talk over one another. Without a doubt such channels
would quickly come to be meeting places for those who still believe in
the "life of the mind," as Alain Finkielkraut nostalgically calls it, and
which are so cruelly lacking in the public sphere, places of safety from
which a sort of foundation or a sanctuary for culture could be discreetly
reestablished in the geographic, virtual, intellectual, and media landscape. It would only be right that radio and above all television should
have a chance to repair, through their intelligence and virtue, some of
the many evils they have caused or rather that have, with their aid, been
caused by the hyperdemocratic and sensationalist misuse of the tremendous possibilities they offer. Indeed, all technologies, *technology as such*,
and science itself should make it a point of pride to undo part of what
they have done, to rebuild what they have destroyed, to technically, sci-
entifically, methodically correct the most regrettable marginal effects of
the undeniable, if misguided, progress they have brought.

Some are even more radical in this regard and call into question
the technological revolution itself, obviously starting with the most
significant and spectacular of its contemporary aspects, the cyber-
netic, electronic, and webmatic revolution of the Internet. I do not
myself subscribe to this point of view, having as I do too much faith
in the marvelous new resources that computers and the Internet have
conferred on research, on the preservation and diffusion of texts, on
thought itself, on the *brain* (let us not shrink from the word), on the
very nature of concept and meaning, and thus on philosophy and how

we conceive the world as well as, quite simply, on literature. I cannot therefore plead on behalf of the book and the book alone. Fortunately, the only thing that threatens its existence is the ever-dwindling number of readers. But it would be a mistake to associate culture too narrowly with the book. Literature, to stay with the subject an instant, existed well before the book and, supposing that it survives, could very well exist without it or thanks to other platforms.

Indeed, the immense majority of books (and this is nothing new, even if the proportions keep getting worse) have absolutely nothing to do with literature nor do they claim otherwise. In fact, most of them have nothing to do with thought, art, intelligence, or knowledge. This is one of the points on which the figures advanced by the friends of the disaster – those who claim that "standards are rising," as the now hallowed slogan, at once pathetic and comically sinister, would have it, and that culture is gaining ground – are false. Even when they are not false in themselves, they are false in their supposed implications. Once again with the possible exception of Jack Lang, the friends of the disaster no longer dare report *overall* victories of culture, or victories in its favor, the sole mention of which would render them ridiculous given all the evidence to the contrary. But it is not unheard of for them to boast of *partial* victories, cases in which, here and there, reading has improved, more books are sold, or sought after, or the "school-age population" is consuming more written work. And it is of course quite possible that there are particular cases in which this is not false, although this is certainly not the way things have tended. But the statistics advanced in support of this splendid progress are misleading even when they are correct, for not only do so many books, including many of the most sought after, have nothing to do with culture and add nothing to intelligence, excepting the purely ocular and mental exercise of reading, supposing that they are indeed read; but, particularly when it is children who spend time with them, these books actually diminish knowledge, are an insult to intelligence, and above all permanently distort one's taste.

Indeed, culture – and this holds as much for the culture of an individual as it does for that of a group or a society in its entirety – is not uniquely defined by what it *includes*, by what is a part of it, what in-disputably belongs to and emerges from it. It is also defined – and one grasps here that we are moving closer to something intolerable, un-avowable, appalling – by what it *excludes*, by what is not part of it, what does *not* pertain to it. What characterizes a good library and makes it easier for one to take its measure is as much the books that are not there, that are not worthy of it and that not only would not add any-thing to it but would spoil it, as the books that are there. In the same way, a good museum and, *a fortiori*, a good art gallery, which has less space at its disposal, establishes its quality as much by the works that one does not see there, that it is out of the question that one should see there, as by those that hang on its walls. It is sad to say and dull to recall that each of us only has at his disposal, as I have said before, a narrowly circumscribed time on earth, and all our efforts and all our care will do nothing to render this time indefinitely extendable. And I do not regret having elsewhere proposed, as one of the possible defini-tions of culture, "the clear awareness of the preciousness of time." The cultivated man never has too much time; in fact, he never has enough for everything there is to read, see, hear, know, learn, understand, and love. The intelligible world, by its sheer size, is incommensurable with his intelligence. The existing world, in its immensity, is out of all proportion with his thirst for knowledge and the possibilities of his memory. By its infinitude, that which is worthy of love exceeds his love in every direction. At every moment he must make choices, which is to say abandon certain paths, certain books, certain areas of study, and certain pastimes. And he is what he is as much by virtue of what he reads, what he hears, and what he studies as by what he does not read, what he does not give time to, what he refuses to waste his time on – this time that culture renders precious.

One of the saddest signs of the great deculturation underway is, of course, the endlessly reiterated demand, by ever-larger populations, that they be *given something to do*, by which I do not mean a job, work, or a career, for that is something else altogether. Rather, their demand is for something to occupy their leisure time, to distract them from their encroaching mortality, to kill time. Everyone seems to agree that it is the job of the state and of various local authorities to dispense this essential service, without which young people, in particular, find themselves with nothing to do (if one is to believe their complaints) apart from vegetate in squares, neighborhoods, and building corridors where there is nothing to do and where, because there is nothing to do, they must abandon themselves to the most natural of activities of the human species when it is left to its own devices: that is, disturbing, bothering, vandalizing, destroying, harming, injuring, causing a nuisance – a *nocence* – and everything that is contrary to in-nocence. The patent failure of mass education may be distinctly read in the intensity of this bizarre demand and the quite humiliating grievance that it entails for those who make it, for they are admitting that, in a society in which so many of the pleasures of intelligence are free, they are neither free enough nor accomplished enough to manage time for which they have no use.

It is also hardly a cause for rejoicing, despite the futile jubilation of statistics, to see so many parents rejoice, supposing they concern themselves with these matters, that their children spend their time with books or even just a little bit of time now and then with a book. Books can deculturate them just as much as video games or their iPod – except, of course, and this reservation should be understood as implicitly present throughout this little essay, except, of course, and this is now what is most frequently the case, except, of course, if one gives to *culture* an entirely different meaning from that of intimacy with the best that art, thought, music, and literature have produced from the point of view (which can always be revised and broadened) of history's best judges taken together, except, of course, if one understands and means to convey, in using the word *culture*, generational culture, group culture, street culture, neighborhood culture, the culture of results, etc., which cultures can very well be and are almost by definition so many cultures of ignorance.

It is not surprising, moreover, that, at the heart of the media system, whose mark, within culture understood in its impoverished contemporary sense, has been the replacement of literature by the book (in the best of cases, obviously, for the book itself, it must not be forgotten, is still very threatened), it is *actors* who occupy center stage, to the detriment of *authors*, even when the former are in fact the authors of their books, which, if I understand correctly, is not always the case. Actors and, more generally, *performers* have taken the place of writers as the emblematic protagonists of what passes for cultural life. It falls to them rather than to intellectuals, philosophers, or novelists, to say nothing of poets, to express what is, perhaps not the general sentiment, but the dominant sentiment, the moral sentiment of the media majority, the *conscience* of the age. And it must be admitted that they acquit themselves of this task with rare conviction, as if it had become an inevitable parallel activity in their profession. They acquit themselves of it as citizens, of course; this is something they never let us forget. But they also do so, at a level that does not call their sincerity into question at all, *as actors* (which they remain) and as performers, narrators, storytellers, something that obviously does not in the least entail the same type of relationship to speech as that of the discarded authors and in particular writers among them. An entire society has more or less consciously (but that is not the question) entrusted to actors, that is to say, to people whose job it is to say what they are told to say, the responsibility to publicly express, in the media, what they believe should be said, thought, and felt. Actors are not asked to *certify* what they declare or take full responsibility for it; they are only asked to say it well. It is right, in this sense, that they should be the established idols, intellectually and above all ideologically (though here we may be splitting hairs), of an era marked by a major crisis of words, of words in their fullest sense, by which I mean one's *word of honor*, of an era where commitments commit one to nothing, where statements are only words placed one after the other in an uncertain order, and where promises implicate no one and are all accompanied by the tacit understanding that they need only be kept in the very unlikely event that there is no kind of obstacle to their fulfillment and no inconvenience to those who make them. It is no coincidence that this devaluation of speech, which is observed everywhere (as if, starting with plumbers and politicians, it has spread to the entire social body, such that its consequences are not only moral but social and economic as well), should coincide with a collapse not only of syntax but also, more strangely, with a very un-expected yet systematic inversion, it seems, of what was until now the order of words in the French language.[xxv]

The media's suppression of mediation (of that mediation for which syntax is the linguistic tool, just as it is the tool of incongruity in the person, of the non-coincidence of self with self, of the struggle against *oneselfism* and its barbarisms) can be amusingly observed in the de-mand for mediation itself, which is only one more attempt to forego the mediation of mediations, by which I mean culture, this detour, this way of inquiring among the dead, among books, pine trees, and tombs how things are regarding ourselves, the world, and life. One need only consider the comical and obstinate demand for more arts education and from the earliest grades so often expressed by the very people who have destroyed the school system! What might an arts education be, one wonders, in an age of great deculturation, when words have no meaning, when names mean nothing, when the very awareness of time, of there having been time before us, centuries of time, has not been aroused by the slightest transmission and is not perceptible in the most meager inheritance? What might an arts education be if it is not grafted onto (as indeed it should be) some suggestion of general culture, some chronological structure, some framework of normative appreciation, some, dare I say, notion of *hierarchy*? In fact, we know all too well what such an arts education consists of and we are all too familiar with the art that it produces – it is that which long ago leapt from kindergarten into the halls of schools of Fine Arts, not without adorning the naves of our poor churches along the way, the walls, seats, and windows of the metro, the corridors and stairwells of our univer-sities. I have named this delight of child psychiatry, this official art of glorified *oneselfism*, this mobilization of the citizen-horde, be it casual or devoted, the *child's drawing*. And what indeed can the arts teacher teach to students who have learned nothing from their French teacher or history teacher, to say nothing of the priest (we shall not mention the cultivated parent here, if only to signal our virtue and remain in the realm of statistical plausibility)? He can only teach them how to be themselves, the poor wretches, to be literally themselves *above all*, as if they were not already sufficiently so, and encourage them to express themselves, as if they had something to express, something other than their incapacity to do so, for want of training – an incapacity that can be moving, even pitiful and, it cannot be denied, shocking but that is of dubious artistic value.

It is as "*mediators*," moreover, that these guides, attendants and speakers in museums and exhibitions are officially known, their task being to present the unprepared crowds with the works they find themselves looking at. In short, they perform on their behalf, in their stead, and in a great rush, the work of mediation that the great deculturation has dissuaded, exempted, or prevented them from doing, all while hastening them, by every species of advertising, toward the most media-hyped and mediatized places of high culture. The goal is always to use culture and its effect to attract audiences who would not "naturally" be so attracted – which is to say, of course, "culturally" attracted – to sites, rites, habits, cultural practices, or cultural behaviors. Post-cultural society does not believe in personal mediation, in working on oneself (except of course if the intent is to become even more oneself), no more than it believes in long meditation, education, or cultural heritage. Or rather yes, it would like to believe in these things but it considers it possible, quite possible, to get by without them. This society does not even think that mediation by desire is indispensable. It thinks that desire can always come later. It wants the act first, in the hope that this will be what triggers desire, just as ancient religions taught that one must begin by throwing oneself at the foot of the altar and faith would come afterward.

In fact, there are many domains in which the numbers alleged by those who deny the great deculturation or even earnestly maintain that the last decades have witnessed progress and development in culture (for there is always someone who will do so) – there are many domains, then, in which these numbers are indeed rising and even rising spectacularly. Admittedly, there are fewer and fewer people attending classical music concerts; admittedly, there are fewer and fewer bookstores; admittedly, the modest success in book sales represents a number of copies sold far inferior to what was the case in the past. But, as the friends of the disaster never fail to remind us, there are infinitely more students in high school, more students in the universities and ten times, twenty times, even one hundred times more people in museums. Be it libraries, theaters, opera houses, historical monuments, or art galleries (and it is no different when it comes to mountain hiking trails), the goal is to always draw in more and more people, people who otherwise would not have had much interest, if any, in going and would never have thought of taking the initiative on their own. This goal is well-intended, one would hope. Those who nurture it probably believe that these people will benefit from the experience they wish to share with them, that their lives will be enriched by it and their horizons broadened. This is not totally guaranteed, for what culture offers – and, in a broad sense, what nature offers, the appreciation of which is highly cultural – can hardly be appreciated without at least some cultural resources, which the schools, in theory, are expected to provide. There are, of course, examples of what one might call a *miracle*: examples of abrupt conversion to art or the love of knowledge. These are not exceedingly rare but they are infrequent and their results often disappointing. A little less exceptional are the cases of brief and transient wonder, of the favorable first impression, a mixture of surprise and respect for convention, which is dissolved in what is perhaps a grateful return to routine. What seems to be most common by far is nevertheless a shameful fiasco, measurable by the failure of isolated cultural experience to have any effect on people's lives, on their ways of seeing and living. These people, whom clever marketing has encouraged to go into raptures before a Velasquez or a Degas, are more easily measured in the quality and the reality of their ecstasy than one would like to admit, if only by their *other* ecstasies and their *other* tastes, such as they are manifested internally, for example, or in the nature of the memories they bring back with them from their trips. It is significant that the Louvre, that temple of beauty and artistic excellence, which houses some of the highest expressions of human genius and thus some of the most precious objects of culture, has begotten, ever since it became a museum for the masses, an entire neighborhood dedicated to ugliness and the trade in ugliness. Admittedly, in the era when museums were still essentially a bourgeois affair, travelers might gladly return from Florence or a Venetian honeymoon with reproductions that were not always in the best taste or evidence of any very sure grasp of the masterpieces they had glimpsed. But one did not see great institutions of cultural preservation propagate vulgarity in abundance, generating or rather secreting around themselves the antithesis of their raison d'être; thereby also insinuating that they are not fulfilling their mission and that the isolated, one-off frequentation of their rooms and galleries has absolutely no effect on people who have no appreciation and have been educated to no appreciation of culture as a total experience.

Readily assuming the tone and attitude of a Fouquier-Tinville[xxvi] so as to frighten and dissuade anyone as soon as they seem on the point of recognizing their protégé for what he is, the friends of the disaster will not fail to ask by what right one can permit oneself to judge the quality of another's aesthetic appreciation, an intimate matter by definition, or even claim to know anything about it at all. They will speak of *contempt*, as they are always so quick to do and as they have always done with such great ballistic efficacy, for in hyperdemocratic society no one can safely allow themselves to be convinced to despise anyone or anything whatsoever, with the obvious exception of the duly catalogued forces of evil, themselves the object of ritual denunciation. And if it is indeed true that we poor mortals are in no position to sound out another person's soul or loins, those who clamor that "standards are rising" and other professionals of sociocultural optimism are doubtless not wrong to question our ability and standing, as simple amateurs, to evaluate the degree and nature of the public's feeling before a given masterpiece. In this instance, one must nevertheless be careful not to underestimate, whether out of conformism or fear, our capacity to know or measure. It is doubtless true that we cannot claim to dependably judge, from one individual to the next, the quality of a facial expression or its internal resonances. Barthes, it is often said, took pride in his ability, when sitting in a café, to *hear* his neighbors at the next table "not understand one another." If so, we can certainly boast of our ability to *see* museum visitors *not see*, even to *hear* them *not look* – often a majority of them, even a sizeable majority.

And perhaps this is not so worrisome after all. These hordes who are thrust into museums without the least preparation or possibility of deriving any benefit from them and who spend two or three hours there because this is what has been planned for them by their tour operator (who thereby keeps them busy without excessive cost to himself, all the while enhancing the prestige of his tours and outings and giving them the best sort of cultural alibi), these multitudes do not have much to lose apart from some time they would have spent elsewhere on something more amusing but less symbolically profitable. And it is not at all impossible – it is even quite probable, proven, vouched for, and demonstrated – that, in the midst of this flood, a few individuals, whose proportion remains to be determined, take pleasure, feeling, or instruction from the experience and are forever enriched by it. In other words, this is not where the danger lies. Nor is the danger to the works themselves, though the crush does put them at greater risk (and this even without considering the fact that, among so many visitors, if such is the word, there is a much greater likelihood that various madmen, vandals, heedless people, misfits, and troublemakers will be found among them and that these latter might without a second thought and even with satisfaction, pleasure, and a sense of justice served contemplate committing the kind of material damage to which paintings, sculptures, and other precious objects are by their nature vulnerable, when they are not outright destroyed). The losers in this mass incursion into what were once sanctuaries of silence, meditation and individual intimacy with art and thought are the old regulars, who no longer recognize the places they once haunted and end up becoming sick of them. These people are dying, it will be said, or will be soon enough. Yes, but even so, they were a species, a human type, supremely precious to civilization. And with them a certain kind of relationship to painting, art, and nature is disappearing, the very relationship that constituted culture and proceeded from it: this type of relationship is dissolving because it no longer has a space of its own, having had to share it with hundreds of thousands of people who are not only totally unprepared to draw enjoyment or enrichment from it but feel no desire to do so.

In the field of culture, which is all hills and valleys, nuance, differences in levels of quality, merit, and talent, there can only be equality
from the bottom up. The movement is always the same, whether we are
talking about teaching or art, music, scholarship, science or cultural
life: on the pretext of equality, hyperdemocracy, which is structurally
incapable of raising the middling and inferior cultural levels, only wins
democratic victories by lowering the higher level, to the point of having
nearly made it disappear altogether along with the cultured class that
was as much its condition as its expression.

Chateaubriand believed there were secret affinities between equality and tyranny. There are others between hyperdemocracy – that is to
say (and I repeat) between the implementation of equality in domains
where it has no business – and the reign of money, submission to the
powers of money, and avaricious docility before the laws of the market.
Thus, by attracting millions of visitors to museums and claiming to
bring in ever more, not only does it become impossible for museums
to fulfill the mission for which they were created, but one ends up
with masses of people who, in the places that advertising has encouraged them to go, have no idea what to do, see, understand, or love and
must be kept occupied in one way or another, especially since there are
immense profits to be extracted from them. Hence the proliferation
around great museums (and now lesser ones) of shopping malls, bou-
tiques, restaurants, cafeterias, and gift shops, where the average visitor
probably spends more time than he does with the artworks themselves.

These invasive sideshows bring in a lot of money but they also cost
a lot, though not always to the same people or the same institutions.
In fact, the curators, directors, and presidents of major museums are
very anxious to see to it that the gigantic investments they have had
to make and which they must constantly continue and renew in the
frantic pursuit of "cash flow" do not go to waste for themselves or for
the legal entities they oversee. Chosen as much for their mastery of the
established ideological jargon, readiness to use it on every occasion,
and demonstrated willingness to enthusiastically submit to the hyperdemocratic demands of the powers that be (and in this case it does
not matter whether the former are "democratic," "on the left," or "on

the right" since the desire for "social cohesion" is a bipartisan affair) as they are for their artistic or "scientific" skills, they find themselves in a situation where the qualities they are expected to display are more those of the businessman or skilled administrator than they are those of the scientist, researcher, historian, or art expert.

It is significant and indicative of the lack of connection between hyperdemocracy and democracy that, wherever hyperdemocracy is to be found (and it is to be found everywhere), men of culture are turned into corporate managers or replaced by them. In a neat paradox, as soon as equality exits its legitimate domain (equality of rights from birth among citizens and equal opportunity), business, money, and the struggle of great interests are everywhere to be found. This is true of museums and it is even more so of television, which we have seen become ever more commercial, that is to say, ever less cultural and ever more sensationalistic as it became widespread among the general public and television sets appeared in every home, subjecting the entire population to advertising, which naturally demanded ever baser programming, programming that was ever less demanding in a cultural sense and ever more immediately pleasing and in keeping with the requirements of the majority since it is this majority that brings in the most money, thus rendering what Patrick Le Lay, former head of TF1, infamously called "available human brain time" ever more valuable.

As soon as everyone had access to television and to the same television programming, it was inevitable, not only that the medium would abandon all cultural pretense or posture whatsoever, wiping itself clean of culture, but also that it would become ever more thoroughly steeped in money, the one phenomenon supporting the other and vice versa. Nor has hyperdemocracy, inspired as it officially is by an ideal of economic equality and the rejection of monied privilege, prevented institutions of learning from making their bed with trade and high finance.

Ever since the arrival of mass education, the school system has been a leading terrain for the competition and conquest of "brands," presenting as it does a nearly limitless supply of choice victims – students, who are learning less and less – for their marketing and lifetime conditioning campaigns. Books are always too expensive for parents but not shoes, or backpacks, or hooded jackets bearing the most sought-after logos. And if many teachers, the oh-so renowned "profs,"[xxvii] are treated with contempt or fail to earn the *respect* so vehemently demanded of *them* by their students, it is not merely due to their all-too-frequent abandonment of formality in speech, dress, and bearing, not merely due to their inability to maintain a proper distance in the pedagogical relationship, not merely due to their social and cultural proletarianization, however glaring and headlong it may be; it is also quite simply due to the comparative modesty of their remuneration, though one must immediately qualify this by adding that the relationship is not as strong as one might believe since the great deculturation is no less conspicuous in much better remunerated professions, such as surgery and law.

In truth, it is not so much culture that is expensive. Democratic progress, the true progress of true democracy, long ago made entire domains of culture, even the most precious ones, accessible to the very poor – without always, it is true, showing them how to make the most of the advantages on offer or enrich themselves thereby. What is ruinously expensive is the exhausting need to keep ignorance occupied, amusing it, channeling it, and satisfying it for reasons of social peace, safety, and profit. This demand is excessively costly but we must grant that it can also be very lucrative. It obviously requires great investments but such investments are generally very profitable.

Ignorance is boring by definition and is thus always hungry for novelty, even cultural novelty if necessary, but it is not the culture but the novelty itself that matters. In the days gone by when culture still kept peacefully to its little corner, only speaking to its "natural" audience (I trust it is unnecessary to indefinitely repeat the obligatory precautionary parentheses here), it could rest on its laurels, even making do with them brilliantly, for its *laurels* were precisely its raw – or "natural," I was about to write – material, "naturally" and constantly replenishing and broadening itself at the margins or cutting edge. Yet under the reign of that oxymoron, hyperdemocratic culture, the representatives of culture must constantly offer up something new. It is now everywhere taken as a self-evident truth – and quite wrongly,

I believe – that a museum, site, garden, or even a historical monument that wishes to be considered "vibrant" must every year or even several times a year offer a new exhibit, a new showing, a seasonal "theme," a new entertainment center, or an interactive area suddenly deemed indispensable. That which was stable *par excellence* and served as a reference and a fixed point is caught up in a perpetual motion machine, a ruinous headlong rush. Yet this is not at all what culture in the true sense demands. Culture was perfectly satisfied with yesterday's museums, which were calm, silent, nearly deserted, and entirely devoted to the unending contemplation of works of art and their meditation. Culture required innovation, of course – exhibitions, for example, and among them exhibitions of new artists, without which culture would have become a frozen conservatory. Yet a conservatory is what culture primarily is, even if never exclusively: innovation has always served to shine new light on what has come before, to incessantly make new discoveries in what was thought settled, something to which everything that has been established as *classical* so eminently lends itself. Among other things, that which was established, museum-worthy, *classical* served to endlessly inspire and spark innovation. But the two roles were quite distinct and the second never threatened the first. Today, by contrast, museums are obliged to dedicate ever more of their space to temporary exhibitions, to the point that very often one can no longer even see or can only see poorly and in a much-diminished way their permanent collections, which are driven into storerooms by the whirlwind of different "activities" taking place around them. And, in an entirely parallel fashion, literary production finds itself caught up in an uninterrupted series of nervous seasonal agitations and "ephemeral sensations," depriving writers of the time they need to establish themselves, books of the time they need to develop, bookstores of the space they need to build up their inventories, and critics of any ambition to investigate or pursue literary history.

Culture used to love castles and parks for what they were – castles and parks – and in no way asked that zoos, entertainment centers, or Ferris wheels be grafted onto them. What requires ever more massive injections of public money is the desire to create desires that do not exist and needs that are not expressed on their own because they are not felt and which one must therefore permanently seek to arouse. All the places of high culture are retrofitted for the sole benefit of ignorance and, as a result, they are rendered inaccessible to culture or are stripped of all appeal, virtue, and educational value. One nevertheless expects a proper return on these expenditures – and not just a cultural one, to be sure. Investors make no attempt to hide this, seeing it rather as a point of pride and an entirely justified one at that. The goal, in their jargon, is to leverage the *economic potential* of a site or monument that passing travelers and tourists had always had the bad habit of ignoring, whereas in fact it is essential to the economic well-being of the county, department, or even region, of its restaurateurs, innkeepers, souvenir merchants, pastry chefs, donkey renters, and show business operators that foreign visitors should now linger a while longer, stay the night in the neighborhood or spend two or three days there rather than a single afternoon. To pick just one example among many: one can thus imagine the regional council of Centre Val-de-Loire deciding that the Chateau of Chambord[xxviii] must be given a theme park or tourist center implicitly inspired by Disneyland or Parc Astérix but nevertheless embellished with stronger educational and "artistic" pretentions, if only to put up a brave face and pacify homegrown curmudgeons. And little matter if the Chateau, caught between these lakes of parasitic commercialism and entertainment, loses all interest and especially all seductive appeal for those who loved it as it once was and only asked that it be preserved as thoroughly as possible.

Just as the Middle Ages were never medieval enough for the troubadour's tastes, Byzantium never Byzantine enough for the Byzantinists, and the Orient never picturesque enough for the Orientalists, culture is never welcoming enough for the ignorant, never sufficiently approachable, visible, or identifiable as such – in a word, never "cultural" enough. The latter must endlessly improve the former, alter it, service it, offer more convincing, recognizable, and narcissistically gratifying imitations of it. But soon all these variations on Las Vegas, large and small, no longer suffice, for a sense of honor and pride in authenticity takes hold of ignorance and all the merchants who work between the cardboard columns of its temples, boasting of their philanthropy and philological scruple, demand that great works of art – Chambord, the Louvre in Paris and the Louvre in Abu-Dhabi—more closely resemble their doubles, that they participate (for a fee) in their commercial and recreational reconstitutions, that they imitate their imitations. All of which is perfectly in keeping, by the way, with the general suburbanization of reality, the world's *suburb-becoming*, the conversion of its cities into amusement parks and its countryside into subdivisions, shopping malls, and priority development zones.[xxix]

Develop: that's the magic word. Develop for crowds, develop for new audiences, develop for those who would never of their own accord come to the castle, set foot in the museum, never think of plunging themselves into the solitude of seaside or mountain, presuming enough of it still remains after so much thoughtful "development." There is no point in remarking here that what has been rejected is mediation via a school or educational system that continues to fulfill the mission once entrusted to it. But they no longer fulfill this mission, having themselves been far too "developed" for their "new audiences" to still possess the strength and rigor needed to grapple with their duty. In this way, having despaired of attracting new audiences to their properties from a taste and desire, instilled by the school system and university, for beautiful things, great works of art, beautiful landscapes, for monuments to the mind or to history, developers instead develop so as to attract those who would have no inclination to visit their showrooms, galleries, parks, beaches, evergreen forests, and other solitary places as they are but who will (perhaps) agree to come if they are also offered and, soon enough, mainly offered what they really desire, that is, whatever sustains and diverts their ignorance. In most cases, *to develop* is to snatch one away from poetry, silence, and discrimination – that supreme virtue of intelligence and wisdom, now become a dirty word – so as to surrender one to entertainment and profit. While this may not precisely be to destroy, it is to waste or discard.

Cultural investments cost a great deal but generate great financial returns. They generate great financial returns but first they cost a great deal. Cultural hyperdemocracy injects massive amounts of money into the circuits of culture. It is up to the directors of cultural institutions to find this money, all the more so as public funding is always diminishing. They have no other means for doing so than lobbying, *fundraising,* perpetually begging for money from private enterprise, thinly veiled advertising campaigns, or commerce, whether overt or covert, real or disguised – in a word, by renting out their collections. The Louvre, as we said at the beginning, has succumbed to these barely disguised loans in its relationships with Atlanta and Abu Dhabi.[4] These rentals have been justifiably and very politely condemned or, rather, loathed and ridiculed by the head curator of the New York Metropolitan Museum of Art, Patrick Montebello, who rightly draws attention to the ratchet effect created by this massive introduction of commercial and para-commercial practices in the domain of cultural exchange. Those who do not embrace these practices are rapidly put at a financial disadvantage relative to those who do, just as television channels without advertising or that severely restrict advertising are put at a disadvantage relative to those with high advertising revenue when they are forced to compete with the latter. For those who hold to the old ways, it can be difficult to resist. Organizing major exhibitions becomes ever more costly, making the appeal to advertising and media hype ever more necessary in order to attract an ever-larger audience, whose presence alone is capable of minimizing losses or ensuring the financial success of the operation through the purchase of tickets and, above all, the scramble to buy the inevitable "merchandise." In this way, the organizers of major exhibitions find themselves increasingly obliged to focus on the number of visitors and past records in this regard –

---

4. From a January 8th, 2008, article in *Le Monde* entitled "The Minister of Culture and Tourism of the Emirate [of Abu Dhabi] Discusses the Development of the Museum Project that France Will Deliver." *Le Monde*: "The worry, in France, is also artistic. Art is sometimes meant to be provocative. Will it be possible to show everything in the Louvre of Abu Dhabi?" *Minister*: "Our approach is simple: the works must respond to public demand. *I would even dare say to market demand.* We have a history, a culture. Not everything can be done too brutally. But for me there is no taboo." *Le Monde*: "Not even the representation of nudity?" *Minister:* "I think I was pretty clear. My criteria are pragmatic. *We want to attract the maximum number of visitors to our museums.* We will take our cultural constraints into account. *But, little by little, the market will triumph.*" [author's italics]

records that must be beaten all over again. The exhibitions themselves become little more than an organized pandemonium, ever more difficult to negotiate for the last lovers of art. More often than not, the latter must make do with the catalog, when they can afford it, and tell themselves that they will go see this or that painting at the other end of the world if ever they get the chance and if it does not belong to some mysterious and inaccessible "private collection" or other.

I said that cultural investment could yield major profits. This is true but it should be made clear that these profits are in general not of a cultural order and do not necessarily or directly go to the source of these investments. They go, for example, to the tourist industry, whose close ties with culture are always highly suspect. The beneficiaries in this case will be hotel owners, restaurateurs, promoters, and so on, who, attached as they understandably are to their profits, will lobby in favor of cultural programs, whether they be festivals or exhibitions, that attract an ever-greater number of spectators and visitors, who are for them so many potential clients. It is in precisely the same way that buyers of television advertising space, that is, of "available human brain time," pressure channels to adopt programming that can draw ever-larger audiences – that is, programming that is ever more focused on entertainment and ever less on culture. One might have thought this goal was achieved long ago but reality proves that, in this instance, the worst can always get worse. Indeed, it is likely that the above-mentioned buyers do not even need to exert pressure. Programing executives strive hard to anticipate their wishes so that they may boast to them of their ever-growing audiences. That is, so that they can ask more money of them and charge a higher price for the handful of minutes in question. Yet we know only too well how these ever-larger audiences are obtained.

In fact, money has no more to do with culture than it does with education or the quality of life in suburban housing projects. I am not saying that it has *nothing* to do with them; rather, I believe it is mistaken to present or look upon money as the solution to all of the problems that are present in these various domains and to describe its absence or insufficiency as the sole source of all evils only so as to spare oneself from having to look elsewhere, on yet more sensitive terrain. It is true that money has a great deal to do with the production of art and artistic creation in general, which has always been very costly. There is no need to mention those princes who ruined themselves and depleted the coffers of state in order to buy paintings, sculptures, or ancient relics, commission great works by great (or minor) artists and erect grand and sumptuous buildings. That is not what is at issue here. Rather, it is the diffusion of culture among the general public and, let's be frank, among the masses. Yet this is less a matter of money than of education and that is above all the job of schools. And education itself is less a matter of money than a matter of method, of system, of educational, moral, ideological, political, and, one might be tempted to write, *anthropological* system.

There is something touching about the resolutions that various authorities make during times of social crisis, each more violent than the last or more visible than the permanent general crisis, to inject even more money into an already ruinously expensive system that, even if one were to double or triple expenditures, would not yield any better results since its failure is entirely pre-programmed by the absence of selectivity, the lack of authority, the aberration of curricula, the lack of conviction, and the low average quality of the proletarianized teaching corps, the great majority of which today has itself been trained in a system that has been in crisis and decay as long as these crises have lasted and from which it has retained a few great lessons, namely: militant hyperdemocracy; a horror of formality, distance, and mediation; inflamed *oneselfism*, as observable in speech as it is in dress; and of course dogmatic antiracism, which is less a moral code than a corpus of ideological precepts and a great principle of willful blindness. The same holds for all those fine and ambitious "suburban renewal projects." More money will not raise anyone's level when none of the principles of true education prevail. More money will not reduce violence or make the suburbs more congenial when there is no social or national compact among populations, no contract of in-nocence, no similitude, and doubtless no compatibility among the different ways of cohabiting buildings, apartments, and neighborhoods, and probably no chance of "community harmony."

In hyperdemocratic society, money is presented as the solution to everything, sometimes by the rulers themselves, who promise "more neighborhood investment" or to "put more money into culture," as is their elegant way of putting things, and always by the citizens, some of whom are persuaded they will receive more stylish buildings, more peaceful neighborhoods, more "high-performing" schools, while others believe that the various organizations tasked with maintaining a semblance of calm will be more prosperous and their leaders more satisfied. Money being everywhere taken as the sole solution to everything, all that remains between rich and poor, as Nicolas Gomez Davila[xxx] very rightly notes, is money.

Within the single, immense petty-bourgeois cultural class, the privileged are nothing more than poor people who happen to have money: membership in the so-called "middle class" or "bourgeoisie" is nothing more than a question of income and purchasing power, which makes classification easier for statisticians and sociologists. And the truth is that the rich correspond ever more closely to what might once have appeared the grotesque, ill-informed image familiar from popular television programming (to risk being redundant). Their image, ever truer to reality and so admirably illustrated by the Head of the State, is that of a caste that is ostentatious, brutal, and phony, one that often shares many traits with the underworld, a mafia, or a camarilla, and whose main privilege – that most precious in their eyes and in those of their millions of envious and spellbound admirers – is the ability to satisfy all of their whims, starting with the most eccentric among them, thanks to their money. When constructing, publicizing, and maintaining their myth in the eyes of the general public, this immediate satisfaction of whims is without fail underscored by luxury hotels, which have little choice in the matter since all of their clients now come from this caste. And this is also the totally disproportionate possibility offered by the promotion of gambling and the lottery: you will be able to do whatever you please, starting with whatever is most preposterous, and little matter if its "vulgarity would disgust the Canebière," as Bernanos, that good son of the North, put it.[xxxi] To the contrary, the uglier, flashier, and more idiotic a thing is, the better show it will make in the eyes of the world of the most precious power that money and power bestow on you: that of doing or making someone do whatever might strike your fancy without taking the least account of other people's judgment, the power, that is, to be exactly "yourself" (and there is no greater privilege in hyperdemocratic, *oneselfist* society).

Indeed, the new privileged class appears to be mainly composed of people who have acquired their fortune thanks to some winning lottery ticket. Not in the sense that they do not seem to have earned their present opulence through hard work and intelligence, brilliance of mind, or a happy coincidence of their particular genius and the specific genius of the age, but in the sense that they do not seem to have had the time to get used to their riches and use them in exactly the same way poor people would were millions to rain down on their heads overnight. The only rich people left are *nouveaux riches*. And if, by chance, they are not *nouveaux riches*, their children will be soon enough as there is no longer any cultural transmission. The hyperdemocratic education system sees to this, making it a point of hyperdemocratic pride to prevent this transmission, even when there is some risk that it might occur "naturally."

"Give me your children," says the system to parents of all backgrounds. "Little matter that they are rich or poor or that you yourself are cultivated or ignorant: I will turn them into proletarianized petty bourgeois like everyone else, ignorant, useless, unintelligible, self-righteous, antiracist, and well-integrated."

Among several other unexpected consequences, the fact that the only remaining difference between rich and poor is money entails considerably greater social precarity among the privileged classes themselves, who, precisely for this reason, no longer have the time to be *classes* nor, as a result, to fulfill their social and cultural roles. In times past, a family that had for a certain time belonged to the privileged class could maintain this status over several generations even after the collapse of its economic standing. In the time of the nobility but also that of the bourgeoisie – which is to say, until the last third of the last century – ruin did not entail social demotion or did so only very slowly, since class membership was not uniquely determined by income level but also by cultural level and the greater or lesser mastery of certain codes governing bearing, dress, and, above all, language. By contrast, in a deculturated, or post-cultural, or "neo-cultural" society – if one may use this expression to describe a society in which the word *culture* has totally changed meaning, now only referring to people's habits and especially their habits relating to leisure and entertainment – in such a society, the economic collapse of a family *ipso facto* entails its immediate social collapse or at least does so within a generation. The son of a "distinguished" and cultivated family, if he has not applied himself in his studies, lacks intelligence, and fails at school, may very easily be led to contemplate, sometimes with impatience and even envy, becoming a sales clerk in a shoe store or head waiter in a restaurant and request, should he die, that a recording of Sheila or Dalida[xxxii] be played at his funeral.

That said – and this is perhaps a consolation for those concerned – while it much more rigorously brings about social and cultural demotion than was the case in the past, a drop in income or in professional standing, from one generation to the next, is far from being the only thing that can produce this effect, especially at the strictly *cultural* level. Within the formerly privileged classes, a loss of cultural level and the social attitudes pertaining to it is the *norm*, even in the absence of reduced income or a deterioration in professional status or educational attainment. Even if these young people happen to be college-educated and hold the same degrees as their parents, the son or daughter of college-educated parents will have the cultural level and social attitudes characteristic of a level of educational attainment shared by thirty or forty percent of the population, whereas their parents or grandparents had those entailed by a level of educational attainment shared by three or five percent of the population. Here we come up against another one of those strange social or mathematical laws, which we already observed in other, barely distinguishable forms: the real level of a diploma's quality and the social repercussions it entails does not in the least depend on its name or even on the number of years of study it requires but on the number of those who earn it and their proportion within the social body. A baccalaureate degree obtained by eighty percent of an age cohort corresponds *mutatis mutandis* (the material taught no longer being the same) to the level of knowledge attained by eighty percent of an age cohort in other eras. And so on for the other diplomas.

I have spoken elsewhere of the general "petty bourgeoisification" of existence and society and of the "dictatorship of the petty bourgeoisie" insofar as this class, having swallowed up all others and constantly fattening itself on the remains, serving as the meeting place for every neighborhood, suburb, and even the remote countryside, always presents its views as so many self-evident facts, facts that are not only generally accepted but brook no possible contradiction, for by their nature they are unable to imagine, envision, or even conceive of this possibility. The result is that no alternative exists for thought under this regime, it has no exterior, whether in terms of space, which is entirely subjugated to it, starting with that of the media, the only true public space, or in terms of time, which is regularly reduced to the present alone and its values, which are presented as both timeless (and therefore retroactive) and universal. Within this now largely consummated transition to the petty bourgeoisification of the world and its inhabitants, however, within this sprawling *petty-bourgeoisie-becoming* that is life in a post-cultural and especially post-literary regime ("This means," says Agamben, "that the planetary petty bourgeoisie is very likely the form in which humanity is advancing toward its own destruction"),[xxxiii] within this predominant tropism, and therefore accelerating and accentuating it, there is to be observed a very perceptible impetus toward proletarianization, as I have already suggested.

It is easy to spot in students, for example, when they appear on television, or at university protests, or directly if one should venture onto their campuses, which often seem to have more in common with a garbage dumb or the infamous Cour des Miracles[xxxiv] than they do with the proletarian spirit properly so-called (in Rome, let it be noted, the *proletarius* was "he who is only considered useful for the children he begets"). The famous "lack of resources" is ritually invoked in this connection and there is no question that the French university system indeed subsists under conditions of great poverty and paradoxical neglect. Indeed, one would be forgiven for thinking that a society determined, against all good sense, to turn all or nearly all its "young people" into "students" would have made it a point of pride to dedicate to this undertaking sums proportional to its stated ambition. As we know, nothing of the sort has happened. But as goes it with the dilapidation one observes in places of higher learning, a few elite schools excepted, so goes it with certain "disadvantaged" neighborhoods. The dilapidation one encounters there is in large part of the *active* variety. It is caused by the very people or a portion of those very people who are its victims and results as much from vandalism, financial difficulty, negligence, destitution, horror of beauty, contempt for order, and distrust and resentment towards cleanliness as it does from a reprehensible neglect on the part of the authorities (who, well aware that any new investments will suffer the same fate, are understandably not much inclined to overcome their misgivings in regard to such vain expenditures).

Whether we are speaking of places of learning or living environments, campuses or suburbs, lecture halls or "at-risk housing projects," poor upkeep depends at least as much and without doubt more on the degree of socialization, culture, civilization, civic-mindedness, civility, and the tendency towards either nocence or in-nocence of those who frequent or inhabit them as it does on the sums of money allotted to their maintenance. On the other hand, and reciprocally, these places, depending on the state of their upkeep, unquestionably have an effect on the people who frequent them, whether they be at home or at work. One cannot expect that the rainbow-colored slums in which many French students are educated, crammed together with their uncouth companions, should produce the same kinds of individuals and culture that the architectural splendor and environmental nobility of the old universities of Oxford, Cambridge, Salamanca, and Pavia were able to generate. In this respect, one must doubtless acknowledge among the factors contributing to the great deculturation the abandonment or near-abandonment required by the hyperdemocratic massification of education, higher education included – even if *higher* in name only – of the former places and precincts of knowledge, which have been traded for buildings and sites that for the most part have no architectural, artistic, or historical dignity and, if they did, would in any case be rapidly stripped of it by the aggressive crudeness and slap-dash vandalism of a portion of their users.

These proletarian and often lumpen-proletarian spaces naturally and unsurprisingly produce proletarians or at best petty bourgeois and little matter in that case if they go on to become doctors, lawyers, businessmen, high school teachers, or even university professors. They produce, though now *en masse*, that tragic human type long ago identified and described by literature: the uncultured graduate, instructed but not educated, the bourgeois without a bourgeoisie, the manager type, the "B.A." (or the M.A. or the PhD). They produce cultural proletarians *en masse*, civilizational proletarians, proletarians in the ways of the world and above all in the ways of language. The only thing they do not produce are *true* proletarians, proletarians still prepared to do the work of proletarians. Mass education, without breeding a broader elite or even ensuring – far from it, in fact – the replenishment or maintenance of the former elite, is gradually eradicating, as surely as it eradicated the cultivated class, the working class, whose traditional functions are more or less provided – but how long can this go on? – by offshoring (whereby the work is done elsewhere), on the one hand, and immigration (whereby the work is done at home by newcomers), on the other.

Since it began, immigration and its progeny have themselves, with help from hyperdemocracy, been drawn into mass education and have had no small part in making it even more massified and even less educational. The opportunity offered by history as well as democratic and technological progress has been squandered. The increasing mechanization of essential subaltern tasks might have been entrusted to a better educated and better paid native working class. A *truly* democratic educational system (that is to say, one that was socially and politically democratic but intellectually selective and meritocratic) could have reliably offered their most gifted offspring the real possibility of social and cultural advancement, the very thing that the hyperdemocratic regime excludes, forbids, makes impossible, having under its reign flattened social standards and reduced them to simple (but considerable) differences in economic status. Dogmatic antiracism for its part quietly ensures that a steady stream of foreign workers is steered toward tasks that natives have been taught are unworthy of them, foreigners whose children are trained by the same system to disdain the same tasks. In this way, Brecht's famous quip may finally be taken literally, for successive governments have well and truly succeeded, through a mixture of recklessness, frightened self-righteousness, ignorance, and short-term opportunism, in "replacing the people."[xxxv]

The prevailing proletarianization, which is so culturally palpable in all the precincts and subsections of the vast central petty bourgeoisie, makes spectacular emblematic appearances in the very heart of power, in the language of government ministers, several of whom deliberately forego the now apparently abandoned obligation to use *third-person* language in the exercise of their functions, and make a show of their enthusiastic *oneselfism* by specifically offering their unique concern with being and remaining themselves (one might have thought this was perfectly secondary to ministerial dignity, if not thoroughly contrary to it) as the motive or justification for their loose phrasing and foul language. In its cultural form (in the so eagerly *countercultural* sense of the term), it is manifested even at the highest levels of state, not just in the President of the Republic's vaunted friendship with the most prominent actors of popular and commercial cinema or his cozy intimacy with a milieu that would formerly have been called Saturday night television (but now Saturday night is every night on television and all day long as well), but even in his most formal speeches, such as the one he gave beneath the dome of the Capitol in Washington, D.C., in which he invoked Elvis Presley and Marylin Monroe to underscore the attachment of his generation (which, like him, was swept along by the same rhetorical movement of petty-bourgeois cultural imperialism) to the United States of America. The proletarianizing cultural tropism is here all the more evident to the degree that we hear and see it in the mouth of the leader of an old nation known for its grand high culture, a leader who, as we are constantly reminded, has aristocratic origins (albeit not especially impressive ones).

The only thing egalitarian about our cultural situation is its disastrousness. It affects, with little variation, all of the old classes and it is precisely this that makes the differences between them essentially economic, thereby depriving them of any true class existence. The old culturally disadvantaged classes are barely less disadvantaged and may be even more so depending on whether one takes into account, in observing them, an indisputably greater dexterity in handling the instruments of communication (even if these show themselves to be, by virtue of their use, fearsome vectors of deculturation) or instead bases one's opinion on the collapse of basic cultural knowledge, which the old system used to lavish on children of the peasantry and the old working class, children who, having now become elderly, show infinitely better mastery, in general, of what are now called "the basics" than do their grandchildren or great-grandchildren. The old culturally advantaged classes for their part – and this is a great victory for hyperdemocracy – are in the process of completely losing, if they have not already lost, the privilege they used to enjoy, a reality that is hardly concealed by their enthusiastic embrace of the so-called "cultural" tools and practices of the Internet revolution. It can be noted in passing that the international prestige and unique standing of truly "French" culture, being highly aristocratic in its origins and, through its timeless exemplars, unapologetically elitist in character (as are most great cultures), have been dealt a fatal blow by petty-bourgeois and proletarianizing democratization, as can be observed everywhere. The world used to be happily enchanted with the France of Proust, Cézanne, Bergson, Ravel, and the Collège de France but the France of Christine Angot, Jean-Paul Chambas, Michel Onfray, and "Cultures & Dépendances"[xxxvi] leaves it quite unmoved. It has the same thing at home.

In this debacle, there is only hope for culture *à la Beckett*, a sort of *Happy Days*[xxxvii] hope: a hope against all hope, a pure, desperate will to continue for the sake of continuing, to persevere in one's being in spite of all reason, because each day gained is an eternity, each victory a negation of the worst, and because the only alternative to this stubborn obstinacy is death. The idea has been advanced elsewhere, apropos of the educational system – and since it seems certain that public schooling as a whole cannot be comprehensively reformed for lack of a single, shared diagnosis, sufficient will, selfishness, and corporatist automatism – of establishing isolated, pioneering, secessionist institutions, which would nonetheless be called upon to serve as examples and places of training and that would depend on three distinct forms of voluntarism: that of teachers, that of parents, and that of students. In what regards culture in general, yet more flexible and finely tuned procedures could doubtlessly be implemented in the form of simple, closely circumscribed agreements between isolated individuals (in post-cultural society, to be cultivated is necessarily to be isolated) for pre-determined goals or instead more solidly built alliances centered on broader objectives. The model, the mythic reference, and the only presently conceivable form of a miniscule, distant hope are the monasteries of the High Middle Ages, where as many scraps of ancient civilization as could be preserved, as best one could, once found shelter amid violence and barbarity in the hypothetical expectation of better days ahead. Our monasteries, which will be secular and cultural, will doubtlessly not be *real*, for isolation is no longer possible in the entirely delimited, commercialized, trivialized, developed, serviced, and *subsumed* territory of the universal suburb. By contrast and provided there is no cataclysmic collapse of this system, it is entirely incumbent upon us to make such sanctuaries *virtual* and never in the history of humanity has the virtual been interlaced with so much reality and substance. Every day, we see the Internet, that brilliant invention, misused as were so many others before it, serve both as an instrument of and window on the great deculturation. It is entirely incumbent upon us, that is, upon those of us who desire to do so, to transform it, as we have already begun to, into a means of rescue, an instrument of preservation, and a witness to survival.

Knowledge, thought, literature, art, and the poetic mode of inhabiting the earth now exist only on the fringes of the fringes, within the gaps of the system, its moments of inattention, the fragmented territory of its lapses, which are fortunately quite numerous. Amid this re-savaging of the world that culture's erasure has ushered in, culture must take as its surest ally the neglectful contempt in which it is held. In the dangerous lulls of the decivilization now underway and amid the violence that the coincidence of self with self is everywhere fomenting (which is precisely what culture had so desperately tried to prevent, with all its skill and strength), it must exist by surprise, in the hours, seasons, cantons, and byways that, for scorn of its weakness and ignorance of its true visage, the powers that be and their bands of assassins have not yet thought to clear of its last traces.

The Great Replacement [2010]¹

Ladies and gentlemen,²

It's very odd to find myself in Lunel to talk about the Great Replacement, for it was precisely here, about fifteen years ago, that the starkness of the phenomenon struck me in all its force and that I coined the expression. At the time, I was working on a book that was published soon afterward by P.O.L. and that was devoted to – indeed, this is its title – the *Département de l'Hérault*.ⁱ

I live in the countryside, spend most of my days at my desk, and am at a certain remove from what are typically called "social movements." Let's just say they're not right under my nose. When I do take notice of them, it may be that I see them more clearly than would be the case if I lived in their midst. I knew the French population had changed a great deal. I was aware of what is politely called "the suburban problem." Countless times, I had passed through those peri-urban zones where all the evils of violence and delinquency seem to congregate, exacerbating those of unemployment and academic underachievement. But what I noticed in Hérault's coastal areas – and how could one not? – was quite different. I was not traveling through the *projects* [nb. *cité*], as they say – and as they say poorly to refer to zones that manage precisely

---

1. "Le Grand Remplacement (conférence de Lunel, 26 novembre 2010)," in *Le Grand Remplacement: Introduction au remplacisme global*. (Paris, La Nouvelle Librairie, 2021), pp. 99-156.
2. This speech was delivered in Lunel on November 26th, 2010, at the invitation of two philosophy professors, one "on the left" and the other "on the right." It took the form of an improvised talk. In transcribing it for publication, I have expanded on certain points but without changing the point of view implied by its date.

not to become *projects*[ii] – but we will have a chance to see how antiphrasis, verbal sleight-of-hand, euphemism of euphemism, and simple lies preside over what is happening in order to make us believe that it is not happening. And when it has actually taken place, when it is so obvious it can no longer be denied, the same people who said nothing was happening will declare that the thing that has indeed come to pass is now *irreversible* and accuse those who would like a chance to at least once discuss things of nostalgia, defensiveness, and lack of realism. But here I am getting ahead of myself. My apologies.

So I was in some old villages of Hérault, big, round, fortified villages, with narrow streets, their lopsided houses squeezed tightly together. Already in the year 1000, many of them had stood in the same spot for some time. That was before France, some will say. Perhaps. Whatever the case, one might have thought that it was now *after* France. For at the windows and doorways of these old houses, the length of these very old streets, there almost exclusively appeared a population never before seen in these parts, which by its dress, demeanor and even language seemed not to belong there but rather to another people, another culture, another history. And in Lunel, which is not a village, there was this very same unsettling impression of having changed worlds without having left the old one, without having quit the streets and squares of our country, with their statues, churches, familiar old landmarks. How many of us have the same feeling every day and not just in Hérault, Gard, or Vaucluse, not just in Seine-Saint-Denis when we still hazard to venture there, not just in the Nord or Pas-de-Calais, but in every part of France, along the sidewalks of our cities, on public transportation, in the Parisian metro, faced with the images and reality of our schools and universities? It's as if, over the space of our lifetimes – less than that! – France has been in the process of changing its people; one sees one people, takes a nap, and there's another or *several* other peoples who appear to belong to other shores, other skies, other architectures, other customs – and who seem to think the same thing themselves.

It will be said – well, perhaps not by *you* since you are here this evening – but in any case we are constantly told, it is official doctrine, radio and television endlessly harangue us about it, indeed no longer even need to harangue us about it such is the extent to which it is taken for granted, such is the extent that it goes without saying, that no one will dare make a peep, it will be said that it is still the same people and that all of them are French, that they are the French people of today. It is always Lichtenberg's knife: one changes the haft, then the blade, but it's still the same knife.

Even according to administrative and legal criteria, however, this remark regarding the designation and official nationality of these people is not entirely accurate. For in the midst of this constantly changing population undergoing radical, irreversible transformation are many foreigners, non-citizens. Admittedly, they do not remain so for long. But as they become French, officially, new ones endlessly step forward such that the proportion of non-citizens remains roughly the same and even keeps increasing despite these headlong naturalizations. To which official doctrine replies – I am not speaking of the law here but of the unspoken media consensus, which dictates to the law what the latter must decree, to judges how they must judge, to reality how it must present itself, to events and news items what they must mean, no matter how implausible it may be – to which official doctrine replies that the distinction between citizen and non-citizen is ever more pointless and without meaning and that what counts is being there, *those who are there*, no matter their status or of course number, and that, to the contrary, we must constantly work to diminish this distinction until we have almost done away with it or done away with it altogether.

It will be vainly objected that this distinction is at the foundation of the social contract and of the incorporation of any human group whatsoever into a state: there is no such thing as citizenship unless non-citizenship exists; there is no treaty between parties unless those who did not sign the treaty are not in the same legal situation as those who did, for otherwise it has no meaning or purpose. Opposing as it often does today's dominant trend, the Party of In-nocence, which I chair, argues for maximally increasing the difference in status and treatment between citizens and non-citizens. It knows that of which it speaks since its very name refers to a foundational pact, one that, like the social contract or the Hobbesian *covenant*, is of course mythical, but that is of the same type as them: that is, the pact of in-nocence, of *non-nocence*. In exchange for a symmetrical commitment on the part of all others, each citizen agrees to not cause harm or even disturbance. This is the principle of *less for more*: everyone commits to being a little less *himself* in exchange for the leisure to be much more and to become, thanks to the liberty afforded him by the reciprocal commitment of all others to not harm, *nocere*, disturb, or impede that which does not harm, everything there is in him of positive potential for being and accomplishment.

Yet I'm not here to talk about the Party of In-nocence, of which I am, as you've just learned or been reminded, the candidate for President of the Republic. Nor am I here to speak about its name or the nature of its commitments, even though they often puzzle, amuse, or irritate those who hear about them for the first time. I have been invited to talk to you about the Great Replacement, which is certainly one of the major themes of this party along with the catastrophic situation of the schools, the crisis of cultural transmission, and the Great Deculturation. But we will no doubt have a chance to say a word about that as well as about what we call, for lack of a better term, the *suburbanization* of the world, or rather its *suburbanification*, its *suburb-becoming*.

I was saying that one factor contributing to the Great Replacement is the permanent influx of newcomers, immigrants, and non-citizens and their massive presence across the country. *Massive* and often illegal, quite an odd combination, but no more so than the strange status of the aforementioned "undocumented" migrants who have broken the law since they officially have no right to be here but are here nonetheless and who – and this is the most extraordinary part of it – may lay claim to rights *by virtue of the very fact that they have broken the law*. From a logical and legal point of view alike, it is an astonishing situation given that the criminal act is here the source of rights. As it happens, these media-friendly illegal immigrants, who have the police against them (somewhat) but (media-political) power on their side, were quick to make a practice of blaming France and the French should anything unfortunate befall them. One even has the impression they are reading from a script they memorized upon or even before their arrival and that, however strange it seemed to them, these hateful diatribes, full of disgust, were what French journalists and officials expected and, moreover, always delivered the best results. One thinks of burglars who sue a landlord because they break a leg in his poorly lit stairwell or get an electric shock from contact with a loose socket not up to code. Alas, when it comes to immigration, the French are so used to this twisted, Rantanplan logic[iii] that it does not even surprise them anymore.

Yet observing that there has been a change of people requires us to venture onto more delicate terrain than the question of the latest and entirely provisional *foreigners.* I'm referring to the question of *what a people is*, a vast subject that we will not fully exhaust. In the thriving traffic in statistics relating to the Great Replacement, one of the most effective tools has an undeniable legal foundation. It takes refuge there, as one might take refuge in an impregnable fortress, and it is quite right to do so. For, to a certain degree, it is just that. I am speaking of the claim according to which there is only one kind of French person and its well-known and particularly fearsome polemical variant, that no one is more French than anyone else. Thus a veiled woman with a shaky command of our language, entirely ignorant of our culture and, worse yet, overflowing with vindictiveness and animosity, if not hatred, for our history and civilization will be perfectly able to say – and she usually does not miss the chance, particularly when she finds herself on television – to a native Frenchman with a passionate interest in Roman churches, the finer points of vocabulary and syntax, Montaigne, Jean-Jacques Rousseau, Burgundy wine, and Proust and whose family has for several generations lived in the same little valley of the Vivarais or Périgord, from which it has observed or suffered through the many twists and turns of our history, this veiled woman can thus perfectly well say and usually not in a very friendly way: "I am just as French as you are," if indeed it's not *"more French"*, as I believe I have heard on such occasions.

And legally speaking, if this person is of French nationality, she is perfectly right. It would certainly be unwise to contradict her, in any case.[iv] And yet it is absurd. More than that: it is oppressive. I will not go so far as to say that it is meaningless. But, to return to a distinction I explored at length in my book *Du sens*,[3] which I borrowed from Plato's *Cratylus*, I will say that this woman's assertion has a *Hermogenian* meaning, that is, one of pure convention as Hermogenes asserts is true of the meaning of words in Plato's dialogue. But it has no *Cratylian* meaning, that is, one long-inscribed in the archeology of vocables, indeed in their origin and the origin of this origin. Law can settle for Hermogenian meaning. I will even say that it *must*, for this is its grandeur, its sacrifice and nobility, like a priest who renounces the ways of the flesh. But life for its part, the life of the mind no less than that of society, cannot do so, and culture even less so, to say nothing of literature, which owes everything to Cratylus and nothing to Hermogenes apart from a few comic effects now and then. If this lady is right, being French is nothing: it is a mockery, a bad joke that has fallen flat, a rubber stamp on an administrative document. Understand me well: I am not saying that the rubber stamp is nothing. I have too much respect for language, for honoring one's commitments, for the law to deny its legal import. But I believe that the law goes astray when it wanders too far from the reality of things, when it contradicts this reality, when it pretends to replace it, when, contrary to the literary sense of the world (which is in such bad shape), it sacrifices to Hermogenes as to a single god and refuses to acknowledge the least debt towards Cratylus.

It is hard to imagine but barely forty years ago Georges Pompidou still spoke – and at Sciences Po,[v] no less! – of the *genius of our race*. Of our *what*? As we know, this word has long been taboo in our language despite having naturally flourished there without incident for several centuries, a word used by Léon Blum and Barrès, Victor Hugo and Racine, albeit each time with a slightly different meaning, so broad was its palette. The language police, a fearsome caste whose decrees cause more fear and trembling than a criminal court, only allow it the meaning given to it by patent, pseudo-scientific racists. And so they have banished it from the polity, from its radio waves and its galley proofs, without any consideration for the very deep and broad place it occupies

---

3.   *Du sens* (in its relation to origin, time, history, etymology, morality, culture, literature, education, nationality, immigration, the Camus affair, etc.), P.O.L., 2002.

in our language or the richness of its semantic range. And now we miss it. For as the immense majority of the world's peoples perceive all too well, a people is also a *race*: by this I have in mind less a hypothetical community or biological kinship than a long-shared history. What I have in mind is more about culture and heritage than it is about heredity. To this I would also add desire, will, love. Individuals who so wish can always join a people out of love for its language, literature, its *art de vivre* or its landscapes. But peoples who remain peoples cannot join other peoples. They can only conquer them, submerge them, replace them.

Many of our new compatriots call us *the French* if not the *faces de craie*[vi] and other such courteous terms. And they say *the French* because they do not think of themselves as being French and clearly have no desire to be so. For some of them, who very explicitly reject it, one might think that the very idea horrifies them. I should point out that the platform of the Party of In-nocence recommends that they be taken literally, that a literal account be kept of their declarations and repudiations and that, if they say they are only French on paper rather than in their heart, soul, or sense of belonging, if they feel less French than something else, consider their country of origin to be their true homeland or dance and shout for joy while waving a foreign flag when France is beaten or humiliated in some sporting event – well, we ought to grant them their wish, align administrative fact with proclaimed and perceptible reality, and relieve them of this Frenchness that they only value for reasons of self-interest or, as we saw above, as a polemical weapon.

After Georges Pompidou, must I go back a little further in time to a more powerful mind and quote Charles de Gaulle? You all know these words full of wisdom and common sense, words that today, in the Fifth Republic, would get its founder censored and pilloried, if not fined or imprisoned:

"It is good that there are yellow Frenchmen, black Frenchmen, and brown Frenchmen. They show that France is open to all races and has a universal calling. But only on the condition that they stay a small minority. If not, France will no longer be France. In the end, we remain a European people of the white race, Greek and Latin culture, and

Christian religion. Let us not deceive ourselves! Have you been to see the Muslims? Have you seen them with their turbans and djellabas? You see perfectly well that they are not French! Those who push for integration have hummingbird brains even if they are very learned. Try integrating oil and vinegar. Shake the bottle. After a moment they will separate again. Arabs are Arabs and Frenchmen are Frenchmen. Do you think the French population can absorb ten million Muslims, who tomorrow will be twenty million and forty the day after that? If we set about integrating them, if all the Arabs and Berbers of Algeria were to be considered French, how would they be prevented from coming and settling on the mainland, where the standard of living is so much higher? My village would no longer be called Colombey of the two Churches but Colombey of the two Mosques!"[vii]

You will pardon me if I once again quote these well-worn words. In today's climate, doing so has the drawback that, rather than comforting the adversaries of the Great Replacement and further raising the figure of General De Gaulle in our esteem by virtue of the accuracy of their analysis and their incredibly, not to say tragically, prescient character, they instead demean him, compromising his posthumous stature and leading him, of all people, to be accused of racism for no other reason than that he believed in the existence of races and the age-old legitimacy of the meaning of this word, its link to what makes a people a people. Instead, in an echo of Hermogenes, it is the opposite that is drummed into us and our children on every occasion: a people is created by a daily act of will and nothing else; it is no more than a convention and a shared desire to live together. One might superficially object that, if that is indeed the definition, things in our country are off to a very poor start. For this desire to live together does not exist, as anyone can see from the generalized disorder, the lack of harmony in social relations, the constant aggression and what the press amusingly refers to, with its familiar genius for naming things obliquely so as not to name them, for misnaming them so as not to speak of them, as *incivilities* – an infinitely euphemistic term that, despite itself, is not completely irrelevant as it is precisely *civitas*, or the social body, that is made a mockery of by these behaviors, to say nothing of civilization itself.

And yet this oh-so Hermogenian definition of the people, linked only to the will and dismissive of origins, is said to be typically French. Indeed, it is even said to be the glory of France, one of the major contributions of the French Revolution. Of course, a contribution of the Revolution, be it major or minor, should not be confused with the essence or genius of France. For there is, I hope, no question of limiting France to the Revolution and what came after, no question of pretending that our country began in 1789, or 1792, or 1793. To do so would amount to abandoning the cathedrals, Enguerrand Quarton, the chateaus of the Loire, Montaigne, Valentin de Boulogne, Racine, Marivaux, *La Religieuse portugaise*, the quays of Bordeaux, and what have you.

Alas, there is some truth to France's megalomaniacal obsession with universality, which today is costing us so dearly. The truth of the matter is that it began as a vain conceit, a fantasy in which the Legislature indulged without, I believe, for one second imagining that it would someday be taken literally. Above all, it was originally intended to allow certain prominent figures, such as Franklin or Washington – or, to cite the example of August 24th, 1792, Thomas Paine and Anacharsis Cloots, foreign sympathizers of the Revolution and deputies to the Convention, who, in a gesture of singular gracelessness, would be expelled one year later *as foreigner*s – it was intended to allow them to become French in the same way that cities appoint honorary citizens so as to make a show of their supposed patronage.

Even so, the people's representatives had too strong a sense of what it is to be a people (a sure sign of this: they did not even think to raise the question) to imagine for a single instant that the whole Earth might one day cite their reckless law to claim a universal right to Frenchness. In the meantime, they opened a breach, which over time has become a yawning abyss in which our disaster is being consummated. As long as its dimensions did not threaten the equilibrium and finally the very existence of the polity, the nation, and the people as a living and embodied entity, that breach made infinitely precious contributions to France: one need only think of Apollinaire, Marie Curie, Levinas (to name a figure closer to our time), and many others – Jews, Germans,

Poles, Italians, Orthodox Christians after the Soviet revolution, heroes of liberty and national independence in all the world's countries. But one should not exaggerate the specific character of this way of becoming French.

It is true that the emancipation of the Jews, which our country was the first to promulgate, on September 28th, 1791, lent France a special attraction in the eyes of many oppressed Jews throughout Europe and the world. And I am well aware that this aspect of things particularly resonates in a town like Lunel, with its very ancient and very brilliant Jewish culture. If they took advantage of the possibility offered them to become French, it is of course because they were oppressed elsewhere. But it was also out of love, gratitude, and admiration for France. Is there any need to recall that this love was on occasion atrociously disappointed in the years that our defeated country lived under foreign yoke? Yet it was never extinguished. But we should remember that this love was hardly less great for Germany itself, for Italy, for England, the last of which, at least, never betrayed it. Was not Disraeli himself, though a convert, Prime Minister of Great Britain in the middle of the nineteenth century and bestowed with every honor one could imagine?

That country boasts less than France of its supposed universality and it tends to find our pretentions in this domain laughable. Nonetheless, it has welcomed as many foreigners as France has and owes them just as much of its grandeur and prestige. One need only think of Van Dyck, Handel, the Herschels, Rosetti and Joseph Conrad, to say nothing of all those who found refuge across the Channel as if in exile without willingly abandoning anything of their culture or nationality of origin: the Italians of the Risorgimento such as Foscolo and Manzoni; the Libertadores of Latin America such as Miranda; Marx and Bakunin, the founding fathers of communism and anarchism; and later the innumerable refugees of Nazism including Pevsner, Freud, and Wittgenstein, who was already a habitué of Cambridge at the time of the Anschluss. One could fill an entire dictionary with their names.

What I am trying to show is that there is nothing historically so specific in the French understanding of nationality that we should insist on it. I would even go so far as to say that we are here to a large extent dealing with a sort of modern myth. The dogmatic antiracist doxa is always ready to denounce the nation's grand narrative but its criticism above all consists in writing new, generally less-flattering chapters, which it then substitutes for the old ones. This is another form of Great Replacement. And notwithstanding the universalist aspirations of which so much has been made these past forty years, the idea of a people remains more or less the same in France as in other countries and for other peoples: one is French essentially by birth, ancestry, and family; along the fringes of this very predominant core may be incorporated men and women whose particular love for France has given them a desire to live here or who, through tragic circumstances or random chance, have been brought to settle in our country, where they felt at home and built a life. These men and women may have played a considerable role in the country's affairs but were very few in number, at least until the end of the nineteenth century.

As an antidote to the succession of self-serving historiographical fads, I rely on two major sources of evidence – architecture and literature – both of which are difficult to distort. In what regards the numerical extent of the wealthy bourgeoisie during the Belle Époque (a class constantly described as a narrow caste of privileged profiteers), the true state of the peasantry during the time of Bien-Aimé,[viii] or the comparative lifestyles of the middle and upper classes in France and Italy during the Baroque age or the neo-classical era, I look more to architecture (including vernacular architecture, of course, with its simple buildings, what one might call architecture without an architect) than to the alternating theories of ideological and ideologized historians, as tyrannical as Molière's doctors. Likewise, in what concerns how one should conceive of what makes a people a people (both in general and in the French case), notions of belonging, or feelings of national community, I put more faith in literature than in the *a posteriori* reconstructions of organic intellectuals.

And on this point literature is clear: until roughly 1970, until the onset of our present crisis of belonging and the first waves of mass migration, which forced us to ask what it meant to be French and obliged us to answer that question in the most convoluted ways, subject as we were to the imperious need to say what was expected of us and nothing more, being French was certainly different in content from being English, Spanish, or Danish but it was not at all different in form. We should recognize, however, that literature's silence on this question is its most convincing testimony. Nine times out of ten and with the exception of times of war or foreign travel, the heroes and heralds of literature simply took the answer for granted. For literature and its readers alike, it was a quietly obvious fact and as such not worthy of introspection, much less definition – for unless you are a dictionary or a legal code, what is the point of defining what everyone understands perfectly well from birth?

I remember going to Belgium as a young writer to speak in bookstores and other places and being very surprised to learn that being Belgian – the state of *Belgitude*, that is, the fact of belonging to the Belgian nation, to the Belgian people – was a source of endless debate. Being Belgian seemed like a fulltime job and it still does. I was delighted that there was nothing so time-consuming about being French. Shall I admit it? It just didn't make much difference to me. Oh, I was as patriotic as the next person but not at all chauvinistic; I still believe that I am not. I did not think the French countryside more beautiful than Scotland's or rank French literature above English literature, French thought above German thought, Berlioz and Fauré above Brahms and Mahler, the mansions of the Faubourg Saint-Germain above the palaces of Italy, Poussin above Titian or Velasquez, or the tradition of freedom and the rule of law in France above that of Great Britain and the United States. I recall being determined to do my duty, if necessary, but I did not think about being French every day and would never have thought to boast about it.

Alas, my delight was premature, for there quickly came a time when being French was just as problematic as being Belgian, just as ambiguous and prey to endless aggressive and perilous disputation. I am nostalgic for a simple and self-evident sense of identity, which does not require perpetual self-interrogation. I would like to be French like the Arabs are Arab, the Jews are Jewish, the Japanese are Japanese, or the Poles are Polish and not to have to think about it except as one occasionally notices a quietly obvious fact that is not constantly created and recreated. The paradox is that those Frenchmen and women whose culture hardly seems French and who are so quick to wield that absolute weapon of language against me – "I am as French as you are" – are often very well-ensconced in another identity (Arab, for example), the solidity, relevance, and depth of which they never for a single moment question even as they radically deny the legitimacy and existence of my own. To repeat: if they are just as French as I am then *French* does not mean much.

The adjective carries about as much weight in this instance as *American* does whenever a terrorist commits an attack in the United States and the television news virtuously persists in saying he is *American* or "born in the United States." It's this "born in the United States" that gets one thinking, for Americans are often born in the United States. Why specify that fact in this person's case? One must await the very end of the "segment" to learn that this amateur chemist is named, for example, Muhammad Walif (for example). In this case, the word *American* is not the most *performative* information: its hermeneutic power is at best weak. But in our dogmatic antiracist regime, the permanent censorship imposed on discourse by the media-political complex, making all speech resemble the movement of a chessboard knight, has this great, didactic advantage: we have all of us become formidable semioticians. I long dreamed of writing a play or opera libretto called *Underprivileged Neighborhoods*. In it, an Underprivileged Youth falls in love with a Privileged Youth, one of the families hosts a great ball, rival gangs come to blows, a silk ladder drops from a tower . . .

And here is the paradox I mentioned: as the French sense of belonging, now reduced to the state of a masochistic madhouse, becomes something so feeble, so disjointed, so purely elective, and, to stick with my terminology, so purely *Hermogenian*, other peoples' sense of belonging, whether it be national, religious, or ethnic, does not seem to have been affected in the least. Quite the contrary, in fact: this type of belonging continues to holds sway over the vast majority of the Earth's surface. To be French, to be English, even more so to be British, to be American – these things are increasingly meaningless and purely formalistic. But being Arab, Chechen, Muslim, Jewish, Korean, Wolof, or Armenian remains what it has always been: a kind of intangible identity that has become natural by dint of having so long been cultural.

In France, a rather moving illustration of the unequal intensity and integrative power of identities may be found in the growing number of young native Frenchmen and women who convert to Islam, thereby simultaneously underscoring and accelerating the Great Replacement. I have no doubt that some of these conversions proceed from a deep spiritual yearning, long reflection mulled over in the recesses of one's soul, and authentic religious awakening. Such cases are entirely respectable. To hear, see, and listen to those concerned, however, and to the degree that one dares sound their hearts and souls, their brains, their available brain time, most such cases seem to principally originate in a despair of being nothing, post-cultural stupor, consummated de-civilization, a respect for strength, a need for belonging, the herd instinct, an impatient desire for submission, and a sense of fatalism.

I am convinced that, for the generations that preceded our own, being French was of a similar nature to these simple and strong identities that we see quietly persevere and prosper around us. Ours, meanwhile, languishes, withers, shrinks, apologizing for its existence while endlessly babbling on about its verbose, pretentious, and disembodied reasons for existing.

What I mean to say is that we have been told many lies – enormous lies. And we have been lied to *sincerely*, I would like to think, out of ideological conviction and the natural inclination of organic intellectuals to tell society and, more precisely, its authorities (in this case the media-political complex) what they want to hear. We are treated every day to enormous lies, lies only made possible by the Great Deculturation, of course. Indeed, the teaching of forgetting must have already broadly achieved its goals for historians to say and repeat, with a straight face and in that tone of hysterical and paranoid threat that is typical of perpetual indoctrination (they always speak *in spite of the bad guys,* expressing eternal truths we all know deep down but that only obsess a clutch of conspiring *old fogeys* [I will call my memoirs

Old Fogey: A Life]), they will say and repeat that France has *always* been a country of immigration. The truth, since that is what we are talking about, is that for roughly fifteen centuries, up until the end of the nineteenth century, France experienced practically *no* immigration. She naturally took in immigrants, foreigners who came on an individual basis and often played, either directly or through their children, a significant role in our country's political and cultural history. I am thinking, for example, of Mazarin, Lully, Law, or Zola's father. But these foreigners did not an immigration make, though we are asked to believe – and we can only believe it by being very ignorant, which is why so many arrangements have been made to guarantee our ignorance and that of our children – that the nation was only ever made of and by them, that they are the essence of France. This is one of the ideological foundations of the famous phrase, "I am just as French as you are." Indeed, *if not more so, if not more so*, since I am of foreign origin.

As for France . . . it is more or less agreed that France is little more than a term of geography, like Italy for Metternich. We have in this way taken the same historical route as the peninsula at the time of the Risorgimento but taken it *backwards*, marching toward *disunity*. Or rather no, since apparently there has never been any unity. Indeed, it is no longer enough for the media-political complex and its somewhat ridiculous enforcement arm, the network of state-subsidized antiracist organizations, to convince the French that they are not a people or are only a people in the purely administrative sense of the term. No, adding insult to injury, they must persuade them that *they never have been* a people, that their shared history was but a dream, that even their past existence, for which they might feel nostalgic, is a mirage, a pure fantasy, an optical illusion, and mental construct. In short, like so many other things they are nevertheless certain they distinctly remember or experience day after day – violence, insecurity, enforced stupidity, the disastrous educational system – *it's all in their heads* and must be actively rooted out by our civic-minded experts. This is what is called *education*.

As I understand it, the dominant theory today – if not in serious history than at least among what the language police retain from it and distill – has it that the Great War and the ordeal of the trenches marked the birth of the French people, who had not existed before except as a hodgepodge of dialects, patois, provinces, regions, and even villages that existed in perfect ignorance of one another except when engaging in one of their interminable rustic punch-ups. And far be it for me to claim that the French people emerged fully armed from Jupiter's thigh, clambered over the walls of Troy in flames, or descended ready-made for history from the lakeside stilt-houses of the Gallic village. Like most other peoples and probably even a little more so, its origins are diverse. The fact remains that, between the fall of the Roman Empire and the great migrations of the twentieth century, it showed itself to be a remarkably stable compound animated by a precocious and growing sense of national unity.

It is here that contemporary historiography and its vulgar translation in the media (though the two are often one and the same, unfortunately) are most clearly at odds with literature. For my part I prefer to trust the latter, especially when it is contemporaneous with the facts. It is shameful to have to recall that France is already present in the *Song of Roland* and Bernart de Ventadour; that France and even the best of her is in Montaigne, who may have been a Jew; that she overflows in Malherbe, Corneille, Tallement des Réaux, Saint-Simon, Marivaux, *Memories from beyond the Grave*, *The Three Musketeers*, and *In Search of Lost Time*. France and the awareness of being French – indeed, not even an awareness but an immediate union of body and soul in the very nature of things (happy days they were . . .)

By dating the true birth of national sentiment to the First World War – that is to say, by absurdly delaying its advent by two, three, four, five, ten centuries or more, depending on the region, social class, and level of culture – the media-political complex or, more specifically, its ideological assembly plant, kills two birds with one stone, for the chosen date follows the first waves of Belgian and Italian immigration, which though they were not cases of *mass* immigration were nevertheless of real statistical and social significance. On this account, France only became France and the French people only discovered the truth about its social conventions, will, and perpetual self-invention after immigration came bearing the spark of life, at last allowing it to achieve its constituent authenticity.

This viewpoint is corroborated by a comical inversion of the history of art. In the past, we naively believed that, in point of its richness, power, and, the word must be said, genius, art in France – I am trying not to say *French art* in order to spare those easily offended – had achieved such international prestige that it outstripped Munich, London, and Berlin, preceding New York by nearly a century, to become the universal capital of the arts, like Rome in the seventeenth century or Florence or Venice even earlier, though the world was narrower then. This prestige allowed it to attract artists from around the world, who came to take advantage of its teaching, unique atmosphere, and the creative ferment of its talent. But we have been disabused of this error and learned the hard way that this picture must be inverted and viewed upside down. It was not France's prestige or that of its art that attracted foreign artists; rather, it was the presence of large numbers of foreign artists that gave our country its artistic prestige and was the essence of its art.

I remember seeing a grand and beautiful exhibition in Paris that clearly explained how foreign artists had made French art. Why they should have chosen Paris as their meeting place went unexplained – doubtless because it was easily accessible to them. The visitor was exhorted in no uncertain terms – as always happens in all domains under a dogmatic antiracist regime, that is, an immigrationist one, that is, today, a replacist one – to educate himself and forthwith draw all of the right moral and ideological lessons.

These lessons only amount to one, moreover, ideology having substituted itself for morality and replaced it (this being another form of replacism). You can be a dim-witted lout, a hateful, loud, boorish liar with your hand in the till; you can disturb your neighbors across the hall or in your building, neighborhood, city, or nation in whatever way you fancy; you can declare yourself exempt from all ethical obligations toward the Earth and your fellow man so long as you also appear and proclaim yourself to be a strictly observant, dogmatic anti-racist; so long as you mindlessly endorse every article of proper doctrine, display your unwavering commitment to it, and support as self-evident every protest favoring illegal immigrants; so long as, finally, you reflexively and unconditionally oppose any effort to manage the tide of immigration and consider abject and "worthy of the darkest hours of our history" the least refusal of a visa. You can even allow yourself a few dispensations or deviations regarding the articles of dogma and, for example, raise Cain so that your children do not have to attend a middle school or high school with too many children of immigrants. So long as holy doctrine is clearly affirmed and reaffirmed on every occasion, questions of morality do not arise – for the doctrine *is* morality.

This is the great triumph of any ideology and for this ideology it is total: *to pass for morality itself.* Or even better: to be, in the eyes of a given society, *the whole* of morality and indistinguishable from it.

Several considerations, however, radically call into question this pretention on the part of dogmatic anti-racism, out-and-out immigrationist and replacist *avant la lettre* as it is, to set itself up as a moral code and even present itself as the ultimate morality.

The first of these concerns its relation to truth. Morality cannot do without truth. If it does, it is not morality. Yet this morality tells enormous lies. Perhaps it lies sincerely, perhaps it is convinced of the truth of its lies – this would only be the more alarming. It lies by omission; it lies by suppressing information and censorship; it lies by constantly minting its counterfeit language, its industrial-scale euphemism. It lies from fear; it lies from love of death; it lies from love of self; it lies from good manners and fear of giving offense (but this fear only applies in what concerns the neo-French, present and future; in what concerns the paleo-French there is no humiliation, blame, accusation, or insult that it does not blithely inflict). It even lies a little bit for self-interest, career advancement, social-climbing, and a desire to move up in the world.

Yet this is only true of its sycophants, propagators, and literary, media, cinematographic, cultural, sociological, and academic propagandists, and their ilk. No matter the profession, one stands little chance of rising to the top of one's office without it. Employers lap it up for the most part: they know very well which side their bread is buttered on and how to guarantee themselves an inexhaustible source of cheap labor. Over the course of history, in any case, concern for the country and its dignity has not always been their chief preoccupation.

And yet, despite the obvious links between this litany and huckster globalism, one hesitates to identify *interest* as the principal motor of replacist ideology and its lies, for one cannot fail to also take into consideration all of the groups that nobly support, promote, and diffuse these deceitful dogmas *against* their own interest, often of the most immediate kind (and who are sometimes just beginning to regret it): Jews, women, homosexuals, secularists, champions of free thought and free expression, all cheerfully busy sawing off the branches on which they sit, alongside the heralds of "diversity," who themselves do not perceive that they are in fact only making more of the same, always more of the same, the undifferentiated universal village or rather the *generalized suburb*, the place where Ilan Halimi crawls in his final hour,[4] violent, wild, deculturated, and decivilized.

Replacism also lies by creation, the invention of myth, the circulation of *topoi*, stereotypes, and set phrases. I have countless times pointed out that, in this period of institutionalized lying, when all words are false, it is no accident that the most platitudinous of all platitudes in this miasma of babble is the expression *it is true that*, so much so that I would not be shocked if our era should be remembered by posterity (supposing there is one and it understands French) as the *it-is-true-ist* period of our history. A time during which, the lie being the rule, all speakers felt obliged, in a desperate effort at perpetual reevaluation, to begin every other sentence with *it is true that*. Every time you hear *it is true that*, you can be sure that deceit is in the air: the old refrain betraying itself by irony.[ix]

I have already said a word about some of the lies of replacist ideology, which is so eager to be a morality and be understood as such: that France has always been a country of immigration but has only really been France since becoming one; that the French have never been a

---

4. Ilan Halimi is that young Jewish shopkeeper kidnapped and tortured to death over three weeks by the "gang of barbarians" led by Youssouf Fofana, in January and February 2006.

people but must answer for all the sins of the Earth. It is always something of the same tea kettle logic, which I will quickly recall should someone in this room no longer remember it: first, you never lent me a tea kettle; second, your tea kettle already had a hole in it when you lent it to me; third, it was in one piece when I returned it to you.

Factual lies, fallacious reasoning, and historiographical myths: the machine that produces them works around the clock. We are all familiar with its most recent production: the highly convenient thesis according to which it was the parents, grandparents, or great-grandparents of our North African immigrants or descendants of North African immigrants who liberated France at the end of the Second World War.[x] Traditionally, this precious exploit was attributed to the Americans, their allies and the internal and external French resistance. Now, we must make a major place in our gratitude for the Moroccan, Algerian, and Tunisian soldiers who landed on the shores of Provence in 1944. The party of In-nocence, which I chair, is all the more inclined to do so as it has repeatedly expressed its horrified indignation at the abject profanation of the graves of Muslims who died for France. It is nevertheless worth recalling, for these points tend to be forgotten by the most recent trends in the history of the country's liberation or by the opportunistic, vulgarized versions thereof offered in the media, that among the troops under French flag who landed in Provence, more than one third consisted of North African Frenchmen, who would later be called *pieds noirs*, another third of Frenchman from France, and a final third of Arab and Berber soldiers, most of whom had little choice in the matter, it is true, though this in no way diminishes their merit nor the recognition we owe them. They served under French command. Their presence in these circumstances, should we wish to congratulate ourselves for it – and how could we fail to do so given the immense value of their contribution? – should be classified among the positive aspects of colonization, at least as far as France is concerned, for without the latter the former would not have been. Let us add without overly lingering on the question that, during their journey to reach Var or Vaucluse, they did not all leave a memory of behavior befitting the representatives of civilization. To remind oneself of this or of the terror they loosed on Italy and, later, Germany, one need merely reread *The Skin* or *Two Women*.[xi] To the loyal, valiant and level-headed combatants among them, there is no question of stinting in our expressions of gratitude.

Another oft-solicited segment of contemporary historiography, this one older, insists on what is nevertheless a more recent aspect of our relations with our new compatriots or virtual compatriots: their role or that of their fathers in reconstructing France after the Second World War. Here again, there is no question of failing to give recognition where it is due and no doubt sometimes it is. One may nonetheless observe that the great waves of North African immigration date from the mid-1970s and that the actual work of reconstruction was by this time largely complete. Nor was it so much the case that these workers were sought out (as some tell it, one might believe they were forcibly brought here!) as that they fought one another for the opportunity to come to France. It was and still is enough to open the door just a crack to receive many more of them than one might wish. A curious conclusion, by the way, to a colonial adventure that the current Algerian president, Monsieur Bouteflika, regularly likens to a genocidal conquest. For it is rather unusual to a see a harshly oppressed people, having just been freed, flock to its oppressor so as to remain under his administration. One would be forgiven for thinking that France had not left such a bad memory on the other side of the Mediterranean after all – hardly had the yoke been lifted than her former subjects, with nothing more pressing to do, rushed to her soil. Or was it as conquerors that they came?

I am thinking specifically of Algerians here. Now, just as they were supposedly getting France back on her feet and doing all the work necessary to bring this about, their own country was sinking into ruin, tyranny, and chaos. Indeed, the country was living off its acquired assets, off what had already been built and *in the furnishings* of French colonization, as it were – living ever less well, to judge by the truth of architecture and urban planning, as I am inclined to do – until the final dilapidation of this inheritance, the victim of corruption and a lack of maintenance. Some will reply that there was money in France and none in Algeria. But this is false: Algeria is a rich country. Had it not been stolen by corrupt despots and all those whose submission they purchased at great expense, its rent from petroleum could have guaranteed prosperity or, at the very least, reasonable affluence for the young nation. If it was to the Algerians of France or their brothers that we owe the relative growth and well-being of our country in the final decades of the twentieth century, it is hard to see why they could not have seen to that of their native land as well.

Of course, there is the fact that Algeria was at the time undergoing out-of-control population growth, a reality hardly compatible with the establishment of a polity founded on rights and liberty or capable of ensuring prosperity, a polity that was itself difficult to square with Muslim civilization in its present state of development. Nevertheless, *Nemo auditur propriam turpitudinem allegans*: no one can invoke his own turpitude as an excuse. And, far from being an inevitability, the country's demographic explosion was encouraged by the authorities, who congratulated themselves for it. I have cited de Gaulle; I will cite Boumediene, his words no less well-known than those of the general as I related them above: "One day, millions of men will leave the southern hemisphere to go to the northern hemisphere. And they will not go there as friends; they will go there to conquer it. And they will conquer it by populating it with their sons. It is our wives' wombs that will give us victory."

It is often said that this famous declaration, delivered from the rostrum of the United Nations in New York on April 10th, 1974, must be placed in its proper context, but doing so only underscores its programmatic character. To be sure, the Algerian president went on to evoke the conquerors' return to their country, but the least one can say is that this return has so far hardly materialized. It is not I who speak of *conquest* but Houari Boumediene. And it must be acknowledged that his remarks are a godsend for those who attribute the ongoing counter-colonization of France by Algeria and of Europe by Africa and its former colonies to a concerted plan. I do not take this path. I am not sure that, one fine day, some individual or assembly of strategists said: "We're going to conquer Europe."

I have no idea. On the other hand, it must be admitted that such would be totally in keeping with the age-old and, as it were, foundational designs of Islam, and that there is no shortage of long-bearded, beslippered prophets loudly and clearly affirming that what is coming to be is in fact what must be done. Ten years ago, they were taken for madmen. Today, they look more like rational forecasters.[5] And I have been told that, in France and Europe, there is no shortage of male or female politicians who believe that what is augured by these beturbaned oracles is inevitable. Little matter, then, whether what is occurring is the result of a duly deliberated plan or no. The important thing is to note that it is indeed occurring.

I have just used the term *counter-colonization*; it is in common use in the terminology of the Party of In-nocence and is among the *elements of our discourse*, to speak in the language of our opponents. We have often been reproached for it on the grounds that it is exaggerated, over-the-top, pointlessly aggressive. I am even told that it dissuades certain people who otherwise share our ideas from joining our ranks due to its too burdensome connotations. Yet it seems to me perfectly justified and – how shall I say? – *observational* . . . I believe it is even more etymologically precise than the term *colonization*, at least as that term is used to describe French colonization.

For, with the possible exception of Algeria and, well before that, Canada and Louisiana, France did not engage in colonization properly speaking. I do not say this to diminish any historical guilt that may be associated with these undertakings. France conquered lands and with them created an empire. In contrast to England in North America, Portugal in Brazil, or Spain in Central and South America, however, she did not strictly speaking establish *colonies*. In Ancient Greece, where the concept originated, colonies were replicas of the metropole, its doubles or external prolongations. It was the same population, only separated. They involved transferring a portion of the metropole's citizenry overseas. For France, in this sense, Senegal, Gabon, the Ivory Coast, Indochina, Tunisia, and Morocco were not really *colonies* in the ancient, original meaning of this term. They were simple dependencies, where the

---

5. See "Que va-t-il se passer?" in *Le Communisme du XXIe siècle*, Xenia, Vevey, 2007; new edition under the title *La Seconde Carrière d'Adolf Hitler*, Renaud Camus, 2016, pp. 41-80.

metropole was represented by a small number of administrators, soldiers, missionaries, educators, and businessmen. For decolonization, this was to prove an essential point. In most regions of the world to which it spread, the French Empire lasted less than a century. When it came to an end, the countries that were subject to it recovered their independence or received it for the first time, and overnight became their own masters. Or at least they did not have large numbers of foreigners dictating how they should conduct their affairs.

It was a different story in Algeria, which, though officially incorporated into the French department system, was at least partly a *colony* in the sense in which the Greeks or Phoenicians understood this word. Or more precisely, it held a large French colony, a million men and women out of a total population of ten or twelve million. Rightly or wrongly, however, the Algerians of that time did not consider the presence of this colony to be compatible with true independence. It was their opinion – and, at the time, no one in the world was surprised by this way of seeing things – that there could be no question of freedom, independence, or authentic control of the territory as long as a foreign population one-tenth the size of the indigenous people remained on the premises. In three weeks, the Frenchmen and women of Algeria, whether they be Christian or Jew, Spanish or French in origin, were thrown into the sea. "The suitcase or the coffin" – that, you may recall, was the graceful operational slogan of this radical action. It did not arouse the slightest indignation within the international community. Even France appeared to agree that one could not truly expect, after all, a population of foreigners one-tenth the size of the Algerian population (even if their families had been there for four or five generations) to be accepted on the soil of an independent Algeria.

Today, France has very well adapted, at least officially, to the presence of four million Algerians and French people of Algerian descent on its own territory, with much more than a tenth of its population – perhaps fifteen percent, some speak of twenty percent – not members of the native people. Perhaps it would be better to speak of the *indigenous* people, if only to remain in the context of counter-colonization, which, with the help of Boumediene, I believe I have shown to be fully justified, even more so than the term "colonization" was in its time.

The conquest by wombs announced by Ben Bella's usurper is exactly what is taking place and, though we do not have exact knowledge of these figures nor the right to know or state them, the relative proportions of the populations of France and their various origins obviously mean nothing so long as they cannot be correlated with the age pyramid. The lower one looks on this statistical monument, the lower the proportion of indigenous people. And, while it is forbidden to count or publish these figures, it is not yet entirely forbidden to believe one's own eyes and one's own daily experience, even though no effort is spared to convince us to substitute, for the judgment of our senses and mind, that of those who are uniquely authorized to speak, the experts, sociologists, and organic intellectuals of the antiracist power, themselves the mouthpieces of state-funded associations. Should we ignore these injunctions and insolently dare to trust in what we ourselves see in our cities' streets, in the cars of the Paris métro or the classes of our elementary and middle schools, where the two or three *céfrans*[xii] who remain increasingly find themselves bullied and mocked, it is not to Boumediene or even de Gaulle that we should turn to understand what is happening but to Chateaubriand:

> "The small tribes of the Orinoco no longer exist; of their dialect there only remain a dozen or so words uttered in the treetops by parakeets that have been freed, like Agrippina's thrush that chirped Greek words from the balustrades of the Roman palaces. Such will be, sooner or later, the fate of our modern tongues, the ruins of Greek and Latin. What raven, freed from a cage, belonging to the last Franco-Gallic priest, will croak, to a foreign people, our successors, from the heights of some ruined bell-tower: 'Hear the accents of a voice once known to you: you will bring an end to all such speech.'
>
> Live on so, Bossuet, that in the end your masterpiece may outlast, in a bird's memory, your language and your remembrance among men!"[xiii]

The vase of Soissons, the morning at Bouvines, "Madame is dying . . . Madame is dead," "Messieurs les Anglais, tirez les premiers!"

"We are here by the will of the people and we will only be dispersed by the force of bayonets!" "So much water, so much water!" "France has lost a battle," "And the solitary string of the marine trumpets . . ." – *the dream of a bird?*[xiv]

An acceptable objection, meanwhile, to the expression *counter-colonization* would be to point out that mass immigration and the change of population it involves are to be observed as much in France, Belgium, the Netherlands, or Great Britain as they are in Western European countries that only briefly had colonial empires (and small ones at that), such as Germany and Italy, or that never had one at all, such as Denmark, Sweden, and Norway. That being the case and taking this objection into account, I see no drawback to speaking of *colonization* period, if that is what one prefers, though this time the protests shall come, not from moderates outraged by the term or its derivative, but from fanatics who judge it too flattering for these masters-in-waiting. For to *colonize* would be to develop, order, give shape and build, all things for which our colonizers have shown no particular inclination . . .

Some wonder about the passive *de facto* acceptance of this endless tide that has for some forty years washed over our shores, of new occupants who permanently settle in this country with their families, establishing their progeny here, radically transforming its appearance and that of its streets, and who in fact perfectly correspond to that immersion the country sought to avoid for fifteen centuries and that it resisted with all its strength. What the independent Algeria of 1962 did not for a moment consider accepting – that ten percent of its population should consist of the representatives of another culture, another civilization, of other ethnic groups, strangers to its religion and to its language (*to a certain extent*, for many of the French people of Algeria, belonging as they did to families that had been there for over a century, spoke Arabic) – France or in any case its authorities, whether they be media or state, blithely accept and indeed in much more acute form, for yesterday's ten percent are today's fifteen or twenty percent and tomorrow's fifty percent, as we have just seen, due to the continuity of the influx, on the one hand, and differential birth rates, on the other.

This latter is naturally denied by the organic intellectuals and certified experts since it is their job to deny it just as they for ages denied, with the same unfailing gusto (often referred to as *"mucchiellism"*[xv] after the most passionate and comical of these professional deniers), falling educational attainment, rising violence, and the disproportionate rate of delinquency among "immigrant-origin young people."

Why does the country, which fourteen centuries ago victoriously fought off invasion at Poitiers and, faced with other invaders, did so again twenty times over in the centuries that followed, now consent to this invasion, barely less threatening in the present and doubtless more so over the long term? It took Spain seven hundred years to free itself from a yoke that it now seems to once again seek, such is the imprudence (though less great than ours) with which it today exposes itself. Yet this is not just a question of Islam. As we have occasion to observe every day, it is division in itself, within a people or between peoples fated or condemned to live on the same territory, that is the constant threat to harmonious social relations and public order. It is this division that our kings took the utmost care to at all costs avoid, even at the price of brutality, for they instinctively knew that nothing could come of it but misfortune for individuals and weakness for the state. And yet they only had to fear division within the same people and the same religion; what if it had been, as it is for us, a matter of several peoples and several religions, several civilizations?

Earlier, I remarked that immigrationists cannot have morality on their side, despite their best efforts to abduct it for themselves, that replacism cannot be a moral code, still less morality itself, due to its frenzied, seemingly obligatory, constituent recourse to falsehood, as if truth were not among the preeminent requirements of morality. But there is another reason that further disqualifies any claim to morality on the part of the practice of dogmatic antiracism: its tremendous propensity to create misfortune.

It tries, for example, to have us take as the very expression of moral law its ritual protests against the expulsion of illegal immigrants, the immense majority of whom, it must be recalled, are in no way political refugees but merely seeking a little more material comfort and to escape the chaos of their country of origin rather than fighting it at home (potentially with France's help), which one might consider to be their historical role and duty.[6] But the moral law should not be confused with a non-dialectical, knee-jerk mawkishness that, without mediation or perspective, shies away from questions of pro and con and that in this instance consists in automatically, mechanically supporting actions the sum effect of which is to bring about more misfortune, a hundred times more, in the form of delinquency, extreme poverty, violence, true racism (though not in the way imagined by these pious works), cultural erasure, and moral offense than these actions themselves prevent. In other words, it is not at all moral to strive out of the goodness of one's heart (and even less so if it for reasons of conformism, cynicism, or self-interest) to establish a hellish society. Should it be discovered – and, for my part, I think this is true ninety-nine times out of a hundred – that the uncontrolled influx of illegal immigrants has a disastrous effect on the whole of society, on the harmony one may observe there, on its educational system, the occupancy rate or overcrowding of its correctional facilities, the safety of its streets and homes, the freedom of its mores, the beauty of its land, or the operation of its social welfare system then the efforts of public authorities to put an end to this influx have strictly nothing immoral about them, no more so than do their (infrequent) attempts to half-heartedly enforce the law. Negligence is the guilty party in this case.

It remains to be determined why this negligence is so great. It remains to be determined why the people and its duly-appointed representatives have suddenly consented to what French people of other eras sought at all costs to avoid and from which they protected the country

---

6. Since this speech was given, the "Arab Spring" has taken place. As it officially seeks to reestablish freedom and the rule of law in the countries concerned, it has been from the beginning been fervently supported by the Party of In-nocence. In its turn, however, it has resulted in massive waves of immigration to France and Europe. the notion that one might flee liberty as a refugee is a novelty of human history, assuming one had not previously collaborated in or served as a henchman for tyranny. So great is the number of those fleeing these events, however, that it is difficult to take them all for former executioners in Mr. Moubarak's or Mr. Ben Ali's secret police.

at the cost of so many sacrifices – I mean, of course, *invasion, counter-colonization*, the *change of people*, the *Great Replacement*.

For a time, I thought that it was to be understood as a distant after-shock of the war and Occupation, of the defeat above all, of the devastating defeat of this country, which for several years following the Armistice had believed itself to be the world's foremost power but that in a few days was reduced to nothing or next to nothing, to a negligible quantity in the titanic conflict then underway. ("What, *the French too*?" exclaimed Keitel during preliminary negotiations at Reims in 1945). I long thought and still do that France never recovered from this humiliation, from the shame that followed, from its compromises and complicities, of which de Gaulle, it is true, had partly cleansed it thanks to his courage, solitude, and genius, but which, once he was gone, resurfaced nearly intact, an incurable, nay mortal wound in collective consciousness. I no longer think nor have I for a long time thought that it is in this *strange defeat* that one must seek the true cause of this astonishing abdication before history, this stupefied consent to the Great Replacement. Great Britain, alas, consents to it no less, and I hasten to point out that the Great Replacement of the English people on its territory, the German people on its, of the Italian in Italy, the foreordained and already well-advanced suffocation of these great cultures and majestic civilizations that gave Europe its incomparable worth, distress me no less than that of the French people in France. The decay of these cultures, the extinction of these ways of life, the massacre of these landscapes are of course not solely due to mass immigration. Rather, they coincide with it as the symptoms of a unique evil that cannot be solely attributed to the humiliation of 1940 and its consequences, since Great Britain did not experience this humiliation but to the contrary heaped glory upon itself by its courage and steely resolve in the face of Nazism.

In the history of the peoples of Europe and several others, Nazism nevertheless remains the common denominator and this independently of whether one fought it, collaborated with its representatives, subscribed to its doctrine, or took part in its crimes. Hitler's murderous madness sullied language, twisted the meaning of words, and altered the course of thought – directly at first and then *indirectly* and more perversely later on, as in a mirror, reversing and inverting its object. This latter period persists to this day. I have called the effect it has upon us the "Second Career of Adolf Hitler." It is less bloody than his first career but longer lasting and hardly less harmful in geopolitical terms. A fatal metonymy is practiced here, the archetypal form of which is the infamous *reductio ad Hitlerum*, the logical absurdity of which, however obvious it may be *in logic* (but it is not on this terrain that the debate takes place), is not enough to protect us. It is as if vegetarianism were a moral monstrosity *mutatis mutandis* on the grounds that Hitler was both a monster and a vegetarian. We have seen the ill-fated word *race*, so beautiful in Bernanos or Racine (*The ancient tombs of the princes of my race . . .*),[xvi] compelled to disappear from law and speech, victim of the absurd meaning given to it by Hitler's followers and henchmen. Poor Bernanos could no longer superbly write, as he did in *The Great Fear of Right-Thinking People* (it is true that he could no longer write that book at all . . .):

"Alas, around the little French boys huddled together over their notebooks, pen in hand, attentive and sticking out their tongues a little, like around young people drunk from their first outing beneath the flowering chestnut trees, in the arms of a young blonde girl, there was in times past that vague and enchanted memory, that dream, that deep murmur in which the race cradles its own."[xvii]

The race no longer cradles its own in any dream. It is no longer a vague and enchanted memory. And it is completely forbidden to hear, under the chestnut trees, its deep murmur. Indeed, the chestnut trees themselves are very ill, except on television. Worse yet: all of the terms and all of the notions that in any way came into contact with the phraseology of the Third Reich have become suspect, as are those who use them. And yet many of them were essential to Europe's system of ontological protection, as indeed they are to that of any other part of the Earth. Deprived of them, the continent is an open city. Their absence and the prohibition that hangs over them because of these intolerable old associations leave Europeans wordless and voiceless faced with all those who consequently see their peninsula as an open-air playground to be used by the rest of the world for expansion, relaxation, and leisure. Just try to pronounce the words *homeland, inheritance, tradition, ancestors, roots, heritage*, or *us*: you will be laughed at before you are loathed.

Even *people* has lost its good standing. In Newspeak, it need hardly be pointed out, *popular*[xviii] [tr. working-class] now means *that which does not belong to the* (indigenous) *people: immigrant, foreigner, French of foreign origin*. It is more or less synonymous with *underprivileged*: *a popular neighborhood, an underprivileged housing project* (that is, a place where the Great Replacement has already happened). Language, which knows all, has already taken note of the thing. Faced with the ongoing colonization, there is no longer an indigenous people, the indigenous are no longer a people or no longer have one: "The candidate's name is Toufik Lassaouï, a fact that should earn him the votes of popular [tr. working-class] neighborhoods."

Let him who has ears hear – and consider himself fortunate not to have read in the same coded language:

". . .the votes of the neighborhoods . . ."

Neighborhood on its own can only be *underprivileged neighborhood*. Only the underprivileged have neighborhoods. For the privileged, there are no neighborhoods.[xix]

For observers who might not be so fond of the idea, the colonization by wombs predicted and endorsed by Houari Boumediene immediately suggests a simple and obvious political and strategic response: have as many children as the colonizer or even more, leaving him no space. Indeed, some even claim that it is falling birthrates in France and in Europe – more precisely, the falling *indigenous* birthrate – that have led to the Great Replacement, paving its way and hastening its arrival. This is a point on which the party of In-nocene and I (who do not always have exactly the same views on everything, though we agree in this case) hold positions that are somewhat difficult to explain and that are not always well received, especially in circles such as yours that are most keenly aware of the ongoing change of people and are the least enthusiastic about this process. For the most part, those who oppose the Great Replacement think that, if we are to resist it, we must have ever more children. This is not our way of seeing things.

It is worth reiterating that we are an ecological party. In-nocence is *non-nocence, non-nuisance, non-pollution*: the battle, which is never entirely won, naturally, and never can be, against everything that harms man, the species, the air, the earth, the landscape, silence, fauna, flora, and the night. And, by far, what most harms man and the planet is the proliferation of man. The Earth has had enough of him. We hold that all environmental policies are perfectly vain if they do not first tackle and tackle without delay uncontrolled demographic growth wherever it is to be found. And we judge irresponsible or mad (the two are not incompatible) the sociologists and economists who, on the pretense that demographic growth has been found on certain occasions to be good for the economy (which in fact is far from always being the case), call for ever more of it, as if this dubious medication could be indefinitely applied, as if there were no limit to the appropriateness of its use, as if, given the state of the world, that limit had not quite obviously been exceeded long ago.

The most advanced peoples have perfectly understood, deep in their hearts and despite the demented entreaties of most demographers, that wisdom lies in demographic stabilization and, better still, decrease. The colonizers long ago sent out by Boumediene doubtless find a dreadful power in the wombs of their womenfolk, and their descendants are carrying out, point by point, the promise made by this statesman and the threat it contained. But we think it would be madness to imitate that power; for, while it is indeed a political, military, conquering, and colonizing power, it is also and at the same time a disaster for the planet, for our country just as much as for the others. At this stage of our human and scientific development, number does not make for power. Just look at the long, solitary resistance of Israel, which finds itself in the midst of a raging ocean of hatred, isolated as its people are among ten or twenty hostile peoples, their population immensely greater than its own. We must not fall into the trap of doing something stupid for the sole reason that those who are conquering us are doing it, that it helps them conquer us, that it is, along with *nocence*, one of the means of their conquest– it is no less stupid for all that. The party of In-nocence is in favor of doing away with pro-natalist policies, the first effect of which, far from protecting us from the Great

Replacement, has indeed been to accelerate it. In lands less favored than our own, in fact, people can hardly believe that there exist in the world countries where one is paid to have children and where one can even, if one knows how to go about it, get by perfectly well without any other occupation than that. And who can be shocked that such people might have nothing more pressing to do than make it to this unbelievable Eldorado as quickly as possible so as to there give birth to five, six, seven, ten, twelve, even seventeen *replacements*, if that's the right word.

As part of a collection entitled *The Communism of the Twenty-First Century*,[7] a title I borrowed from Alain Finkielkraut to refer to the dogmatic antiracist regime and its reign, the media-political complex and its ascendancy, I recently published a short essay called *Worse than Evil*, which addressed the conceivable remedies to counter-colonization, the forms of national resistance that one can bring to bear on it.

It dealt with the subject negatively, for two of these remedies were, in my opinion, *worse than evil*. The first was demographic growth; the second the National Front or, more precisely, Jean-Marie Le Pen. It is difficult to broach this question at the present juncture, for the National Front is obviously undergoing a transformation. We do not know what tomorrow holds for it should Marine Le Pen become its leader, as today seems most likely, what mark she will leave on it if that is the case, how she might possibly change its direction, whether it will even keep its present name or instead adopt a new one in order to bring together all opponents of the Great Replacement, no matter the political family from which they hail. Let us not mortgage the future; let us wait. I will only say that I take it to be one of the great catastrophes of our recent history, of which there have been no shortage, that the only somewhat consistent and explicit resistance to the worst disaster affecting us, the change of people, should for a quarter of a century have been embodied by a man, Jean-Marie Le Pen, whom I can in no way support and to whom it is fundamentally impossible for me to give my vote. One effect of this impossibility and of the impossibility of casting

---

7. "Pire que le mal," in Renaud Camus, *Le Communisme du XXIe siècle*, Xenia (Vevey, 2007), pp. 77-98.

a vote at this decisive moment in our country's history, of being unable to give my vote to anyone, of despairing of my vote, was my decision, in 2002, to found the Party of In-nocence.

The time is passing and I have gone on long enough, so I will very briefly say a word regarding a third remedy, an impossible one in my opinion: to turn or return to Christianity. One strength of the colonizers, doubtless of a majority of them, is Islam – and they are well aware of this, they know perfectly well that this is what most frightens us, that it is their most fearsome weapon, and this is indeed one reason they are so fond of it. Islam is a very dynamic religion, beloved by its faithful and very naturally, almost invincibly geared for conquest. Another religion could have resisted it; it did so in the past and succeeded. Once again, one need only think of Poitiers, Las Navas de Tolosa, Lepanto, Vienna, and so many other battles in which Europe as we know it was founded and affirmed. Some believe that the same faith could render the same services. Alas, faith cannot be compelled. Against a living religion, one that, like all living religions, is less concerned with morality than with dogma, power, submission, and loyalty, a half-dead religion is no match. And I have too much respect and even affection for Christianity, despite its turpitudes, to return to it out of self-interest, strategic considerations, or the simple yet true reason that we would be stronger if the faith still inhabited us. I have often been called a *Maurrasian*, quite haphazardly, by journalists who have read neither Maurras nor me but who found the insult, for of course that is what it is in their minds, fit nicely into their arsenal and could seriously harm their adversary – that is, me. Yet this is a point and there are many others on which I am not Maurrasian to save my life. I would not think it honorable to throw myself and still less others into the arms of a religion that inspires no faith in me.

It inspires affection in me, as I said, and often admiration, though sometimes anger. It is a very intimate part of my culture. I could say as much, despite the great swathes of this beautiful legacy of which I am ignorant, about Greek heritage, Jewish heritage, Celtic heritage, and that of the Enlightenment and free inquiry. The poles of resistance to what is taking place – counter-colonization and the Great Replacement –

are not to be found in demographic growth, or religion, or Jean-Marie Le Pen. They are to be found in culture and political will, political will in the service of culture, primarily French culture: not that it is necessarily superior to English or German culture but because it is ours and we are responsible for it within European culture and all the cultures of the world, towards which it has always been extraordinarily open. It and the civilization that gave birth to it and on which it for centuries cast its light are among the most precious, loftiest and, until recently, most admired cultures and civilizations to have ever graced the Earth or be witnessed by man. We must defend them and promote them from within and without, especially against the ready-made substitutes that are far from equaling them, be it in terms of mildness, intelligence, dignity for man, freedom for woman, or spiritual elevation. I am of course thinking of so-called multiculturalism, which everyday proves itself to be just another code word for our spectacular, market-driven stupefaction, our hyper-democratic hebetude, the Ruquiérization[xx] of our mind, our cabaret politics, our Great Deculturation. To save what can still be saved, to offer the life of the mind, while awaiting something better, a few sanctuaries amid the debacle, the party of In-nocence has from its earliest days demanded the creation of a radio station and television channel dedicated to culture – without the least chauvinism, it must be said, other than that of knowledge, art, science, literature, theater, cinema, and music (and I do not mean a station or channel after the fashion of TF1 or "France Culture").

I just mentioned Israel but I could as easily evoke Quebec, though perhaps the Quebec of the second half of the last century more so than that of today, which alas seems rather inclined to give up, the result, more of mass immigration and so-called "multiculturalism," than of Americanization and federalism, as was the case in the past. The Québécois were an outpost of the French people hemmed in on all sides by pressing conquerors. Now the French are the Québécois or should try to be if they are to withstand, as the former did, denaturation, denaturalization, or however one should name the phenomenon of which deculturation is only one part, at once a symbol, a condition, and the necessary means.

Faced with the massed legions of the Great Replacement, we must ever more firmly assert our desire to keep our culture, our language of course, our *art de vivre* and way of being, our religion or what is left of it, our landscapes or what remains of them, our laws, mores, habits, dishes, and freedoms. France has always been open to those who wished to join her out of love, admiration, or a sincere desire to become integrated into her spirit and way of being on the Earth. She must close herself off completely, however, and should have done so long ago, to those who claim to settle here in order to rebuild on her territory the type of society they have left. She is not an Islamic land, for example, and if it were only up to me, she would absolutely refuse to become one. For a very pious Muslim, one who is strongly attached to the external and collective rites of his religion and even more so if he is a fundamentalist, settling here should in no way be a reasonable objective. It is pitiful and would be funny were it not so tragic that the law of 1905 on secularism, the origins of which were highly anti-clerical, whatever else one might say, serves today, by an extraordinary reversal, as cover for the country's Islamization. Oskar Freysinger and his Helvetians[xxi] have our total support and admiration for their refusal to see Switzerland covered in minarets. We refuse to see them cover France. But the time has grown very late. The presidential election of 2012 is doubtless our last chance to make our passionate opposition to the Great Replacement known.

It is for this reason that I am a candidate in it or a candidate for the candidacy – less from any hope that I will succeed, it must be said, than from an inability to continue doing nothing faced with the tragedy now being perpetrated all around us, a tragedy without precedent in our history. In fifteen centuries, there has not been a single episode, dramatic though some may have been, neither the Hundred Years War nor the German occupation, that has represented a threat as serious, deadly, and virtually definitive in its consequences for our homeland as the change of people. In light of this and however severe today's economic crisis may be, however worrying the issue of debt, however alarming the fate of our most disadvantaged compatriots or those facing the greatest social and economic precarity . . . in light of this, the campaign themes of the other candidates are laughable, I am not afraid to say. Indeed, the crushing preponderance of economic questions over political ones in this debate is an obvious symptom of the Great Deculturation, the Great Decivilization, and the erasure of national sentiment – of the price of petroleum over the fate of the state, of retirement over the retreat from history, of the day-to-day life of individuals, however legitimate a concern that may be, over the fate of the nation, as if the survival of a people as such were less important than the comfort with which it pursued its mad journey toward the dustbins of history.

But I wager this is not the case at all. Peoples die hard. Ours has several times over shown itself capable of making a spectacular recovery. Nations are more resilient than the merchants of available brain time would like. Civilizations as well. They have been known to rise from the grave.

Nocence, Instrument of the Great Replacement[1] [2010][2]

Ladies and Gentleman,

Nocence, Instrument of the Great Replacement: the title that I have chosen for this short speech may seem rather odd, even obscure.

I imagine that you know all too well what the *Great Replacement* is. It is, in fact, the grim realization of Bertolt Brecht's famous quip. You know the original version, "I have learned that the people has 'forfeited the confidence of the government' and 'could win it back only by redoubled efforts.' Would it not be easier in that case for the government to dissolve the people and elect another?" You are even more familiar with its current version: "It is very simple; we will just have to change the people."[i] In his recent book *Egobody*, the philosopher Robert Redeker,[ii] one of the most obvious direct, personal victims of Islamism, which has targeted him with death threats and forced him to spend months in hiding, reflects on the philosophical implications

---

1. This speech was delivered at Paris' Espace Charenton on December 18th, 2010, as part of a Conference on the Islamization of Europe. It was subject to a complaint filed by MRAP, resulting in a trial that earned the author two successive condemnations, one before the 17th Chamber of the Criminal Court of Paris, on April 14th, 2014, and another on April 9th, 2015, before the Paris Court of Appeals, which upheld the earlier ruling.
2. "La Nocence, instrument du Grand Remplacement (18 décembre 2010)," in *Le Grand Remplacement: Introduction au remplacisme global.* (Paris, La Nouvelle Librairie, 2021), pp. 157-170.

of the modern body, all parts of which can be replaced. This is how the replacists see the people: one can indefinitely swap out all of its parts and it will still be the same people or in any case will keep the same name.

I recall one of the first times I was struck by this point of view, which I find astonishing and incomprehensible. It was while listening to the radio, to public radio, a Mecca, like its televisual counterpart, of replacist ideology. It was ten or fifteen years ago and the topic was Spain and the retirement problems it was already having, which were linked to demographic considerations. Some worried that there would soon no longer be enough Spaniards to pay for Spaniards' pensions. But the journalist was completely reassuring. He believed that the problem was a false one. Indeed, one need only bring Moroccans, who could not ask for anything better, Mauritanians, and Malians to Spain, and the matter would be settled. These newcomers would make excellent Spaniards. Except that they would not be Spaniards since they would be Moroccans, Mauritanians, North Africans of all sorts, which is to say, descendants of the very people from whom Spain and Spaniards had spent seven centuries trying to free themselves. Indeed, this was the very subject matter of the *romancero*. Well no, actually. Because for the replacists, if we declared them to be Spanish then they would be Spanish, they would enjoy, crucially, all the privileges of that status, they would be an opportunity for Spain.[iii]

It is hardly worth pointing out that the essential precondition for this mysterious transubstantiation is what I have elsewhere called *The Great Deculturation*. A people who knows its classics does not meekly submit to being led to the dustbins of history. If it is to accept its replacement, it must no longer know who it is, what it is, what it has been. The teaching of forgetting is necessary if national belonging is to become no more than a name. Less than a name: a stamp on a passport, an affiliation to which one lays claims when there is some advantage, economic or strategic, in doing so. This is the famous "I am as French as you are and even more so!" of every respectably rigged debate. But this same affiliation is disavowed at the first opportunity by saying *the French* to refer to those French people to whom one belongs without really belonging while boasting of some recipe from *back home* in reference to Algeria or Morocco or while parading through Marseille waving Algerian flags or smashing everything in one's path because Algeria has won a soccer match (one can only wonder what their distress and discontent would have looked like had Algeria lost . . .).

I first experienced the Great Replacement in Lunel, in the Hérault department, some fifteen years ago, and also in the old, medieval villages of the coastal plain after noticing to my stupefaction one fine day that, in the space of a single generation, the population had completely changed, that it was no longer the same people at the windows or on the sidewalks, that a visual transformation had taken place, that, in the very places of my culture and my civilization, I found myself walking in another culture and another civilization, which I had yet to learn had been adorned with the lovely, deceitful name *multiculturalism*.

And now for *nocence*. I am speaking here on behalf of a party, the Party of In-nocence, which I grant bears an unwieldy name since it has made the difficult wager that it could spread a concept among the public, *in-nocene*, which in two words is not at all the same thing as innocence-in-one-word, for the latter is something that one can lose or is in danger of losing at any time, an object of nostalgia or longing, whereas in-nocence-in-two-words, *non-nocence*, the repudiation of nocence, of harm, is an ideal to be attained, an aspiration, something that is before us rather than behind us. In-nocence-in-two-words posits that nocence, which is to say harm, the act of harming, to make an attempt on another's life or ruin it, defile it, make it unbearable, is prior, that it is always *already there*, that it is that against which one must struggle both within and outside of ourselves. Nocence, of course, is pollution[iv] in the ecological sense of the term: attacks on nature and the quality of life, the quality of the air, the quality of the water, the quality of the landscape, and of our national heritage. It is also all the attacks on person and property (the famous and oh-so-delicately named *incivilities*), up to and including organized crime. As we see it, the great advantage of the concept of *in-nocence* is that it allows us to consider *as a whole* everything that pertains to politics, ecology, day-to-day existence, to daily life, real life, the relations between individuals, citizens, neighbors, fellow citizens, our fellow inhabitants on this planet and in our apartment buildings as well as in our neighborhoods, suburbs, cities, and nations.

Yet to consider *as a whole* is precisely what the media-political complex is incapable of doing. It is exactly what it does not want to do. It is what it strives not to do in the framework of this great undertaking to obfuscate reality, an undertaking indispensable to its own survival because if it showed the world as its lack of foresight has made it, as its incompetence, base calculation, and the interplay of unknown interests have made it, the citizenry would not fail to hold it accountable. Whence this language it has invented so as *not* to say, not to show, to hide what is taking place and has already taken place: *young people* for delinquents, *working-class neighborhoods* for neighborhoods that the indigenous working-class population has had to flee, *disadvantaged neighborhoods* for zones of violence and lawlessness, *multiculturalism* for the great deculturation, *diversity* for the triumph of sameness, for the disappearance of identities, for the universal suburb. And so on. Whence also the unmoving partition it imposes between problems that, as a result, appear to float in the air totally independent of reality and have not the slightest chance of ever finding solutions because they have no explanations, because their explanations are hidden and must remain hidden: the crisis of transmission, the collapse of the educational system, the housing crisis, prison overcrowding, delinquency, violence, insecurity.

One must fight violence, they say, one must fight insecurity, one must fight the delinquency of young people in working-class neighborhoods. But always they partition, isolate, euphemize, and try to render incomprehensible – except to the victims, of course, except to the frontline protagonists, who for their part know what is really going on. On one side is everyday life, the schools, stairwells, neighborhood problems, rioters, smashed storefronts, looting, drugs, drug-dealing – in a word, *nocence*, the enormity of nocence. On the other side and partitioned from it: politics properly so-called, history, the country's future, the fate of the French people, which is to say, to repeat, and to get to the point, the Great Replacement, so-called multiculturalism, which is merely a code word for the Great Deculturation, and, we might as well come out with it, the growing presence of Islam, the growing ascendancy of Islam throughout the territory and landscape, the gradual Islamization of the country.

One side and the other supposedly have nothing to do with each other, one side and the other should remain carefully separated. It would even be *criminal* – a word much-loved by the complex – to draw a line between insecurity and immigration, between violence and so-called multiculturalism, between prison overcrowding and counter-colonization, between the difficulties of educational transmission and the fact that France is now like a spinster who raises other people's children, children who are strangers to her culture and very often her language, and who, in many cases, have learned from their families and places of origin to hate that culture, and that history, and that language, all of which are then to general surprise so difficult to instill in them. I am of course not saying that the *entire* crisis of the educational system is the result of immigration and the Great Replacement. I am of course not saying that these are the source of *all* nocence. I am saying that one must be blind or of unspeakably bad faith to not see and not say, to not want it to be said, that nocence is in league with conquest. Even better – and this is the point to which I wanted to devote this short speech – nocence is, along with demography, though that is another subject, one of the principal instruments of conquest, a resource, one might even call it a military resource: its military wing.

Political leaders make me laugh when, in an effort to reduce or control this floodtide of nocence, this permanent violence, this unbearable insecurity, this headlong deterioration of human and social relations over ever-expanding swathes of what one hesitates to still call *national* territory, these political officials, these mayors, these prefects, these cabinet ministers appeal to the conquerors' religious leaders, hoping that their influence, faith, religion, the mitigating effect of religion on mores, will subdue their aggressiveness and render them as gentle as lambs. These secular leaders have got their religions mixed up. They are confusing the newcomers' religion with their own, that of their ancestors. In what concerns those who are strangers to it, the non-believers, the infidels, the religion they are dealing with and in which they set so much hope for the restoration of public order does not primarily preach gentleness, kindness, in-nocence. This is not at all its first concern. Its first concern, which it very much considers a *moral* concern and this is precisely what misleads us, is its own triumph, the greater glory of its god, assuring itself an ever more secure and wider grip on the world, either by conversion, conquest, or preferably both at the same time. Everything that tends in the direction of this ideal is good, morally good, religiously good. Nothing that tends in the direction of this ideal could possibly be evil. This is what explains the notable weakness, which in our naiveté never fails to shock us, of religious con-demnations of terrorist attacks and crimes committed in the name of the conquering religion, condemnations always uttered, in the best of cases, half-heartedly. This is because, for this religion, the question of means is utterly secondary, as is indeed the case for most religions, which are only very secondarily moral codes, while they are in their ascendant phase. The core of their moral code is to vanquish, to win, to subjugate, to spread. Otherwise, they would betray their raison d'être. They would not be what they are.

Indeed, this religion cannot be separated from a civilization, a civilization that has known extraordinarily brilliant moments, that has made lofty achievements and produced great works in the domains of architecture, poetry, storytelling, mysticism, and music. This civilization has never forgotten its nomadic origins and the close link, the near confusion, that exists in its mind between struggle and taking possession, between fighting and sacking, between war and raiding. Consider that characteristic and almost inevitable moment in recent political demonstrations when the direct intervention of the so-called "opportunities for France" immediately results in smashed windows and looted stores.[v] I ask them to forgive me for speaking here of their violence, for I know that they cannot bear such criticism. It seems ter-ribly unjust to them. It infuriates them. Hardly do they hear it than they smash everything, they loot, they plant bombs.

Do not be fooled, however. You are not dealing with hooligans here; you are dealing with soldiers. Well, they are hooligans, but these hooligans are an army, the military wing of the conquest. Little matter if they are aware of this or not, and indeed I believe they are much more aware of it than one gives them credit for. Nocence, whether it be noise, destruction, the occupation of apartment building halls, and the requirement that one lower one's gaze in passing, be it thefts, burglaries, assault with deadly weapons, drug-dealing, the totality of what is now politely called organized crime and the new, ultraviolent forms it has taken – nocence is the instrument of the Great Replacement, of the change of people, of counter-colonization, of conquest, of the never-ending expansion of areas already subjugated by the neo-colonizers. Those among the newcomers who make life impossible for the natives force them to flee, force them to evacuate the terrain – this is what the Anglo-Saxons call *white flight*, the fleeing of white people – or, worse yet, stay and submit, assimilate to them, convert to their mores, their religion, their way of inhabiting the earth and its suburbs, which are, alas, its future.

I have been reprimanded – I am used to it – for having spoken of *ethnic cleansing* in this connection. Very well, we do not want to make anyone angry: let us speak simply of *housekeeping*, of military house-keeping. These colonizers, who endlessly criticize the natives for not sufficiently welcoming them or welcoming them well enough, seem to have nothing more pressing to do once they have settled in than to take up all the space for themselves and, like all colonizers, dream only of being among themselves, the natives only being good in their eyes for running businesses, perhaps, keeping shop, even if that means the shop will be looted from time to time. While perfectly suited for the initial phase, the famous melting pot, the aforementioned social mixing upon which so much hope was placed has now been largely superseded across broad swathes of the territory. The attacks to which police officers, firefighters, and doctors are subjected as soon as they venture into already subjugated territory speak for themselves: though they are constantly reduced to matters of delinquency and the fight against delinquency, it is in terms of *territory*, of the defense and conquest of territory, that these problems truly present themselves.

I am obviously not saying that *all* newcomers practice nocence. Nor am I saying – far from it – that it is *only* newcomers who practice nocence. What I am saying is that a staggering, improbable, incredibly disproportionate proportion of this nocence is their doing and that, in such proportions, nocence is not a phenomenon that can be left to policing or the courts, whose feebleness is all too familiar, caught up as they are in a web of laws, regulations, European directives, and even international treaties that leave the nation defenseless and turn the polity into an open city, a sort of Troy where the wooden horses are in every public square, cheered on by our overjoyed opinion makers, by the frenzied Friends of the Disaster, by the impatient collaborators of the Great Replacement. Whether one is speaking of law enforcement or the courts, the penal system is impotent in the face of what is to the highest degree a matter for political thought and action, for political action of the most pressing and urgent kind, of a kind most essential to the survival of the state. Every time a native is commanded to lower his gaze and step off the sidewalk, a little bit more of the country's independence and its people's freedom is dragged through the gutter.

The Replaceable Man[1] [2012]

Ladies and Gentleman,

I feared until the last minute that I would not be able to appear before you this evening as planned as I was being detained at the Department of Criminal Investigations. It's the sort of place where you know when you enter but can never be too sure when you'll leave. I was summoned there at the behest of the Deputy District Attorney, Madame de Fontette, in response to a complaint filed against me by MRAP.[i] The paradox, if I may say so, is that this complaint involves a speech I gave in 2010 at the Conference on the Islamization of Our Countries[ii] and that had the same general theme as tonight's, namely the Great Replacement. In other words, they're keeping an eye on me and I'm speaking on eggshells, as it were. I see for that matter that I was mistaken about the subtitle of this talk or that, with everything that is going on – Madame Fontette, Police Officer Miche, the Rue du Château-des-Rentiers – I mixed up my talks. I see that you have written: "Immigration and the Change of People." I had believed it was: "The Replaceable Man." I don't think it's too serious a mistake, for really there's not much difference between them. Alas, it's exactly the same subject.

"To speak is a strange place," said Blanchot. Another particularity of the situation I present to you and which almost prevented me from

---

1. "L'homme remplaçable (conférence devant France-Israël, 8 mars 2012)," in *Le Grand Remplacement: Introduction au remplacisme global.* (Paris, La Nouvelle Librairie, 2021), pp. 193-220.This speech was given in Paris on March 8th, 2012, at the invitation of the France-Israel Association.

addressing you today is that MRAP's complaint against me concerns a *speech*, a speech given more than a year ago now, a speech that has since been published and is now a book or *part* of a book alongside two other speeches, this collection of oratory having been published last fall by David Reinharc Editions under this very title, *The Great Replacement*. Why attack speech when one possesses a written document, which says exactly the same thing since, in this specific instance, it was composed before the speech was ever given and formed the content of the latter? Is this by virtue of an old French tradition – not always respected, admittedly – that would make one think twice before attacking an author qua author for the purpose of silencing him or a book or text he has written, whereas the spoken word is somehow less protected? Perhaps. Or maybe MRAP is simply ill-informed and does not know that this book exists.

Its ignorance would be somewhat excusable, for the press did not do much to bring this volume to its attention or to that of the public. There are two kinds of reasons for this, I believe – let us leave aside a third, which certainly is not inconceivable, which would simply be that the book is bad.

The first reason has to do with the sum total of my books, of which there are now more or less one hundred, with my "literary personality," if that expression is not too ridiculous, with me, in a word: the media and I took an instant dislike to one another. I have always taken the liberty of saying what I think of them, which has not always been entirely favorable. Yet they are the power that never forgives or forgets. A man who has once said something bad about a newspaper no longer exists for that newspaper. Or, should it be impossible to ignore him completely, he is dragged through the mud. Indeed, the two methods are not incompatible: he can be made to disappear beneath the mud. Preferably, however, one will have nothing to do with him, will act as if he did not exist, and will sign off on his certificate of social death, to speak like Tocqueville, whom I cannot resist the bitter, tragic pleasure of citing once more:

> Under the absolute government of one alone, despotism struck
> the body crudely, so as to reach the soul; and the soul, escaping

from those blows, rose gloriously above it; but in democratic republics, tyranny does not proceed in this way; it leaves the body and goes straight for the soul. The master no longer says to you: You shall think as I do or you shall die; he says: you are free not to think as I do; your life, your goods, everything remains to you; but from this day on, you are a stranger among us. You shall keep your privileges in the city, but they will become useless to you; for if you crave the vote of your fellow citizens, they will not grant it to you, and if you demand only their esteem, they will still pretend to refuse it to you. You shall remain among men, but you shall lose your rights of humanity. When you approach those like you, they shall flee you as being impure; and those who believe in your innocence, even they shall abandon you, for one would flee them in their turn. Go in peace, I leave you your life, but I leave it to you worse than death.[iii]

The second reason has to do with the subject of this book, the speech being challenged in court by MRAP, and my remarks to you this evening: The Great Replacement. What I call the Great Replacement is very simple; each one of us here can observe it every day, so long as he has the audacity to believe his own eyes, his daily experience, very often his suffering, which my friend Richard Millet[iv] recently had the courage to acknowledge on television in front of dumbfounded and soon indignant guests when he spoke of his pain at being the only one or almost the only one of his species, of his race, "the only white person," as he said, on the 6 PM subway at Châtelet station. What I call the Great Replacement is the change of people, the substitution of one or several peoples for the people whose ancestral roots are there, whose history had for hundreds or thousands of years coincided with the territory in question.

Should any of you still find this vague and fail to see what I am alluding to, it seems to me that I might, speaking as I am before the France-Israel Association, appeal to an example that should finally convey my meaning: the Great Replacement is what would happen to Israel if, God forbid, we were to accede to the Palestinian demand for the so-called *right of return*. Under such conditions, could Israel remain a

Jewish State, as one says? With another people or several others, would France still be France other than in name, supposing she retains that for very long?

It was ten or fifteen years ago, while listening to a radio program about Spain, that I believe this dilemma first occurred to me. Initially, the journalist pretended to be very worried about the demographic situation of Spain, where the population is aging before one's very eyes. Who was going to pay for Spaniards' pensions, he wondered? Fortunately, an answer was ready at hand. And after having worried us a great deal about the old age of Spaniards, he was ready to fully re-assure us. There, right on Spain's doorstep, was a marvelous resource, tens and hundreds of thousands of Moroccans, Mauritanians, and Malians who would be delighted to come to the country, rapidly re-duce the average age of its population, and, while they were at it, ac-cording to this journalist, fund the pensions of Spaniards old enough to leave the workforce.

In truth, even on this last point – that is, the issue of pensions, secondary and even trivial as they are compared to the destiny of a people, of a nation – one would very quickly learn that the proposed system did not work nearly as well as we had been told it would, that it even tended to worsen the situation. But this was not the reason for my surprise and concern. I could not and still do not understand how, if one were to bring in Moroccans and Mauritanians to substitute for deficient Spaniards, the Spanish demographic situation would be stabi-lized (which, as it stood, did not seem to me threatened at all but that is another topic for debate, which we should perhaps set aside for today). Such stabilization by these means was only possible if one imagined completely abstract men and women, *naked* ones so to speak, reduced to themselves, neutered of all origin, all belonging, and also all culture, for culture is of course not only but is *also* and even *first and foremost*, if only chronologically, the voice of the dead, the inheritance of ances-tors, the memory of great works, customs, rites, and convictions, even if they must be abandoned or only momentarily stifled. Fortunately, neither nature nor culture makes men like this, men who are so mor-ally and intellectually disarmed, so subject to the eternal *da capo*, the constant return to nothing for lack of any heritage. But this is just how the Great Replacement would have them and just how it manufactures them thanks to the industry of stupefaction, which in this is energetically assisted or prepared by the teaching of forgetting.

The issue is very efficiently summed up by Christopher Caldwell in his book, *Reflections on the Revolution in Europe: Immigration, Islam, and the West.*[v] He asks: "*Can you have the same Europe with different people in it?*" At the risk of verging on absurdity and certainly distress, one might just as well ask: "Can you have the same Israel with another people inside its borders?" And, in a much more pressing way since the thing has already in large part happened: "Will you have the same France with one or several other peoples on its territory?" To his own question, Caldwell answers *no* without the least ambiguity. Transposing the same question, as I have, to the case of Israel, I understand that the Israelis and their friends also answer *no* without hesitation. And I, too, answer *no* in what concerns France. In order to answer *yes* to any of these questions, peoples would have to count for nothing, would have to be of a purely administrative substance, with no history, indeed no past, no physical reality, no body, no skin, no blood, no soul.

As I have taken the liberty to draw the comparison, it will be said that France and Israel are not nations built on the same principles and this would be right. It will be said that Israel is the state of the Jewish people whereas France is the state of those who want to be French and this would not be wrong. Yet one would still need to know what this desire to be French means and above all whether it is always there. But this is precisely what one is not supposed to talk about.

What Presiding Judge Delegorgue said time and again during Zola's trial at the time of the Dreyfus Affair[vi] can be said of the Great Replacement now underway: "The question will not be asked."

As you will have noticed, we are in the midst of a presidential election. The Great Replacement is, in my opinion, the most profound and most radical upheaval to confront our country since the beginning of its history: more profound and more radical than the Hundred Years War, more profound and more radical, more permanent in its consequences, than the defeat of 1940. But no, we will go on as if nothing is happening. And if, for once, we agree to put a name on what is taking place and which has been so denied, it will be to observe that what's done is done, that there is no longer any need to talk about it, that one must come to terms with it, that the best thing is to learn to love it. One is familiar with the famous diptych: nothing is happening, nothing is happening, nothing is happening, there has always been immigration, and it is even diminishing. That's at first. And then comes (but they can be simultaneous, that's the best of all): there has been immigration, they are here, French society has been transformed, it is in the past and there's no point in dwelling on it. Earlier this week, the newspaper *Le Monde*, which has been the fervent promoter and unruffled chronicler of the change of people, very calmly mentioned that the last traditional butcher in Pantin, a city of sixty thousand inhabitants, would be shutting its doors, with the butcher handing over the keys to his halal successor, if I may say so. The symbolic import of the event did not seem to have crossed the columnist's mind.

I tend to think for my part that even the crisis, the terrible economic crisis,[vii] the ravages of which I do not in the least underestimate, but which I nevertheless note, on the basis of what one can see with one's own eyes in most parts of the country, is not particularly notable, counts for very little, and is almost an illusion when set against the other crisis, the demographic one, the one that must not be named, the change of people. And, if you will allow me, I will say that, given the present state of the field for the job of head of state, there are three types of candidate. First, there are the four or five major candidates, who we are told are down to two or perhaps four again in the last two or three days. Second, there are ten or twelve *small candidates*, whose numbers continue to diminish as they withdraw from the race and throw their support behind major ones. And third, with all due respect, there is me, small to the point of invisibility, invisible to the point of not existing.

It is an ectoplasm that speaks to you, a phantom, a corpse, an invisible man, a black hole. I am nevertheless a French author, one not totally unknown and who has been translated in several languages. Special numbers of academic journals have been devoted to my work and it has been the object of international colloquia, including one hosted by Yale University. I have nevertheless written about one hundred books, some published by major publishing houses and several of which concern eminently political subjects, including *The Communism of the Twenty-First Century*, *The Great Deculturation*, *Decivilization* and, once again, *The Great Replacement*. I am nevertheless the President of a political party, the Party of In-nocence, two words and a hyphen (if you wish, I will explain this choice of name). While I allow that it is not exactly a mass party, it has devoted activists who are presently going to great trouble to collect the notorious five hundred signatures.[viii] The party is in perfect working order and possesses a good quality journal, the *Cahiers de L'In-nocence*, and a detailed platform, which has also been published in book form care of our friend David Reinharc, who is here with us today.

But to no avail. We are unable to obtain the necessary signatures because the media does not talk about me and the media does not talk about me because they either do not take me seriously, have themselves never heard of me, or, to the contrary, have a score to settle with me, or, finally, because they above all wish to avoid any discussion of the Great Replacement, which is, I repeat, nevertheless by far and whatever one might say to the contrary the single most important historical phenomenon of all the historical phenomena confronting us today, indeed the single most important one that France has experienced in the course of her history since it is bringing that history to an end. It is the eternal story of Lichtenberg's knife. One changes its blade and then its haft: is it the same knife?

The Great Replacement is not or *would not be* my only campaign theme, or at least *would not be* if I were able to properly run for office. The Party of In-nocence and I take just as great an interest in educational issues, and one of the principal measures we are proposing is what we call *school secession*. It is our view that, in its present, debased state, the educational system can no longer be reformed. Of course, there is no shortage of reforms, and counter-reforms, and indeed plans for yet more, but it is all too late. There are too many forces of inertia arrayed against it, too much corporatism, too much abdication baked into the system, too much ideology, a too-great acceptance of impotence, of, dare I say, *anthropological* impotence, so deeply has it taken root in the structures themselves. Nor is it only the schools that are concerned. There is something *below* the schools, something having to do with the family, with the new structures of parenthood, with the relationship between parents and children, with the relations between generations – I have discussed all of this in two of the books I mentioned in passing, *The Great Deculturation* and *Decivilization*.

Nor has the teaching profession escaped unharmed from these phenomena of deculturation and decivilization since they first got underway, far from it. These questions first arose a generation or two ago: the recalcitrant students of yesterday, those who did not learn very much and who received their diplomas because it was hardly conceivable that they not receive them, are now part of the teaching profession. I am not a minister just taking up my duties and obliged to say, as one inevitably does when one is the Minister of the Interior, that the police force is made up of exemplary civil servants *who do a tremendous job*; or, if he is the Minister of Justice, that judges are exceptional people *who do a remarkable job under difficult conditions*; or, if he is the Minister of Education, that teachers display admirable competence and devotion, *and do a sensational job*. I cannot speak to devotion. As for competence, for example as regards language and the quality of language, I sometimes have my doubts. Of course, these doubts do not concern *all* of the individuals in question, very far from it. But they do concern enough of them that I am not sure one can today say of the teaching profession in our country or, for that matter, the judiciary that it is of particularly outstanding quality.

Even so, there are many excellent teachers. There are also – and this point interests us more directly here – many teachers who are in despair over the present situation, over this dreadful waste. As I am when I see so many boys and girls of every social, economic, cultural, and ethnic origin, who could have received an education and made something of it, something for themselves, something for the community, for the common good, and who did not receive this education or were given a mediocre simulacrum because of the advanced state of decay in which the system finds itself.

It is with them in mind, these boys and girls who are aware that they are being robbed of their future, as well as for their parents and the teachers I just mentioned, that we have drawn up what is, I believe, one of the most striking proposals of our platform: *school secession*. This is not at all a matter of moving from public to private schooling and still less of creating some kind of sectarian system. It is a matter of securing, for the secessionists, a number of high schools and other educational institutions proportionate to their number. One such school if there are a thousand of them, one hundred schools if there are one hundred thousand of them, and so on. This system would be based on a kind of triple voluntarism: the voluntary participation of its teachers, the voluntary participation of students' parents, and the voluntary participation of the students themselves. We will also proceed from the assumption that the problems of transmission are not so complicated as is often claimed. We basically and more or less consciously know what kind of education yields results and what kind does not. It is ideology that incessantly complicates matters and stands in the way of getting back to this. For us, the essential point is to make sure no one who wants to learn [*apprendre*], in the two senses of this verb, *to teach* and *to receive knowledge*,[ix] be hindered from doing so. Organic education specialists tell us that it is the child whom they want to place at the center of the system or that they have already placed him there, with the result that the aforementioned system is infantile, chaotic, and violent. But their true golden child, the one around whom all turns and that is the object of all attention, is in fact precisely the *hinderer*: not just he who will not learn because he does not want to learn or is incapable of doing so, but also he who will *hinder* others from learning, above all if there are two, three, or fifteen of these students in the classroom, where they are indeed often in the majority. Our secessionist high schools will be reserved for teachers who want to teach, parents who want their children to learn, and students who want to learn. If these conditions are met, it must be reiterated, everyone will be admitted without distinction of wealth or origin. And those who would like to make the most of this education but have difficulty keeping up with it, for example because they are from a "culturally disadvantaged" background, as the expression goes, will be especially assisted in their efforts by the members of a special educational intervention corps, so to speak, whose mission will be to ensure that no one be condemned to an undesirable or undesired educational situation, and that it can at any moment be improved for the better if the party in question is so willing.

A secessionist education will be available, I repeat, to everyone who *desires* it. The goal, in effect, is to restore to knowledge, instruction, and education the quality with which they are consubstantial and which should never have been lost: that of being a privilege, an opportunity, something eminently *desirable*. It will be given to all who desire it. In this system, however, those who do not desire it will not remain – those who cannot or do not want to take advantage of it, those, above all, who would hinder others from taking advantage of it. Rest assured, the punishment will not be harsh for these students: they will be sent back to the current system, about which so many commentators say so many good things every day or at least say that it can be reformed. They will not find our punishment too severe, for it will be what they so fervently champion. We will leave them to their reforms and to their reforms of reforms – unless the example we offer in its turn inspires their desire and more and more people wish to join the triple voluntarist system, secession becoming the norm. In the meantime, there is nothing to lose. The present system is our safety net, our guarantee to those who reject the experience we offer.

You may be wondering why I am speaking to you about education and the schools in a talk officially dedicated to the Great Replacement, to the change of people, and, more precisely, to the replaceable man, he *who can be replaced*, who is not irreplaceable, that is, he who is not entirely a man or an individual and still less a citizen. It is because there is a close relationship between the change of people and the disaster of the national educational system. This relationship is active in both directions but I will not today insist on the relationship of cause and effect between the change of people in classrooms and the difficulty, nay the impossibility, of teaching in them. Far be it for me to think that the tragedy of the schools is solely due to immigration, though it is a major component of it. Even less do I maintain that the impossibility of transmission is the *cause* of the Great Replacement, which would be absurd. Those I call the Friends of the Disaster – the ex-*standard-risers*, those who formerly assured us that academic "standards are rising" (they have abandoned this pretense somewhat . . .) and who still think and say that culture is spreading, that violence is abating, that immigration is diminishing, that in any case there was never much of it to begin with, that it has been declining for years, that in any case now that it is here the question is no longer whether it is a good thing or a bad thing but rather how to adapt to it and learn to love it, that France has *always* been a country of immigration, that indeed more is needed, that, in general, we need more of what seems to have not worked, more immigration, more pedagogy, more suburban planning, more multiculturalism and ethnic plurality, more disaster, in short, for if it is a disaster it is because we have not gone far enough, have not sufficiently believed in what we were doing, because we have spoiled everything for lack of faith, nostalgia, attachment to outdated values, idealization of the past, and, of course, *racism* (it does not work if we do not add *racism*) – in short, our friends, the Friends of the Disaster, have a theory they adore, what I would call the conspiracy theory theory.

Even though it is well known that they hate the thing, these words, *conspiracy theory*, exert a magical force of attraction on the Friends of the Disaster. They are even a bit gaga on this point. They would do well to update their *elements of discourse*, as I believe it is said. As soon as something or someone displeases them, which is a lot of things and a lot of people, they randomly yet systematically hurl the accusation that one is promoting a *conspiracy theory*. I do not give them this pleasure, for my part, as I do not believe in a conspiracy theory (not that this will prevent them from attributing one to me: the Friends of the Disaster are not very scrupulous philologists . . .). It nevertheless remains the case that I do not believe that, one fine day, twelve or fifteen arch-mandarins got together in a hotel or boardroom or held a conference at the Maison de la Chimie[x] and decided that it was necessary to deculturate the world in order to make way for the Great Replacement, the replacement of certain peoples by certain others. Nor do I believe the converse, that the same arch-mandarins or others got together to decide that only the Great Replacement, the interchangeability of peoples, would make it possible for them to render imbecilic the entire world, would permit its Great Deculturation, its decivilization, and thereby advance their evil plans.

What I do believe, however, and I will go so far as to say that I am sure of it, that I would stake my life on it, is that the two phenomena are linked. I am not saying that the teaching of forgetting was intentional, deliberate, or chosen as one decides on a plan. I am not saying that mass entertainment, which is permanent and impossible to flee, like the noise pollution with which our public spaces are today deliberately saturated, corresponds to a carefully crafted policy. I am saying that they have played an indispensable role in the change of people. As I like to say and to repeat, a people who knows its history and who knows its classics, a people who knows itself and knows what it owes itself, does not let itself be led – except in the case of open tyranny, armed constraint, and rampant terror – into the unspeakable abysses of history. But stupefaction dispenses with the need for terror, intensive entertainment returns patent dictatorship to the prop room. What was required was the disaster of national education, the teaching of forgetting, media-driven decerebration, the stupefaction industry, pedagogical theory, the official repudiation of general culture, systematic changes to the meaning of words (*music, culture, projects, youth, working-class neighborhoods, undocumented migrants*), Laurent Ruquier, Philippe Meirieu, Richard Descoings, Laurent Mucchielli,[xi] the media-political complex, the chorus of the Friends of the Disaster and their canned applause, politics-as-theater, show business as ideological influencer, and their interchangeability – all of this was necessary to make possible the interchangeability of peoples and first of individuals.

No, not *first*. Interchangeability had more modest beginnings. With all due apologies to my friends at MRAP, I have so little enthusiasm for conspiracy theorizing that I believe that everything is linked, that it is impossible to isolate a single causal mechanism that is not itself a piece of some enormous machine that is today ready to grind us to bits. Not that this would matter very much, for we are replaceable men. I would not be surprised if the Great Replacement began with the industrial revolution or perhaps only with its triumphant phase, the advent of scientific management, which Charlie Chaplin and Fritz Lang so clearly recognized and portrayed for what it was. Initially, it was the tools of production that were replaceable, but soon it was the objects produced as well. From dawn to dusk, we are surrounded by and make use of replaceable objects, on the sole condition that we can afford them of course. But their cost is in any case much lower than what it would be should we instead substitute one irreplaceable object for another. The replaceable object costs less for everyone, for the consumer as well as the producer. But alongside this synchronic or, if you will, *horizontal* replaceability must be set another, vertical form of replaceability, a diachronic replaceability that cuts across time and only benefits producers. At the end of a variable but statistically determined period, the objects are expected to once and for all break down. And once they have broken down they can no longer be repaired; everything is arranged so that, for the consumer at least, it is more economical (in the short term, of course) to replace them. More *economical* but certainly not more *ecological*, it goes without saying.

I say *objects* but I could just as well say *houses.* We are the first civilization that constructs buildings to last ten years, twenty years, thirty years perhaps. I recall when one of the regime's great accomplishments, the Millau viaduct, a few dozen kilometers from the Pont du Gard,[xii] was inaugurated a few years ago and we were told, as if it was some great marvel, that it might be in service for *forty years* or more, like a nuclear power plant. And I swear I once heard someone explain the disastrous condition of a high school ravaged by violence and "academic underperformance," as it is politely called, by reference to its dilapidation. Just imagine: *it had been built in 1977*! What can we hope to accomplish, pray tell, what sort of education can possibly be offered, they ask us, in a high school built in 1977? In times past, the older a teaching establishment, the more prestigious it was. Today, if such an establishment is thirty or forty years old, it risks being rejected as obsolete.

I mentioned in passing nuclear power plants but I could also have brought up the ecological situation. Is it because of these threats or

the fact that deadly weapons are in the hands of madmen that the species unconsciously appears to have lost faith in its own survival, that it
seems to only build for death, that it mixes death into all of its materials? For make no mistake: *replaceable* means *perishable* and vice versa.
My friend, the philosopher Robert Redeker,[xiii] the same man who has
for several years lived in hiding under constant police protection, like
Salman Rushdie, after an article of his in *Le Figaro* on Islamic violence
led to death threats, has shown the clear link between replaceability
and thanatocracy, between the cosmetic and the interchangeable. In
keeping with a mindset borrowed from Taylorist industry,[xiv] the body
is first replaced by parts, by pieces. And indeed, there hardly remains
a single part of your body, be it heart, kidney, breast, genitalia, hand,
arm, or face, that surgery cannot now change so long as it has the replacement part at its disposal, an ever-larger stock of which must be
kept on hand until a point is reached where the replacement parts indispensable to the system may themselves be replaced at will, produced
and almost self-produced: artificial hearts, stem cells, savior-siblings.
But the body is then replaced *en masse*, one unit at a time. This is the
advent of the planetary body, promoted by spectator sports and by
the entertainment industry, themselves ever-more indistinguishable
from political activity, which increasingly takes place in stadiums,
arenas, and on the sets of television variety shows. In his alarming
book, *Egobody*, Redeker once again clearly describes the advent of this
planetary body. Having revisited Kant's observation about the ways
in which, even within the white race – Konigsberg's terminology, not
mine – the Danish body differs from the Spanish body, he writes:

> "The difference between bodies overlapped with the difference
> between nations. There was also a difference within nations:
> the body of a Gascon from Tarbes and that of an Alsatian from
> Strasbourg. All these differences have been swept away by the
> inexorable progression of the planetary body promoted by ath-
> letes, models, by the Kens and Barbies presenting television
> news on the little twenty-four-hour news channels but also by
> the stars of the entertainment industry.

The triumph of the planetary body obviously means the end of the difference between bodies."[2]

However, the end of the difference between bodies is a small matter compared to the end of the difference between souls, minds, habits, which is as good as saying between cultures and civilizations as this has been ordained by the demand for general interchangeability, more commonly known as globalization. Globalization can be criticized and sometimes is – this is still permitted. But it has friends and allies in high places who are well-regarded, very popular, very admired and much loved and who are totally off-limits to criticism, by which I mean they are *impossible to criticize* even though they invite it, and their reputation for being above all suspicion protects them by an effect of metonymy.

At the forefront of these allies respected by all: democracy and post-genocidal antiracism.

For democracy, nothing is more precious than equality. This is its "stock and trade," as the advertisers would say. And yet equality is essential to general interchangeability. Consider how difficult, almost impossible, are exchanges between cultures or, it should be said, *civilizations* that do not bestow the same value on human life. In this connection, I have never been able to understand how the Palestinians could accept exchanging one hundred, two hundred, or five hundred of their own for *a single* Israeli, sometimes a dead Israeli. Not only is this in no way democratic but above all it is deeply contrary to equality between . . . between . . . here I am at a loss for words; you will fill in the blanks for me. This kind of exchange strikes me as terribly humiliating for the Palestinians. It seems to me that, when they are freeing a kidnapped Israeli, they should insist that only one imprisoned Palestinian be freed in exchange.

By its very existence, dogmatic antiracism also favors replacist doctrine. I will even venture to say that I have long been pleased to note that my analyses perfectly coincide on this point with those of your

---

2.   Robert Redeker, *Egobody. La fabrique de l'homme nouveau*, Fayard, 2010.

president, Gilles-William Goldnadel.[xv] He and I are in perfect agreement, he most recently in his *Reflections on the White Question*[xvi] and I in a short essay entitled "The Second Career of Adolf Hitler," a text republished in a collection the title of which is itself borrowed from Alain Finkielkraut, *The Communism of the Twenty-First Century*. By this, Finkielkraut and I wish to specifically refer to dogmatic anti-racism, an antiracism that has overflowed the banks of morality to become power and, very quickly, an excessive, repressive, oppressive power. I say that I believe us to be in perfect agreement, Goldnadel and I, in seeing the disaster of all the disasters – the genocide, the death camps – as being the impossibility of defending anything that appears to be even remotely associated with Hitler and the Final Solution, which have irremediably compromised such things. I mean the *state*; I mean *borders*; I mean citizenship insofar as it necessarily entails something that is not itself, non-citizenship, *foreignness*;[3] above all, I mean *country, cultural heritage, national traditions* – let us not even speak of *race*, located as it is at the phosphorescent summit of all that is unspeakable.

"I have above described," writes Monsieur Goldnadel, "the abhorrence in which the Western nation-state and its Holocaust origins are held."

And later, "It is necessary to see this abhorrence of the state as institution, which originated in the shock of the Holocaust, as a mortal threat to the world that is still free and civilized."

By separate paths, he and I arrive at the same images, the same words, and in any case the same name. I speak of the *second career of Hitler*, he speaks of the *last ruse of Hitler . . .* or of the devil.

From this second career, this last ruse, he uncompromisingly deduces the threat that hangs over Israel, a threat that is not properly political or military but ideological and almost ethical. I entirely subscribe to his thesis, which he expresses thus: "And today, Zionism, the desire to see the Jewish people build and preserve a mono-national State, is crashing headlong into the allegedly modern and supposedly

---

3. Renaud Camus, Emmaneul Carrère, and Alain Finkielkraut, *L'Étrangèreté*, "Répliques," Tricorne/France Culture editions, Geneva, 2003.

humanistic conception according to which a people's need for inde-pendence and to militarily defend its borders in the case of threat are outmoded and ethnocratic."

From this second career of Adolf Hitler, this last ruse of the devil, I take no pleasure in deducing the threat that hangs over France, a threat that is not so much political – although it is political as well, just as it is economic – as it is existential and ontological. I would not be surprised and even hope, as a virtual exchange of favors between us, to see Gilles-William Goldnadel lend his support to this way of seeing things, he who admirably summarizes the apparent paradox of our present situation, and this will almost be my conclusion: "Swimming against the political and historical current of our age, a part of the Jewish people wishes to embody the spirit of Western reaction against a notion of progress that sees it as consisting in a world without walls or borders. For the most well-intentioned, the fact that the Jewish people suffered more than any other people from this narrowly retro-grade conception of the nation makes this a betrayal. For the least well-intentioned, it is a confirmation of the chosen people's bias."

I hope you will count me among the most well-intentioned, dear Gilles-William Goldnadel, and I certainly see no betrayal in the appar-ent paradox that you underscore. Moreover, I am too much a disciple of Roland Barthes and too much a practitioner of *bathmology*, that semi-amusing science of the levels of language and its alternating lay-ers of meaning, which he invented as if it were a game and that I take more seriously than he does – in short, I am too much the Barthesian and too much the bathmologist to not see in this lovely semantic rever-sal, in this Moebius strip of reflection on what a nation is, the promise of a new alliance.

Speech Before the 17th Chamber [2014]¹

I might as well admit at the outset that this speech was never given. On February 21ˢᵗ, 2014, at the conclusion of the suit that MRAP had brought against me for "inciting racial hatred," I was asked by the presiding magistrate of the 17ᵗʰ chamber,ⁱ as is customary, whether I had anything to add. Why yes, I did have something to add, absolutely. I had taken notes during the preceding phases of the hearing, in particular during the cross examination of the witnesses by MRAP's attorney and during his closing argument. And I had every intention of expressing the content of these notes, that is, my indignation and my protest. "The defendant has transformed the courtroom into a soapbox," Jérôme Depuis wrote the next day in L'Express, *"and then we witnessed this stupefying spectacle of a defendant publicly putting on trial the attorney who was prosecuting him! [. . .] The court was dumbstruck."*

At the time, however, in my appalled vehemence, I only managed to reel off half of what I meant to say. Here is a reconstructed and, I hope, improved version of that speech.

It goes without saying that I have no idea what the outcome of this trial will be. I would nevertheless like to express my gratitude to the Court for the admirable formality and courtesy with which the proceedings

---

1. "Discours à la XVIIᵉ Chambre (21 février 2014)," in *Le Grand Remplacement: Introduction au remplacisme global.* (Paris, La Nouvelle Libraire, 2021), pp. 335-362.

were conducted. It seems to me, if I may permit myself to say so in the courtroom, that it does honor to the French legal system. The length of this hearing has been perhaps a bit trying for the public, but all parties concerned in these proceedings have had ample opportunity to express themselves. Apart from an episode to which I will return, the various points of view were presented without meeting with either undo indulgence or hostility. These debates have been characterized by proper distance, objective reserve, and a concern to avoid misunderstanding. May the presiding magistrate and her assessors accept my sincere thanks.

It is late, everyone is tired: please be assured that I will try not to be too long since, according to custom, I am the last to speak. I must first respond, a bit belatedly, to a question posed me by one of my judges, who wished to know whether, in the offending speech, "*Nocence, Instrument of the Great Replacement*," any passage specifically repudiated violence; whether any contradicted the charge according to which I could have, by my words, incited violence, aggression, combat, armed conflict, racial hatred; whether any might have dissuaded my listeners from thinking that I was calling upon them to take up arms and use them. I am so unaccustomed, and for good reason, to being reproached for preaching physical confrontation that at the time, and not knowing by heart the text of those already distant remarks, I was not so sure what to answer this judge. Since then, I have had time to peruse my copy of *The Great Replacement*, the book in which the speech that supplies the subject of this trial is contained. And I discovered this passage, which I submit to the member of the Court who sought to question me:

"And now for *nocence*. I am speaking here on behalf of a party, the Party of In-nocence, which I grant bears an unwieldy name since it has made the difficult wager that it could spread a concept among the public, *in-nocene*, which in two words is not at all the same thing as innocence-in-one-word, for the latter is something that one can lose or is in danger of losing at any time, an object of nostalgia or longing, whereas in-nocence-in-two-words, *non-nocence*, the repudiation of no-cence, of harm, is an ideal to be attained, an aspiration, something that is before us rather than behind us. In-nocence-in-two-words posits that nocence, which is to say harm, the act of harming, to make an attempt on another's life or ruin it, defile it, make it unbearable, is prior, that it is always *already there*, that it is that against which one must struggle both within and outside of ourselves. Nocence, of course, is pollution in the ecological sense of the term: attacks on nature and the quality of life, the quality of the air, the quality of the water, the quality of the landscape, and of our national heritage. It is also all the attacks on person and property (the famous and oh-so-delicately named *incivilities*), up to and including organized crime. As we see it, the great advantage of the concept of *in-nocence* is that it allows us to consider *as a whole* everything that pertains to politics, ecology, day-to-day existence, to daily life, real life, the relations between individuals, citizens, neighbors, fellow citizens, our fellow inhabitants on this planet and in our apartment buildings as well as in our neighborhoods, suburbs, cities, and nations."

Now I ask you: do you think that those hearing such remarks could for an instant imagine that the person speaking to them in this way was inciting them to violence? Perhaps to sleeping, or yawning, or drowsiness out of an excess of seriousness; but certainly not to violence. By definition, and even according to this speech which is on another subject, *in-nocence is non-violence.* I have only ever called for *political* action. And for my part it has consisted in founding a *political* party, which is not exactly a large party (so be it), but which anyone is free to join.

By way of example and to make myself better understood, I would in this connection like to refute a polemical and propagandistic legend that has grown up around a book I deeply admire, despite some significant reservations: *The Clash of Civilizations*, by Samuel Huntington. The opinion-makers and their lackeys pretend to believe, and work very hard to make us believe, that this book calls for violence, that it *advocates* violence and desires it. Yet the very opposite is true. Huntington tried to warn his contemporaries of the danger that any too-close, imprudent, and ill-informed contact between civilizations might lead to violence, antagonism, and conflict. These entail the *risk* of a clash, of head-on conflict, which we greatly exacerbate when we choose to ignore it, as our leaders have done for forty years by allowing several very different civilizations, a great many cultures, and a large number of peoples and established communities to settle next to each other on our country's territory, divvying it up between themselves in ever less amicable fashion.

In my own way, I am merely restating Huntington's prediction. Far from calling for violence, but trying on the contrary to avoid it, to drive it away from us, I tirelessly denounce reckless policies – or perhaps policies that are only too aware of what they are doing – these friends of the disaster, these harbingers of misfortune, that day after day create the strict conditions for conflict, tension, animosity, and uncontrollable nocence. It is an ex-Yugoslavia that they are blithely preparing for France and for Europe – a Sudan, a Mali, a Central African Republic, a generalized Lebanon. Indeed, we are alas no longer talking about the simple *conditions* for future violence; for ages now, we have been watching it quietly set up shop, as it were, in our lives. It is not as a prophet that I speak of this but as a chronicler and almost an historian. For the disorders that it brings in its wake are not just a matter for the future; they are already at work among us, as witnessed by the growing brutality of social relations, the unprecedented and sadly justifiable distrust between citizens, rising insecurity, and the worsening of major and minor crime alike. It is absurd to reduce, as it is commonly done, these phenomena to an inexplicable accumulation of random events, a matter for law enforcement or the courts, police intervention or the penal code. This violence and these disorders are not simply a matter for the police, nor even for the criminal justice system. They are matters of policy and of history, of the history of peoples, the relationships between civilizations, the disappearance of some of them, the conquering activities of others, of the collapse or preservation of nations.

But having satisfied, I hope, the request of that member of the Court who wished to know what, in the offending speech, might prevent its listeners from interpreting it as a call to violence – and my answer is *everything*: everything I am, everything that forms the party that I preside, the entirety of the speech itself, and especially the paragraph I just read to you – I would with your permission now like to revisit what seemed to me a great moment of truth during the remarks of the Most Honorable attorney for the prosecution.

I am not alluding here to his closing argument.

His closing argument, and excuse me for saying so in his presence, is something I could have written myself with my eyes closed while composing a sonnet with my other hand. We all knew it by heart before he even began speaking. I am sure that everyone present here today has already heard it a hundred times – a thousand times. It is the doctrinal bath in which we are immersed from dawn till dusk and from dusk till dawn, the ideological and commercial soundtrack of our existence in advanced, dogmatically antiracist society. I would not be shocked to learn that Monsieur Mairat possesses a giant checklist on which, upon hopping out of bed in the morning, he ticks off the boxes of those set expressions that will be useful to him for whatever occasion the day may present. Almost any of them will do the trick; he fills in his boxes with little crosses.

I do not think I heard the famous reference to the "darkest hours of our history," but I may have been distracted for an instant. As for the rest, nothing was missing. The reference to Vichy, for example, was certainly not lacking, thrown out there just in case because that's what's done in these types of situation, and because this is how we have always proceeded. And I assume it would be useless for me to speak of my veneration for General de Gaulle here, for the man and for the speech of June 18th, or challenge anyone to discover in the hundred or so works I have published the least favorable allusion to the Collaboration. As it happens, I belong passionately, at least as a matter of moral and intellectual allegiance, to the other camp: that of the Resistance and the struggle for our country's freedom and survival. But no matter. There is no place for such details in the system of thought whose rigorous demonstration we have just witnessed. This system makes one think irresistibly of Bergson's famous saying regarding laughter: *something mechanical encrusted on the living*. However, apart from the fact that we're not here for our amusement, and myself least of all, we are rather confronted with something mechanical crushing truth as a matter of course, as a duty of state, out of conformity to oneself: an automatic Procrustean bed reducing anything that does not correspond to its pattern to the same tried and true structures.

Monsieur Mairat has opportunely reminded us that today is the seventieth anniversary of the execution of the heroic resistance fighters of *l'Affiche rouge*.[ii] I say *opportunely* because we can never adequately celebrate their sacrifice or memory. Yet why are they appearing here? Might the implication be that I am in one way or another responsible for their suffering and death? That I am on the side of their executioners? That my way of thinking, speaking, writing, and acting would place me among their persecutors? They died for love of France, its independence, and its dignity. Though freedom fighters, they were treated like hooligans. For my part, I denounce – without, moreover, calling for anything other than *political* action, *political* decisions against them – individuals whose nocence, what I call *nocence*, whose delinquency, whether major or minor, is by its accumulation leading to the enslavement of our country, to the conquest of its soil, its cities, its suburbs, its neighborhoods, and to the constant enlargement of its lost territories.

I call these hooligans *soldiers*, which is rather to do them an honor, for, no matter the society, to do so is a promotion in point of dignity. You choose to see them as young Muslims in general. I know this is done to hurt my cause, which you can always use as an excuse. But in this instance, it is you who are indulging – if only to accuse me – in that oh-so familiar *racist amalgam*, as they say. It is not I. I have never said anything about young Muslims *in general*. I spoke of young *delinquents*. Not for an instant are they the same thing in my mind, nor in my speech. As for any parallels between these delinquents and the members of the FTP-MOI,[iii] I find it difficult to convince myself that you are being completely serious on this point, despite the gravity of the subject. In any event, I am not going to make myself look ridiculous before this Court by stressing that these two things have nothing to do with each other, for that would be to once again imagine that there could exist any similarity, however contestable, whereas the very opposite is true.

We are dealing here with conduct that resembles what on the internet is called (and please excuse this recourse to English terminology) *Google bombing*. It consists of almost indiscriminately associating a name that one wants to sully, or a man who one wants to discredit at all costs, with the most ignominious traits, misdeeds, crimes, and words that one can find, so that they crop up as soon as a third party seeks to inquire about this name or that man. And here I am, by an innocent metonymy of this kind, lumped together with those who tortured and killed the martyrs of the Manouchian^{iv} network!

I imagine that Monsieur Mairat possesses, alongside his checklist of set phrases for every time he needs to inveigh against the interchangeable Foul Beast, today wearing my face, a calendar of horrors, an almanac of terror, a martyrology of hostages and the persecuted, which reliably supplies him – the monstrosities of history and the history of monstrosities being what they are – with a dreadful anniversary for *every* day of the year, court holidays excluded. But has he no scruple in ceaselessly summoning and summoning again these poor, swollen-faced dead to serve this task so unworthy of their martyrdom, to silence, beneath their dreadful shadow, all those who venture to speak of what MRAP does not want spoken of, namely, this other horror, the change of people and of civilization, the Great Replacement, *that which is taking place*?

Be that as it may, by the time Monsieur Mairat rose to make his closing argument, he had already, in my opinion, radiantly presented the substance of what he had to tell us, and which had so deeply enlightened us. This was during the questioning of my witnesses and especially the first among them. I say *questions*, but I would do better to say *lessons*, rather harshly administered ones at that. In any case, it was during this cross examination that the magnificent moment of truth to which I earlier alluded occurred. In one stroke, all became perfectly clear.

We thus have a young man, a man who is young, a Frenchman of Moroccan origin, passionately attached to France and its culture, to its literature, which he teaches, or which he taught, at a suburban high school to students who for the most part share his origins, be they Moroccan, Algerian, Tunisian, sub-Saharan or whatever – African in their great majority, in any case, and often Muslim. This young teacher confided in me that, if the majority of his students were any guide, everything I said in the offending speech as regards the sentiment of conquest felt by so many young immigrants and descendants of immigrants fell well short of reality. He quite distinctly said as much here: most of these teenagers believe that France will be Muslim in fifteen or twenty years. And they consider it poetic justice, a well-deserved punishment for France's history of colonial conquest in short, and just compensation for themselves and their loved ones. As the witness told you: his students refer to the French as "the French," as if this were a community to which they did not belong. Sometimes it is "the Gauls" or the "*jambons-beurre*."[v] They find the idea that they themselves might be French laughable. That their teacher speaks to them about the love of France, his or theirs, strikes them as madness. And, were they able to take it seriously, they would see his avowed patriotism as nothing short of treason. Fortunately, they suspect this is just his way of pulling their legs.

This little speech – hardly a speech, a hushed account, almost apologizing for being here, but which was nevertheless assured, pursuing its own path and seeking nothing more than to set out the truth of a lived experience – sent Monsieur Mairat into a cold rage. And we watched, astonished, as this great Parisian attorney, at once counsel for and distinguished member of an association that makes a business of ideological virtue (especially that of others), attempted to *demolish*, as I believe it is said, a witness, a young, modest, polite high school teacher *of diverse background*, as one also says, alas, and not irrelevantly in this instance. He gives him a history lesson, he gives him a lesson in politico-moral rectitude, he gives him a lesson in pedagogy, he teaches him how to do his job, he all but gives him a lesson in literature even though this young teacher is a writer and the author of a lovely book, *Prosopopée*, published by P.O.L.[vi] Oh, let us give this senior lawyer his due: he did not for a moment call into question the testimony itself, the reality of the facts, words, and feelings it related. Doubtless he feared that this might be to invite a thousand similar testimonies, a thousand memories, a thousand lived experiences to corroborate it in people's minds. No, if one was to believe his interrogator, it was in the *interpretation* of the picture he had painted that our apprentice schoolmaster revealed he had understood nothing, did not feel what one is supposed to feel, was guilty of unpardonable blindness.

These teenagers who did not love France, who did not consider themselves to be French, who spoke of *conquest* in connection with our country and congratulated themselves that it was taking place – did their teacher have any notion of the *reasons* they had for seeing things this way, or at least for pretending to for purposes of provocation? Had he ever heard of something called *discrimination*? Could he imagine what it meant for these boys and girls, the children or grandchildren of immigrants, to live in the France we know, with its familiar injustices and lack of opportunity for young people like them, given labor market discrimination and the endemic racism we see every day around us? And he expected them to love France in these conditions and say so? Does it love them? Does it show them that it loves them? Has it shown them in the past? Did it show this love to their parents, their grandparents? Does Sétif, May 8ᵗʰ, 1945, ring a bell?ᵛⁱⁱ Do you have any idea how many people died among the peaceful protesters whose only crime was to believe the promises that had been made to them, and to ask that they be kept? And one hundred and thirty years of state-sanctioned racism in Algeria – are you aware of this? And slavery – you must talk to your students about slavery, no? It's on the syllabus, it seems to me? And none of that helps you understand the sentiments, the attitudes, the feelings you are reporting, just like that, as if they came out of nowhere, as if with this experience, this history, these high schoolers could think any differently? When one is a teacher, one has to think. That's part of your job.

Under this thundering assault, the poor witness might have begun by pointing out that this experience of discrimination in contemporary France, which the attorney offered not as justification but as explanation for his students' less than loving attitude towards the country, was something he was particularly well positioned to understand since he had experienced exactly the same thing himself, his personal history in no way differing from that of the teenagers he taught; and that this same history had led him, not to hate France, but rather to deeply love it, to love its language and culture: there is thus nothing inevitable about it. He refrained from replying thus, doubtless out of courtesy, instead contenting himself with pointing out that he taught literature, not history. And that, in any case, it did not seem to him that it was his job to incessantly revisit France's crimes; rather, it was to inspire love for her, especially for her great books and her great authors, from Villon to Marcel Proust and from Marivaux to Albert Camus.

Alas, it would take more than this to appease the big man from the Paris Bar, who was now on a roll and presenting us with the gist of his way of thinking, which is to say that of MRAP since he is not just a lawyer but also one of its presidents; which is to say, MRAP being one of its darling children, heaped with its favors, the thinking of official France, of the current ideological regime, of what one might call, at the risk of redundancy, the ruling ideology. It is with pleasure that, in passing, I notice that he is no longer disputing facts or feelings. There is no longer even any effort at justification. Monsieur Mairat quite clearly tells us as much: he is not trying to justify the feelings, statements, or attitudes of the teenagers described by the teacher; he is merely seeking to *explain* them, and first of all to the teacher himself. But the explanation is very simple: if France is hated, it is because she is worthy of hatred. Her history is a tangle of horrors, especially in what regards the peoples who today furnish the great contingents of our classrooms.

If France has only ever inflicted hardship, massacre, and indiscriminate injustice on them – Sétif, Charonne, Maurice Papon,[viii] one hundred and thirty years of state-sanctioned racism (if that is the expression) – and contributed absolutely nothing positive to their lives at all, one might obviously wonder why these peoples have specifically chosen our country to live in, to earn a living, and to educate their children. And one might also wonder whether their history, in contrast to our own – *to our own* such as Monsieur Mairat seems to see it and wishes it to be taught – has been nothing but sweetness and light, understanding, affectionate fraternity with neighboring peoples and minorities, finesse in commercial and maritime relations. My first witness was blamed for not taking sufficient account in his opinions (even though he did not to my knowledge offer the least opinion), his classes, and his mind of the institution of slavery and its legacy, its aftermath, its consequences, which could not help but register in the feelings he described for us. Now, the institution of slavery, yes, without a doubt – but which one? Only that institution for which the French are guilty? Or rather *all* instances of slavery, in all the forms it has taken throughout history, with all of its protagonists and as it is still practiced in more than one country in the world, particularly in Africa and the Arab world? But would there not be reason to fear that such a thorough, exhaustive, just, and balanced lesson might give rise to other disagreements among the students, other irreconcilable grievances, other hatreds? Unless it were only the hatreds provoked by France that are truly irreconcilable due to the incommensurable nature of her crimes?

Formerly but still not so long ago, it was Germany's crimes that were held to be incommensurable to any others in the history of humanity. Yet in 1963 – that is, fewer than twenty years after the end of the Second World War – General de Gaulle, the soul and inspiration of the resistance to Hitler's Germanic stranglehold over Europe and our country, called for reconciliation, not just between the two states but between the two peoples as well. And from that time forward it has been nothing but exchange programs on both sides of the Rhine, shared friendship and love between the youth of the two countries, and occasionally even ministerial committees bringing together their two governments. Who could have imagined anything of the sort in 1945? In less than a generation, this hatred and resentment were in this way overcome, transcended, and almost forgotten. Fifty years after the movements for national independence, why should this not be the case of that felt by the descendants of formerly colonized peoples towards France? Are these grievances, these hatreds, these desires for vengeance still so active and powerful that they explain everything, even if they don't *justify* it, as I am grateful to Monsieur Mairat for having repeatedly pointed out? And, first of all, do they explain what has now almost officially begun to be called the *failure of integration*?

And yet, even if the conquest of Algeria or Dahomey (to cite just two examples) was brutal, the French colonial empire never constructed or made use of death camps, carried out no genocides, and did not engage in mass deportations. And while it cannot be denied that they were responsible for acts of torture, especially towards the end, it is no less certain that their opponents hardly showed themselves to be more civilized. Is it really necessary to recall the massacre of the Harkis?[ix] And how, in the space of just a few weeks, eight hundred thousand of our compatriots in Algeria were thrown into the sea because this state, freshly liberated from French tutelage, considered – and in this was perfectly understood by the entire world, which wholly shared its way of seeing things – that it would not be truly independent if a tenth of the population remaining on its territory was not of the same origin and same religion as the majority?

Should you now object that the war with Germany lasted six years and the occupation of Algeria one hundred and thirty-two, I will reply that, at the time of reconciliation, the Germans had been the hereditary enemy of the French for almost a century and that the one-sided sort of war that had pitted them against each other since 1870 had between them resulted in the deaths of millions of people – a number infinitely greater than that of the victims of the colonial wars or of colonization itself. Is this the place to underscore that, over the course of France's much-discussed one hundred and thirty-two year presence in Algeria, the indigenous population of that country increased from three to ten million inhabitants, that certain endemic diseases disappeared, that a great number of hospitals were built, that a school system was established – a very inegalitarian one, to be sure, but efficient enough to educate all the elites of postcolonial Algeria, which, I recognize, is not necessarily a recommendation? The architectural and urban appearance that this country to this day presents was given to it by colonization. And one often has the impression that, despite its petroleum windfall, which should have made it a rich country, it continues to live in the dilapidated remains of the French presence. Yet, if one is to believe Monsieur Mairat, there have been, in France's attitude toward Algeria, as toward all the countries she once colonized and administered, as toward the peoples of these countries, be it on their own territory or, more recently, on that of the metropole – that

there have been sufficient grounds in its injustice, cruelty, cynical per-
secution, and racism to explain the refusal or inability of young people
born in France and of French nationality to feel French; and grounds
to account for their desire, their hope, and even their avowed certainty
that our country will very soon be conquered by its former colonial
subjects; and grounds for understanding without surprise or bitterness, but with the appropriate resignation, the ever so striking rate of
nocence encountered among such a curiously high proportion of their
peers.

What France is suffering from, in short, is what she has made others suffer. What she is enduring in point of hateful delinquency, rude-
ness, aggression, petty and not-so-petty violence, and *nocence*, to use
a word of my own invention, is the fateful price of her own crimes. In
other, strangely familiar words – but I'd rather not make a mistake
I elsewhere denounce and further belabor old Vichy and the Moral
Order . . . – in other words, her misfortunes are the inevitable fruit of
her sins. She can only alleviate them by ever-greater repentance. Just
look at the proliferation of all these masochistic museums, one for each
of our sins, and which, as sanctuaries of repentance, are the secular, lay
equivalent of Montmartre's Sacré-Cœur.ˣ And the African slave trade,
does that ring a bell? You had better speak to your students about the
African slave trade, don't you think?

In his fervor, Monsieur Mairat went on to cite Frantz Fanon,ˣⁱ extol-
ling his continued relevance, his relevance today. Fanon's thought, he
told us, holds not just for the Antilles in the middle of the last century,
for colonial and postcolonial Algeria, for the exploited Third World
and the oppressed peoples and races who aspired to independence and
freedom in the heyday of the Cuban revolution and Éditions Maspero;ˣⁱⁱ
it holds for twenty-first century France as well. Ah, Monsieur Mairat
has no idea how right he is! Nor does he realize to what extent he
is preaching to the choir in my case! Or that, on its website and fo-
rums, in its deliberations and activity, the little party over which I
preside, L'In-nocence, gives pride of place to these words by Fanon:
"The enslavement, in the strictest sense, of the native population is the
prime necessity. For this, its systems of reference have to be broken.

Expropriation, spoliation, raids, objective murder, are matched by the sacking of cultural patterns, or at least condition such sacking. The social panorama is destructured; values are flaunted, crushed, emptied."[xiii]

Monsieur Mairat is right: a more exact description of what is now taking place can hardly be found. He asks us to transpose it; alas, he himself does not transpose enough. His argument applies to schemas and processes that are seventy years old, as are most of his references: L'Affiche rouge, Sétif, and the sinister early career of Maurice Papon. His interpretation of what is happening is one war behind the times. In listening to him, one is reminded of those French generals of 1940 who, right up to and beyond the disaster, continued to meticulously prepare for the battles of 1916. He was kind enough to explain to us that, in 1977, the meaning of the acronym "MRAP" was changed from the *Movement against Racism, Anti-Semitism and for Peace*, the original name given it in 1949, to the *Movement against Racism and for Friendship between Peoples*. Had he not himself drawn attention to this onomastic development, I certainly would not allow myself this remark, but he is doubtless not unaware that the same four letters are now commonly understood to designate the *Movement for the Accelerated Replacement of the People.*[xiv]

By dint of focusing on conflicts that have fortunately lost much of their relevance, the organization has blinded itself to the far more significant and heartbreaking tragedy unfolding before its eyes, which it indeed stokes by reflexively diverting attention from it – an old habit – when it does not simply deny it outright. This explains the terribly mechanical nature, so striking and which I noted above, of the closing argument that we heard. No matter how much its impeccable gears seized on every occasion to invoke the most tragic shadows and the most noble spirits, this impressive machine, designed to impress and even to frighten, to intimate whomever dare raise the least objection, now turns in a vacuum: it is not only a refusal to see, but a resolute desire to *prevent* one from seeing and, of course, from naming what one has seen – hence my presence here today.

This refusal to see and above all to hear is shared by broad swathes of our society, rightly traumatized as they are by these references that you, Sir, so prodigally dispense and by the very well-founded fear – proof of which you have just supplied – that clear-sightedness regarding ethnic substitution and the dogmatic antiracism that today promotes it will in some way or other be likened to complacency, even complicity, vis-à-vis the racist fanaticism of yesterday. For governments, civilizations, and individual consciences, caught as they are between an antiracism that has become suicidal from excessive self-hatred and a still-murderous racism, with no path to safety, no emergency exit, no way out, the result of this obsessive fear has been paralysis. This paralysis, I have taken the liberty of calling *the second career of Adolf Hitler*: his inverted career, a photographic negative prolonging his misdeeds through his role as foil to anything that would claim to defend the nation, the native people, the national culture, and that is immediately associated, beyond all refutation, with unspeakable crime – a role posthumously conferred upon him by the very conduct you have so perfectly illustrated in this courtroom. It is a double constraint, a ridgeline between two abysses, a *double bind*, as we used to say in my youth: one would swear there is no other possible reaction to the grip of these vertigo-inducing pincers than silence and resignation, abdication, impotence, and relinquishment. You yourself seemed to confirm this by your reaction, or absence thereof, in this instance, to the testimony of my second witness.

It was a quiet man, calm, level-headed, and cultivated, who presented before the Court, without hatred but not without emotion, one imagines, the reasons he and his family felt obliged to move out of a city, neighborhood, and home where they had been peacefully living for years, and which they loved. This man is of the same ideological origin, if you will allow me the expression, as you and I are, as are the vast majority of this country's good citizens, raised as we all were on the antiracist milk of the liberal, progressive France open to others of the long postwar period, the France of "never again." It is frightening to note the degree to which this irrefutable slogan has been, by virtue of its very irrefutability, the necessary condition of this terrible "second career" to which I alluded a moment ago. In this newly inverted, top-to-tail role, less criminal than its predecessor, no doubt, but with hardly less disastrous consequences, Hitler's ghost, elevated to the status of *terminus ad quem* of every objective observation, leaves Europe and its civilization absolutely defenseless against what is killing it. The continent is like a patient who has had a cancer, Hitlerism, and who, to prevent any chance of relapse, is operated on and reoperated on by his surgeons, of whom Professor MRAP is one of the most renowned, in such a thorough manner that they one by one deprive him of all vital functions. He will die, no doubt, but at least it will not be of Nazism, fascism, racism, or anti-Semitism.

The second of my witnesses told you (to drastically abridge his misfortunes) of how he had watched with pleasure and interest as men and women from elsewhere began to appear in his suburban neighborhood, which in his view, as in that of the overwhelming majority of us at that time, recommended it and aroused his favorable consideration; of how he had amicably welcomed them; of how he had become close with some of them; of how, for a number of years, everything had gone harmoniously in the midst of what was not yet called *vivre-ensemble*; of how later, as the population changed more rapidly, and as the population that had "always" been there became proportionately smaller (I am being as brief as possible), everything gradually went downhill and then rapidly went downhill, finally turning into a nightmare – the area itself, the streets, the sidewalks, the shops, human relations, living conditions, especially for women, spouses, daughters, who were constantly insulted, provoked, threatened; of how life, local life, life as it had always been, had little by little become intolerable, due to endless burglaries, abuse, assaults, the impotence or indifference of the police, indifference by dint of impotence; of how the first hints that the time had come to pack up and leave came from declared enemies; then of how these were followed by friendly advice on the part of longtime neighbors, friends from the early days of diversity, as it is now called, to leave, to not be stubborn, to not take pointless risks, to accept that the game was up; and of how in the end, despite the promises they had made to never to leave the premises, to never accept that, forlorn resignation came over them and they left without taking particular pains to determine if they were being watched by the victors.

This story of a man and his family driven from their home by the change of people, and more specifically by the aggressions of every kind and every degree of seriousness that were its expression, is the exact, literal, almost word-for-word illustration of what I am criticized for having set forth in this speech, "*Nocence*, Instrument of the Great Replacement," which has brought me before this court today. Yet, in regard to this story of ten years in a man's life, in regard to this restrained presentation, free of pathos, of a forced exodus, this poignant statement of the upending of an existence – an account that thousands of French men and women could give, though doubtless with less restraint – in regard to what we have just heard Monsieur Mairat had no questions to ask, no comment to make. Nothing in him was inclined to receive this testimony. One would have sworn that nothing in him permitted him to even *hear* it, to became aware of it, to register it as the observation of a proliferating reality. He could well have endeavored to take the person who gave it to task, to discredit this witness like he tried so hard to discredit the preceding one, but, apart from the fact that this would have been no easy task, he no doubt concluded that any such undertaking would have been redundant with what MRAP saw as the very purpose of this trial. For this witness and I are saying exactly the same thing: he on the basis of a painfully lived experience of the most palpable reality, which, one imagines, will stay with him forever; and I in a more general and abstract manner. He is answered by silence; I am answered by an attempt to impose silence.

I have said and I continue to say that, in the painful scene with the young teacher, Monsieur Mairat's comments clearly revealed to our minds a totally ideological vision of the world in which France's crimes and misdeeds, treated as if they were her entire history and what set that history apart from others, serve as the interpretive key to everything, including and above all her misfortunes, the humiliations and *nocences* to which she is daily subjected and about which, sorry, she has no right to complain, just as no one has a right to complain on her behalf. There is indeed a vision here, one more coherent than can be said. But it is a vision to prevent us from seeing.

Exchange with Alain Finkielkraut on Migrants [2015][1]

The publication of a communiqué[2] by the Party of In-nocence, whose President is Renaud Camus, sparked protest from Mr. Alain Finkielkraut, giving rise to the following exchange:

Alain Finkielkraut: How can you say, my dear Renaud, that the people fleeing the bombing in Syria and open-ended military service in Eritrea are pseudo-refugees?

Must one be European to be a true refugee?

Can we not simultaneously conceive of their distress and our own?

---

1. "Échange avec Alain Finkielkraut sur les migrants (août 2015)," in *Le Grand Remplacement: Introduction au remplacisme global.* (Paris, La Nouvelle Librairie, 2021), pp. 437-450.
2. Communiqué no. 1860, 14 August 2015, *On the New Behavior of Illegal Immigrants*:

    The Party of In-nocene and NON have remarked that, as their ranks swell and they become stronger, as they become more aware of the passivity of the native population and its leaders' penchant for collaboration, migrants, illegal immigrants, so-called refugees, or whatever one wishes to call them are, simultaneously and in many parts of the European continent, becoming more violent, more aggressive, surer of themselves, and are physically lashing out at law enforcement. In this way they are revealing their true face as invaders and conquerors. And yet the political class, facing the worst invasion that Europe has suffered in centuries, continues, after the fashion of the President of the Senate, Mr. Gérard Larcher, to absurdly talk of a "humanitarian crisis." At this rate, it would not be surprising should history textbooks, with the replacist servility for which they are known, begin to speak of the centuries of the Barbarian Invasions as "the time of Humanitarian Crises."

It is incumbent upon politics to confront tragedy, not flee it into some ready-made past, whether it be it that of the 1930s or the Barbarian Invasions. If we are going to take a firmer hand in what regards immigration, we must also, it seems to me, avoid hateful short cuts. It is essential to control the flow of migrants. But it is shameful to denounce the barbarian hordes now washing over France.

In friendship,
Alain

Renaud Camus: Dear Alain,

The communiqué you mention does not specifically target "the people fleeing bombing in Syria and open-ended military service in Eritrea," so neither it nor I am saying what you say.

Your second question: "Must one be European to be a true refugee?" nicely illustrates the exaggerated and, I would say, polemical nature of your questions. It is certainly not necessary to be European to be a true refugee, but this concept is totally powerless to account for the gigantic waves of migration that are now submerging Europe and destroying it. And if there are indeed so many true refugees within this huge influx, why do they not take advantage of their numbers to become actors in their own history, like every other people before them and before a continent beyond history comes into existence, a peoples' rest home, that is veering towards chaos as a result of their influx?

"Can we not simultaneously conceive of their distress and our own?" Conceiving of their distress should not consist of removing them from history as we claim to remove ourselves, even at the price of becoming passive objects, playthings, and victims. Conceiving of their distress should not consist in making it our own, in immersing ourselves in it out of some suicidal solidarity. The reasoning at work here is of exactly the same type as that which destroyed the educational system: some children receive a good education and others receive a bad one or receive none at all, so let's put the latter together *en masse* with the former, in this way there will no longer be any education and everyone will be, if not happy, at least equal in stupidity. There is misfortune and there is happiness, so let's put misfortune (or incompetence, or lack of public spirit, or barbarity) in the country of happiness (or the rule of law), and that way everyone will be unhappy, which will be much more just. The operating principle of this sort of thinking is: Destroy, she said. To persist against all reason in seeing the invasion as a humanitarian problem and nothing else is to destroy Europe. May the brutality and savagery that so many so-called refugees have begun to exhibit (I imagine that the true ones are more peaceful and less demanding . . .) open the eyes of this full-up continent, which is eager to have done with itself.

In all friendship,
Renaud Camus

A.F.: Dear Renaud,

You may not be specifically targeting the people who are fleeing fighting in Syria, those escaping the Eritrean prison state, or, for that matter, the persecuted Christians of the Near East, but you are also targeting them, encompassing them. And that is the problem. You often say that to think is to make distinctions. In this communiqué, which I do not believe I wrongly attribute to you, you have fallen short of this requirement.

You object that, if there are so many true refugees, they should take advantage of their numbers to become actors in their own history. Is this the sort of reasoning that German and Polish Jews should have followed during the interwar period? And, as you well know, I am not arguing for opening the borders. I persist in wishing to see firmness uncoupled from disgust and hatred.

Your friend,
Alain

R.C.: Dear Alain,

You ask me to make distinctions, and indeed how could I not hear your call. And yet you yourself, immediately thereafter, draw the classic parallel – I daren't say amalgam[i] – between today's situation and that of the 1930s. We here find ourselves at the heart of what is causing our downfall. Europe is dying from its fantasy of replaying the previous war. This is what I took the liberty of calling "the Second Career of Adolf Hitler" in a volume whose title I borrowed from you yourself (*The Communism of the Twenty-First Century*). Hitler is on the tip of every tongue and every thought, and this obsessive reference is paralyzing us. The continent, as I have often written, is like a patient who has been so operated and re-operated upon for the Hitlerian cancer that, as a precaution and due to what is now an entirely imaginary fear that there might be a recrudescence of this disease, he has been deprived of all vital functions and left defenseless against other horrors. He no longer has a heart, brain, loins, will, or eyes. He does not even see the invasion to which he is subject and which he takes, like the President of the Senate, for a humanitarian crisis. We are mistaking giants for windmills.

Among the mass of migrants, there are true refugees, you say, and refugees from the worst kind of horrors. Certainly. But there are so many of these refugees that they are peoples. The Party of In-nocence and I have always insisted on and proclaimed the necessity and duty, for France and for Europe, to support peoples against their tyrants. In contrast to many of our friends, we are not in the least anti-interventionist. To the contrary, we have constantly called upon Europe to rearm and once again become a great power, an essential actor of history. It cannot be said that our positions are incoherent. We have long advocated the creation of a Christian state in the Near East, a sort of Greater Lebanon; we advocate, that is, the decolonization of a part of the Arab-Muslim colonial empire, precisely the only one that has never been decolonized but which, to the contrary, is in the process of conquering Europe and progressing on all fronts. Eritrea is an abject prison state, so let us help these people against their torturers. Let us not offer them our country.

In all friendship,
Renaud

A.F.: Dear Renaud,

I agree with you: the reference to the 1930s is today disarming Europe. Even so: we cannot act as if the twentieth century never took place. It is because there was no room left on the boat in Switzerland, in particular, that refugee law exists today. This is not something to be erased with the stroke of a pen. It is up to us to join firmness with perspicacity. It is also up to us to not yield to the temptation to see all those whom we turn away as invaders.

In all friendship,
Alain

R.C.: Dear Alain,

As we see it, it is not a matter of ending refugee law with the stroke of a pen but of very thoroughly revising it so as to strictly refocus it on the right to asylum, just like we want to refocus "culture" and the "cultural industries" on culture. Your formulation suits me perfectly, and I very gladly subscribe to it: "to not see all those whom we turn away as invaders." I would be even more liberal than you and would really like to not see some (a very small number) of those who we do not turn away as invaders. There nevertheless really is an invasion taking place under the cover of "refugee law," which has become a very bad farce. And this invasion no longer even bothers trying to appear pitiful, friendly, and peaceful. It is becoming what it is: aggressive, violent, and conquering.

Yours,
Renaud

A.F. Dear Renaud,

If one wanted to curb the current destructive process for everyone, it would be necessary, not just to wage a ruthless war against the human traffickers, but also to intervene in Libya and perhaps Eritrea – a prospect about which the progressive camp, the identitarian-sovereigntist camp, and right-thinking European opinion refuse to hear a word. This is deplorable. But let us not convert our impotence into vengeance against the wretched people landing on our shores.

Thank you for driving me into a corner.

R.C.: Dear Alain,

The wretched people landing on our shores, as you say, are for the most part not so wretched as all that. Many have paid twenty or thirty thousand euros to reach us, sometimes more – something of which I myself would be incapable. If they truly are refugees, a tenth of that money would have sufficed a thousand times over to arrange for that status before violating our borders, an act that, in all civilizations of the Earth, has always made criminals out of foreigners. Yet, far from behaving in a guilty or grateful manner, they boast of their spectacularly illegal status, they are more and more aggressive and bellicose, and a considerable part of the *nocence* not resulting from preceding waves of immigration is due to them. Faced with which, Europe constantly wonders what new rights she could give them, while a growing number of her own citizens live in extreme poverty.

That the progressive, identitarian-sovereigntist, right-thinking European, and, I would add, Putin-worshipping camps refuse to contemplate the overall geopolitical aspects of the situation is, I quite agree with you, worth lamenting. For my part, I continue to use my little voice to call for Europe to return to history, starting with an army and force of intervention worthy of the name.

Your friend and admirer,
Renaud Camus

A.F.: Dear Renaud,

There is a lot of arrogance in the "working class neighborhoods" but I do not discern any among the migrants who have sold all their belongings in order to cram themselves into old tubs in the Mediterranean or who risk their lives to reach England.

I spent a fascinating day in your company, in any case, and hope you will not forget me in the course of your next visit to Paris.

Your friend and faithful reader,

R.C.: Dear Alain,

And here we are back at our starting point, the communiqué of In-nocence – which, for its part, discerns a great deal of arrogance among many migrants, and this is what it calls their "new behaviors," which it finds highly revealing. In Kos, they attack the police and spread fear in the port. In Italy, they demonstrate for food that is more in keeping with their tradition and complain about the presence of women among the people tasked with assisting them. In Paris and Calais, they throw themselves at police officers. At the entrance to the Chunnel, they control access. They everywhere march openly with banners of protest, even though they should not be here at all, of course. Throughout Europe, they have been involved in a growing number of rapes and assaults. And I am not speaking of their catastrophic effect on the environment in the most material and immediate sense of the term: any place they congregate immediately assumes the aspect of a garbage dump. We are far removed from the "asylum seekers" of previous eras. Let us not blame origins and cultures, but number. As soon as number makes for strength, it is strength and the spirit of conquest that steps forth.

I will be in Paris in early September and will of course see you again with the greatest pleasure.

In all friendship,

A.F.: Dear Renaud,

Number, indeed. As Leopold Kohr, Ivan Illich's intellectual mentor, once said: "It seems there is only one cause behind all social woes: excessive size. Excessive size seems to be the sole and unique problem permeating all creation. Wherever something is amiss, something is too big."

It nevertheless remains the case that the invasion of which we are speaking is also and inextricably a humanitarian tragedy, as many other examples in addition to the ones you cite attest. To attempt to welcome all the wretched of the Earth would be suicidal. But do we really need to deny its reality to give ourselves courage?

In all friendship.

R.C.: My dear Alain,

You are right in thinking that I am one hundred percent of the same mind as you and Leopold Kohr concerning the excessive size of everything, of cities, museums, populations, institutions, fields, of cow, pork, and veal factory farms. This is one of the many points on which there is not the least disagreement between us. Gigantism entails normalization, normalization interchangeability, interchangeability *replacism,* and *replacism* the Great Replacement.

I do not believe I am one to be reproached for denying the reality of anything whatsoever and certainly not humanitarian tragedies or even, I would say, human ones to the extent that they follow from the practice of *replacism.* That today's immense crisis has a humanitarian aspect and that this is a matter for international mutual aid is undeniable. It is a question of between two and five percent of it, I would say. To reduce this crisis to that share alone, to choose to only see and address this aspect of its sheer scale, is pure madness, criminal blindness, at best a certain penchant of the right-thinking soul who does not want to depart from familiar ways of speaking, at worst abject complicity in the abandonment of a people and a civilization.

I take the liberty of attaching to this letter a recent contribution on the subject by Mr. Francis Marche at the forum of In-nocence.[3]

Be assured of my very Kohrian friendship,
Renaud

---

3. Francis Marche (*Forum de l'In-nocence,* August 2015): The man comes from Pakistan, he has just landed on the Greek island of Kos. Pakistan is not in a civil war, there is no bombing of the civilian population in this country, and it is not experiencing any more mass atrocities than the France of François Hollande.

    His commentary on the manner in which he was received, a reproachful tirade interspersed with moralizing criticism ("This is no way to treat people"), conveys the essence of the problematic attitude of these migrants, who believe that Europe owes them everything Europeans enjoy in addition to having to take their word regarding their personal situation in their country of origin, a privilege that France, for example, does not grant its own citizens, who are obligated to furnish dozens of "supporting documents" for absolutely everything that has anything whatsoever to do with a benefit, the granting of an exemption, the provision of a service.

    The problem is real and it is objective. It is not a matter of "hatred" against illegal immigrants shouting about their rights and our obligations but of considering the situation as it is, beyond the emotive confusion that is stoked by an agitated media.

The Apartment: Response to Emmanuel Carrère [2017][1]

When there appeared in French a collection of articles and criticism by Emmanuel Carrère, *Il est avantageux d'avoir où aller*,[i] our mutual friend Alain Finkielkraut suggested that the two of us should discuss it on the radio, since in his book Carrère vigorously criticizes my positions by way of an open letter addressed to me several years earlier.[2] I have known Emmanuel Carrère since forever, as they say. I have much affection and admiration for him. But I found it a little unfair of him to refuse this public debate since he is, quite rightly, the media's favorite son, worshipped by them and invited everywhere, appearing on the cover of all the magazines, whereas I am – and not without reason – their bête noire, banished everywhere and, in France at least, now deprived of all means of expression other than my self-published books. As I might have been able to respond for once, it seems to me that he should not have refused me this opportunity.

But now that his book has been published in Italy, *Verità*[ii] has given me the chance to do just that: respond. It would be churlish of me to refuse.

The letter that Carrère sent me, to be published in what was then my magazine, and which he includes in his collection is entirely organized around the theme of *the apartment*. One would think one was

---

1. "L'Appartement (21 mars 2017)," in *Le Grand Remplacement: Introduction au remplacisme global.* (Paris, La Nouvelle Librairie, 2021), pp. 507-514.
2. Carrère's letter to Camus is reprinted in appendix to this volume.

reading Leibniz' Theodicy: "Thereupon the Goddess led Theodorus into one of the apartments of the palace: when he was within, it was no longer an apartment, it was a world, *solemque suum, sua sidera norat.*"

And indeed, Carrère's apartment *is* the world. It is at once a metaphor for the world and a real apartment, a *beautiful* apartment, he says, in the tenth arrondissement of Paris.

Carrère has the rare courage to admit that he is a *bobo*, a "bourgeois bohemian," one of the most universally reviled social categories in France, both by those who do not belong to it and by many of those who do. Almost singlehandedly, Carrère defends the bourgeois bohemian, the comfortably well-off bourgeois bohemian, nicely settled in his life, liberal, progressive, generous, a man of the Left or close enough – there he is, the bourgeois bohemian in his large, bright, well-lit apartment, up in the sky, and not so expensive as one might think since it is located in a neighborhood already largely given over to "diversity," as it is generally known. That is where he was living, in any case, with his wife and two children, when he wrote me the aforementioned letter in 2011. He nevertheless declares: "What I meant to say is that, should I tomorrow be ordered by decree to live with my family in only one room of this beautiful apartment and give up the others to those hordes of Kurds and Afghans who camp in the street four stories below, I would find it extremely unpleasant, I would seek to leave and make arrangements elsewhere, if that was still possible, for a life more befitting my tastes, but I would not consider the steps taken against me to be unjust."

One notes very much in passing the splendid lack of class consciousness here displayed by Carrère, who "would seek to leave and make arrangements elsewhere" and who without a doubt could easily do so, so long, that is, as an *elsewhere* exists. Yet this is precisely what millions of our fellow countrymen cannot do, forced as they are for lack of money to stay put and become, in an awful twist of fate, foreigners in their own land among newcomers of different cultures, mores, and civilizations who are not always so affable or easy to live with.

But let us not linger on this point, for there is worse to come. We here find ourselves at the heart of replacist ideology, which seeks to convince native Europeans that they have law and morality *against* them. They can drag their feet a bit if they want, but they know deep down that it is their duty to make way for the others. And why is it their duty? Because there are fewer of them. If there is a family with seventeen children in the street below, a family with only two must hand over their big, bright, beautiful apartment to them or at least hole up in a single room and try to lay low. This is not just the heart of replacist ideology but also a description of its technique, its instruction manual, for ethnic substitution, what the poet Aimé Césaire very rightly named, apropos of Martinique and therefore in an entirely different context, *genocide by substitution*. I do not know about Italy, but in France, at least, pro-natalist legislation, originally intended to protect the existence of the French people, has over time proven itself to be one of the most effective tools for the change of people.

This supreme refinement – the consent of the victims – was unknown to other genocides, those that preceded that of the Europeans. I have referred to replacism, the ideology of general substitution, as *the communism of the twenty-first century*. The legitimation by Europeans themselves of their own elimination is the precise, replacist equivalent of Stalinist self-criticism. The Great Replacement is a long Stalinist show trial, that of the purges. Emmanuel Carrère tells us why we must step aside, why we are guilty for existing and taking up too much space in what has always been our native land.

"I see no reason," Carrère writes, "why little Liré should belong to us any more than to the miserable wretches of Sudan."[iii]

And why should these Sudanese have the same rights as we do – that is to say, more than we do – *in the land of our forebears*? Because there are more of them. In contrast to the most familiar forms of replacist self-criticism, which is in fact a type of self-hatred, Carrère does not invoke the crimes of Europeans. No, he invokes demography. To believe him, what gives Africans a greater claim to our beautiful apartment is the fact that they have seventeen children or seven, whereas we only have two or none at all.

It is my opinion, however, that the earth has had enough of man, as have other species; that the population explosion is the greatest danger threatening the planet; that all ecological policies are perfectly vain so long as population growth has not been brought under control; that the old European peoples, whose numbers have never been so great, have despite the exhortations of insane demographers shown great and profound wisdom in quite sensibly seeing to their own demographic decrease, whereas African demography is for its part a dreadful time bomb.

Yet for Carrère, it is this madness, this total planetary irresponsibility, that of uncontrolled birth rates, that confers rights. It is because they have more children that non-Europeans should have the right, according to him, to invade the territory of Europeans and make themselves at home in their beautiful apartment. In short, he encourages vice and punishes virtue. He makes irresponsibility the foundation of rights and responsibility an instrument of death or elimination.

Along the way and very significantly, he abolishes the right to property, that persona non grata of the modern legal conscience. Apartments, to follow his reasoning, belong to those who most need them. This is yet another point of commonality between global replacism and communism. In Western Europe, the most enduring legacy of the Soviet experiment is the *kommounalka*, the shared collective apartment, like in Moscow and Saint Petersburg in the era of Stalin and Brezhnev. Except that, in coming West, the *kommounalka* became continental in scale. Our *kommounalka* is the dreadful *vivre-ensemble*,[iv] the forced cohabitation of different peoples, the most natural, inevitable expression of which, apart from permanent tension and terrorism, is the *state of emergency.*

Given the increasing frequency with which natives are expelled for the benefit of so-called refugees and unoccupied apartments are requisitioned for their use, it becomes a bit more apparent, every day, everywhere in Europe, that the right to property is in the crosshairs of global replacism. This is an occasion to recall that, despite its bad press, the right to property has always been regarded as a foundational element of civilization, freedom, and even human rights – and this for peoples no less than for individuals. It is perfectly logical that the ideologies of human replacement and the interchangeability of peoples should see it as an impediment and wish to reduce it, do away with it, for like races, classes, sexes, generations, levels of language and of culture, names,[3] formality and proper distance, it is an obstacle to the industrial production of UHM, Undifferentiated Human Matter.

---

3. See *La Civilisation des prénoms*, the author, 2018.

Appeal of Colombey [2017][1]

Immigration has become invasion, and invasion, migratory submersion.[2]

France and Europe are one hundred times more colonized and more seriously so than they ever themselves colonized. Irreversible colonization is *demographic* colonization by population transfer.

Some say there is no colonization because there has been no military conquest. They are mistaken. It is delinquents, petty and not-so-petty, who are the army of conquest, all those who make life impossible for French people by harming them in every imaginable way, from the oft-cited incivilities to terrorism, which is merely their continuation. The perpetrators of attacks all first cut their teeth in common law crime. Indeed, there are no terrorists. There is an occupier who, from time to time, executes a few hostages – us – as occupiers have always done. I call occupiers all those who declare themselves such or show themselves to be such by their behavior.

The change of people – ethnic substitution, the Great Replacement – is the most important event in the history of our country since its inception, for, with another people, its history, if it continues, will no longer be that of France. France has always wonderfully assimilated

---

1. "Appel de Colombey (9 novembre 2017)," in *Le Grand Remplacement: Introduction au remplacisme global.* (Paris, La Nouvelle Librairie, 2021), pp. 553-560.
2. This appeal was issued on November 9th, 2017, anniversary of the death of General de Gaulle, in Colombey-les-Deux-Églises, not far from his tomb. It resulted in the creation of the National Council of European Resistance, presided by Renaud Camus, and that of the movement of its sympathizers and supporters, the group Résistance, presided by Karim Ouchikh.

individuals who wished to be assimilated, but it cannot assimilate peoples and even less so hostile, vindictive, indeed hate-filled and conquering peoples. One must be unspeakably vain and utterly ignorant of what a people is to imagine that, with a changed population, France would still be France. All words are deceitful but the most deceitful of all, alas, is *French*. There are no French jihadists, for example. If they are jihadists, they are not French.

To believe that there are only French people in France is a total illusion. There are the invaders and the invaded, colonizers and colonized, occupiers and occupied.

One does not put an end to colonization without the departure of the colonist: Algeria, in its time, sufficiently demonstrated this to us, alas – it is for us a good opportunity, by the way, to underscore the difference of civilization.

One does not put an end to an occupation without the departure of the occupier. There is no other way out than remigration. The same people who claim it is impractical want forty million migrants to come to Europe, when it is not two hundred million. They claim that man has entered an era of general migration. Let him migrate and remigrate, then. What is possible in one direction must obviously be possible in the other, more gently and with greater resources.

The time is no longer for politics, elections, parties. 2022 is too far away, the change of people will by then be too advanced, the replacers will be the arbiters of the situation, assuming they are not already its masters. And in any case, no game can ever be won when one's opponent holds all the cards and has made all the rules. Power – its banks, judges, and media – wants ethnic substitution. They are not protecting us from it; they are overseeing and promoting it. They have drugged the people into accepting it through the teaching of forgetting, deculturation, censorship, repression, and continuous injections of self-loathing. They are not importing workers, especially as there is no work to be had and will be less and less of it. They are importing future consumers, whom they no longer even bother to pass off as refugees since the overwhelming majority of these migrants come from countries where there is not the least war: orphans, sick people, adventurous or conquering youth, adolescents who have quarreled with their parents or got into trouble with the police, shopkeepers whose businesses have failed.

You say these future consumers have no money. Do not deceive yourself, tomorrow they will have yours, because the so-called "social transfers" are in truth little more than ethnic transfers. Europe is the first continent to pay for its own colonization.

A specter is haunting Europe and the world. It is replacism, the tendency to replace everything with its normalized, standardized, interchangeable double: the original by its copy, the authentic by its imitation, the true by the false, mothers by surrogate mothers, culture by leisure activities and entertainment, knowledge by diplomas, the countryside and city by the universal suburb, the native by the non-native, Europe by Africa, men by women, men and women by robots, peoples by other peoples, humanity by a savage, undifferentiated, standardized, infinitely interchangeable posthumanity.

Of all genetic manipulations, the Great Replacement, a sort of surrogacy implemented at the scale of the whole planet, is the worst. Genocide by substitution, in the phrase of Aimé Césaire, is the crime against humanity of the twenty-first century. And indeed, it is quite remarkable that, in their laudable concern for biodiversity, the ecologists should stop with man.

Replacism now considers itself strong enough to directly take on responsibility for managing the human park in the absence of any intermediary. In France, Emmanuel Macron, who alongside Justin Trudeau is its most perfect representative, has already neutralized the microcosm, discharged from their duties the leading actors of French political life of the past thirty years, populated the National Assembly with puppets in his pay, assembled a government of casual encounters, split all the great parties asunder. He does not govern, he manages, as he would a bank or a corporation.

He exits politics by way of economics, finance, and business management. We want to exit it by way of history. The question of the independence or subservience of a great nation, of the survival or disappearance of a great civilization, is not a matter of politics; it is a matter of history. Charles de Gaulle, whom we celebrate today not far from his tomb, on the anniversary of his death, Charles de Gaulle in London was not politics.ⁱ Jean Moulin in Lyon was not politics. Neither was Joan of Arc in Chinon or Gandhi in Calcutta, nor any of those who have risen up for the independence of their country and the dignity of their people.

What we need today is not a new party, nor even a union of the right: the rejection of replacist totalitarianism concerns the left no less than the right. What we need is for all those who oppose a great NO to Islamization and African conquest to come together. What is needed is a National Council of Resistance, of *European* resistance, for all European nations are invited to fight alongside us for the salvation of our common civilization, at once Celtic, Slavic, Greco-Roman, Judeo-Christian, and free-thinking.

My friend Karim Ouchikh, president of SIEL, and I, Renaud Camus, have decided to establish just that, a *CNR* [*Conseil National de Résistance*], or CNRE [*Conseil National de Résistance Européenne*]. We publicly ask all the well-known figures who seem driven by the same desire to save our country that they join us, and in this way, we will enlarge our committee via cooptation. But all the French people and all the Europeans who think as we do are invited to contact us and give us their support. Our objective is to amass such strength that, ideally, we will never need to use it.

That said, if by some misfortune the only alternative left us is submission or war, we choose war, a hundred times war. And there would be nothing *civil* about it, despite the numerous traitors and collaborators. It would instead be in keeping with the great tradition of struggles for the right of peoples to determine their own fates, for the liberation of their territory, and for decolonization. We must finally exit the colonial period, about which our colonizers speak so much evil even as they colonize us. Once and for all, and if possible above the Mediterranean, we must stop the mad pendulum of colonization and counter-colonization.

Long live free France. Long live European civilization.

Appendix

The present text was sent to the Italian magazine *La Verità* on 21 March 2017. Here is the letter from Emmanuel Carrère to which it is a reply:

Le Levron, in Valais, Friday 21 October 2011

My dear Renaud,

Knowing how sharp your ear is, I am sure you noticed my embarrassment on the telephone when you suggested I write a text on Soviet dissidence for the Party of In-nocence's new journal. To gain time, I asked for a few days to think it over. This is the result.

I admire you and think of you as a friend. In a recent entry of your journal, there was a rather melancholic passage in which you lament that so many of your friendships are inactive, unactualized, ghost-like, and you mention me among these ghost-friends. This saddened me, first because it is true, next because it is not altogether true. After all, I have spent an average of one week per year for twenty-five years reading your journal and in recent years as much reading *Demeures de l'esprit*, thereby informing myself in detail of what has happened to you, of what you have seen, heard, thought, felt, sometimes suffered, day after day. My curiosity in this regard has not diminished, the moments of irritation do not make a dent in it, for, in the case of the people one really loves, even their flaws are qualities, and for my part, when I am writing a book, you are one of the readers of whom I think, one of those whose reactions I anticipate and from whom I impatiently await a letter, a letter that, by turns funny, understanding, and affectionate, never fails to arrive. So, yes, of course we don't see one another, we don't call one another, we haven't gotten into these habits, but if I think about it, I realize I don't have many friends with whom I have such intimate exchanges or who occupy so prominent a place in my mind.

By chance, I happen to now be reading Nietzsche and often, in reading him, I think of you. Of your sincerity, your freedom, your altitude. Of your sense of "the happy form," which is the opposite of the form by means of which, now as before, one makes one's way in the world: a compact philosophical system, a nicely done little novel. Of your extraordinary talent for burning your bridges, sawing off the branches upon which you sit, always moving yourself further away. Of your moustache, of the Engadin, which even if you do not frequent it suits you so well. Of the almost grandiose contrast between the size of your oeuvre and the silence with which it is greeted. I sometimes see myself, without too much bitterness, as one of those simple writers, widely read and appreciated in their lifetimes, who only go down in history as footnotes because they occupy a little place in the correspondence or journal of the misunderstood genius of his time, whose fame has constantly grown until it takes up all the space. When one sees oneself in this role, one would like to strike a good figure: to have been clear-sighted, faithful, and I hope I am. Yet what bothers me (and after having considered, out of cowardice or politeness, the idea of excusing myself for lack of time, I tell myself that your proposal has made this clarification necessary) is the turn your work and destiny, driven as they are by solitude, has taken when that work and destiny finds, I will not say readers, but what is very different, disciples – those people whose calling it is to immobilize dancing thought in ponderous certitude. I love Nietzsche but not the Nietzscheans, as Nietzsche loved Wagner but not the Wagnerians, and I must say that, as much as I love Renaud Camus, I am ill at ease with the Party of In-nocence.

I almost entirely agree with everything you say for the simple reason that it is you who says it, unfurls it, stratifies it, bathmologizes it, and that it is the meteorology of your mind, not a discourse of truth. I do not agree with anything your party says, even and above all when that intersects word for word with what you yourself say. Even and above all – above all even more – when something somewhere inside me agrees.

For example: I believe my ear is as almost as attuned as yours to the impoverishments and trivialities of contemporary speech, and you can reprise as often as you like your famous generalized Noël Roquevert number and always find an appreciative audience in me. But when people gather under your leadership to share their pitying disdain for those of their fellow creatures who say "no worries," "it's true that," or "le Gersss," and, worse yet, bubble over with enthusiasm in distinguishing themselves from these plebes, I find it all too much. I even find – forgive me, I am going to moralize a little – that freeing oneself from this disdain and this caste pride is a matter of spiritual and moral progress, reveling in it a mistake, the same with which the Gospel reproached the Pharisees. I am myself inclined to make this mistake. Practically from birth, I have been one of those people who raises an eyebrow when the unfortunate Arnaud Montebourg says "applicant" for "candidate" and who look down their noses at the young women, with their diamond-studded nostrils, speaking very loudly into their cell phones, but I try to correct myself and have no desire to join those who make of this error – because I am sure that that is what it is – a cause and rallying cry.

Since I'm on the subject, I will continue, and tell you what I think of the most insistent theme of In-nocence, which is the great replacement, reverse colonization, the foreigners in our country who should behave like well-mannered guests, loving our language, practicing our religion – or theirs, but discreetly, and in showing gratitude towards us for our indulgence. Sincerely, Renaud, I think that none of this means anything anymore, for the simple reason that there are today more than six billion (or is it seven?) of us on Earth, which is obviously far too many and which will only get worse and will necessarily render life – I agree with you here a thousand times over – less sweet, the neighbors more numerous, louder, more noxious, but short of hoping that a cataclysm decimates three quarters of the planet (and that one

206 ENEMY OF THE DISASTER

belongs to the quarter that remains), what can one do about it other than move over to make room?

Hélène and I very much like the apartment in which we live and you would, too, I think, if you would give us the pleasure of coming to see us in the course of your next trip to Paris. It is large, bright, supernaturally quiet: no neighbors above us, no neighbors beneath us, we feel good here. The thing is that, in the 10th arrondissement, the population of which is divided between Arabs and Pakistanis running industrious little shops, there are Kurds and Afghans who bum around the Gare du Nord while hoping to get to England, street people and bums of various nationalities, who piss on the walls – bobos like us, in short. There is much to be said about the bobo, doubtless the most disparaged (including by its own representatives) social type there is. And I, who am one, the real deal, exhibit-grade, I would gladly come to his defense – and, at the same time, that of the "politically correct," which is also so disparaged and that no one is willing to personify. In short: as a good bobo, I came to live here, not only because one can find beautiful, large apartments for less than one pays in the swankier arrondissements, but also because, all things considered, I like it. I like what Jean-Christophe Bailly, in *Le Dépaysement*, calls the "multicolor" (If you haven't read it, I highly recommend *Le Dépaysement*, which ranges the breadth of the French countryside, describing it with an acuity of attention comparable to yours but reaches other conclusions, ones with which I find myself to be in greater sympathy.) But that is not what I wanted to say. What I wanted to say is that, should I tomorrow be ordered by decree to live with my family in only one room of this beautiful apartment and give up the others to those hordes of Kurds and Afghans who camp out in the street four stories below, I would find it extremely unpleasant, I would seek to leave and make arrangements elsewhere, if that was still possible, for a life more befitting my tastes, but I would not consider the steps taken against me to be unjust . . . Of course, I am not totally mad, I know that justice counts less than relations of power, and that, if the wretched of the Earth are right, from their point of view, to besiege our peaceful retreats, we are for our part right to defend them every inch of the way. But I think that the argument: "This is my home, not yours," can be justified in what we may call ethological terms (Konrad Lorenz, the Greylag Goose, the herd, all that . . .), but not in all due justice, and even less so in all due globalized justice. Like you, I like or rather I liked the little countries, the Syldavias, Bordurias, Caronias, I liked them all the more as my own suited me fine, in short, I had come at the right moment, but, on reflection, I see no convincing reason why little Liré should belong to us rather than to the miserable wretches of Sudan. In which respect I am more pessimistic than you since, even as I largely share your ideal (a civilized, bourgeois life spent enjoying Bonnard, Toulet, leafy monasteries, and the moon going down over what was once a temple), while hoping that the circumstances that allow me to lead this life last a little while longer, I do not believe I possess the right to defend them, rather the contrary.

Ultimately, it is this conviction of being in one's right – that of the Frenchman, the man who knows how to speak, the knowledgeable man – that stops me in my tracks, not in your writings, where you never cease drilling down into and excavating what you think, but in what I have been able to read of the Party of In-nocence. This is why, without moving away from you, I do not want to associate with it or its journal. That said, should you think it appropriate to publish, in place of the requested article, this letter detailing the reasons for which I do not want to write it, I have nothing against it.

I hope, my dear Renaud, that these disagreements and the liberty I have taken in presenting them in no way damage our friendship. However ghostly, it is for me priceless.

Emmanuel

Contributors

Renaud Camus

A native of Chamalières in the Auvergne region of central France, Renaud Camus (b. 1946) is one of France's most brilliant stylists and the author of more than 150 books. *Tricks*, his first and only work to be translated into English until now, appeared in 1979 and was prefaced by Roland Barthes, one of twentieth-century France's greatest literary critics and Camus' mentor. In addition to the political essays collected in *Enemy of the Disaster*, Camus is also known for works of fiction, philosophy, travel writing, art criticism, and the extensive diary he has kept and published for over forty years. He lives in the Chateau de Plieux in the village of Plieux in southwestern France and is the president of a small political party, the *Party of In-nocence*, which advocates immigration and education reform and the promotion of civic peace.

Louis Betty

Louis Betty is Associate Professor of French at the University of Wisconsin-Whitewater. In addition to his work on Renaud Camus, he is also the author of *Without God: Michel Houellebecq and Materialist Horror* (Penn State Press, 2016) as well as numerous scholarly articles. He received his PhD from Vanderbilt University in 2011 and lives in Madison, WI.

Ethan Rundell

Ethan Rundell is a translator, journalist, and alumnus of UC, Berkeley, and Paris' School for Advanced Studies in the Social Sciences (EHESS). Rundell has translated over a dozen books as well as scores of academic articles. He lives in North Carolina.

Notes

The Communism of the Twenty-First Century

i. Camus is here referring to the controversy surrounding an interview Finkielkraut gave to the Israeli newspaper *Haaretz* in the fall of 2005 after a period of widespread suburban rioting in France on the part of predominantly ethnically north-African, Muslim youth. The interview, in which Finkielkraut contended that the spirit of revolt in the suburbs had a religious and ethnic character rather than a merely social or economic one, drew criticism from the left-wing press but was defended by Nicolas Sarkozy, who at the time was minister of the interior under president Jacques Chirac. It was in the same interview that Finkielkraut claimed that antiracism could be considered "the communism of the twenty-first century."

ii. Presumably a reference to a proposed referendum to ban the construction of new minarets in Switzerland, which was widely criticized in the international press. In 2009, the referendum passed with 57.5% of the vote.

iii. Jean-Paul Sartre upon returning from a trip to the Soviet Union in 1954. See Jean-Paul Sartre, *Situations, IV* (Paris, Gallimard, 1964), pp. 248-249.

iv. A translation of the French euphemism "zone d'éducation prioritaire," which refers to underperforming school districts targeted for special investment.

v. A reference to the Stakhanovite movement of Soviet Russia. Modeling themselves after Alexei Stakhanov, a miner renowned for his prodigious productivity, Stakhanovites took pride in producing more than was required of them by the state. The Stakhanovite movement began in the 1930s in the coal industry but later spread to other areas of Soviet industrial production, though it eventually came to be criticized for placing too great a burden of expectation on workers. A "Stakhanovite of pleasure" would thus be someone who both pursues sexual pleasure in great quantity and also manages to achieve it, potentially prompting criticism for excessive sexual "productivity."

vi. A reference to a popular French televised talent show and singing competition than ran from 2001 to 2008 and was reprised in 2022. American equivalents are shows such as *American Idol* and *America's Got Talent*.

vii. Translation of "c'est vrai que." Elsewhere, Camus approvingly uses the expression "il est vrai que," also translated as "it is true that" but lacking the ironic connotation of "c'est vrai que." When one hears the words "c'est vrai que" (during a televised political debate, for example), it is almost certain, Camus insists, that what follows will be precisely not the truth – hence the need for an emphatic expression to conceal one's impending dishonesty. Even minimal attention paid to French television will reveal to the viewer the ubiquity of this verbal tic.

viii. An intentional shift to the demotic. Camus is mocking what he sees as lazy speech, syntax, pronunciation, and spelling on French television and radio and in text messaging. "That's whatcha gotta understand" is our translation of "c'est ça qu'vous avez qu'i faut bien comprendre." "Whatcha mean" is our rendering of "Cékoi" [C'est quoi?]. The generalized degradation of written and spoken language is, in Camus' view, a major vector of deculturation in France and also one of its principal symptoms.

ix. The Roissy Detention Center (Centre de rétention administrative) is located near the Charles de Gaulle Airport in the northern suburbs of Paris. It is used, among other things, to house foreign nationals awaiting deportation to their country of origin.

x. "Green" here is an allusion to Islam, for which it is often considered the "official color," figuring prominently as it does in many of the flags of Islamic nations. Camus is calling attention to the imposition of Islam as the dominant worldview in neighborhoods where communists ("reds") once supplied the prevailing ideology.

xi. *L'Humanité* was originally a socialist newspaper founded by Jean Jaurès in 1904. In 1920, it was taken over by the French Communist Party (PCF – *Parti communiste français*) and is still in circulation. Waldeck Rochet and Roland Leroy were French communist politicians of the 20th century.

xii. George Marchais (1920-1997) led the French Communist Party from 1972 to 1994.

xiii. One of Camus' best-known neologisms, which can be roughly translated as "non-harm" or "non-nuisance" (*nocere* in Latin meaning "to harm," and from which the English word "nuisance" is derived). The hyphenated character of the term is intended to note the sense in which innocence is secondary to "nocence." In other words, since the natural human inclination is to damage, destroy, bother, and pollute – in a word, to be a nuisance – a person has to work at "in-nocenting" himself, at becoming civilized and therefore harmless.

xiv. An expression denoting an idea or discovery that, in hindsight, seems simple or obvious.

xv. The French term for affirmative action. Whereas the American term is euphemistic, the French equivalent is strikingly literal (one discriminates but for a good cause, a positive result). The French have more recently introduced euphemistic terms such as "action positive," "mesures correctrices d'inégalités," and "dédiscrimination."

The Second Career of Adolf Hitler

i. Laure Adler (b. 1950) is a French journalist and essayist and was the director of the radio station *France Culture* from 1999 to 2005. She thus held this post during the "Camus affair." In 2000, Camus published *La Campagne de France*, certain passages of which had criticized the uniform ethno-religious composition (in this case, Jewish) of the contributors to a 1994 *France Culture* panel discussion on immigration and national identity (see section 2 of the introduction to this volume). MRAP (*Mouvement contre le racisme et pour l'amitié entre les peuples* – "Movement against Racism and for Friendship among Peoples") is a French non-governmental organization founded in 1949. MRAP successfully sued Camus in 2014 for comments he made in a speech during the *Assises internationales sur l'Islamisation* (International Conference on Islamization) in Paris in 2010.

ii. Inner-ring suburbs ("banlieues") in French cities roughly correspond to inner-city "ghettos" in the United States in terms of poverty, crime, and physical blight and in the flight of white residents. While in the United States the phenomenon of "white flight" has historically been from inner cities to suburbs, white flight in French cities is from inner to outer suburban rings, posh city centers being generally unaffordable for *banlieusards*, or "suburbanites."

iii. Likely a reference to a December 11th, 2006, speech given by former Iranian president Mahmoud Ahmadinejad at the *International Conference to Review the Global Vision of the Holocaust and Other Controversies*.

iv. The expressions "Nique ta race" (Fuck your race) or "Nique ta mère la race" (Fuck your mother's race) are common (albeit shocking) insults in French.

v. Vacher de Lapouge (1854-1936) was a French anthropologist whose racial typology emphasized the superiority of Anglo-Saxon and Nordic peoples to Jews and other European peoples. Lapouge's ideas found favor after his death in Nazi-occupied France. The reference to Chamberlain is to Houston Stewart Chamberlain (1855-1927), a British-German philosopher whose two-volume work *The Foundations of the Nineteenth Century* (1899) influenced the German *Völkische* movement and anti-Semitic racial policy under the Nazi regime. Finally, Camus' reference to Rosenberg is to Alfred Ernst Rosenberg (1893-1946), a Nazi theorist and author of the book *The Myth of the Twentieth Century* (1930). Rosenberg was executed by hanging in 1946 after being convicted of crimes against humanity at the Nuremberg trials.

vi. A reference to Frederick Winslow Taylor (1856-1915), the creator of the theory of scientific management. "Fordist" is a reference to Henry Ford.

vii. Impossible, that is, because of the prevalence of Muslim students who believe that Jews, and in particular Israeli Jews, take advantage of the Holocaust in order to dominate and oppress Palestinian Muslims. For a canonical treatment of the rise of antisemitism in the French suburbs, readers should consult Georges Bensoussan's *Les Territoires perdus de la République* (The Lost Territories of the Republic) (Paris, Mille et une nuits, 2002, reissued in 2015).

viii. Presumably a reference to issues surrounding the wearing of Islamic dress in public schools (the wearing of ostensibly religious clothing or symbols in public schools was outlawed in 2005), which is commonly interpreted as an antisemitic (and therefore racist) provocation.

ix. "Ce mode de pensée angelo-bleu-blanc-beur, donc, bellâmo-benettonien, répressivo-touche-pas-à-mon-potiste . . ." A simultaneous evocation of the multicultural- and diversity-themed advertisements of the Benetton Group and the slogan "Touche pas à mon pote!" (Hands off my buddy!) launched by the French association SOS Racisme in 1985 to fight discrimination and promote the integration of young people of North African origin into French society.

x. The Avenue Paul Doumer traverses Paris's posh 16th arrondissement. Clichy-sous-Bois is an urban municipality on Paris's eastern periphery that was the epicenter of the suburban riots of 2005.

xi. Houari Boumediane (1932-1978), president of Algeria from 1967 to 1978; Abdelaziz Bouteflika (1937-2021), president of Algeria from 1999 to 2019.

The Great Deculturation

    i. A reference to several French booksellers with physical locations in France.

    ii. Catherine Clément (b. 1939) is a French philosopher, essayist, novelist, and journalist known among other things for a controversial book on bullfighting, *Torero d'or* (Paris, Hachette,1981).

    iii. This is a pejorative play on the term "français de souche," which appears several lines above in the main text and means, roughly, a native Frenchman (English equivalents of the word "souche" being "stock," "stump," "root," or other related words denoting the starting point of organic growth). "Souchien," as Camus notes, combines the word "sous," meaning "under" or "beneath," and "chien," meaning "dog," to suggest that native Frenchmen are of less value than dogs ("sous-chiens").

    iv. In contrast to its English cognate, "popular," the French adjective "populaire" possesses strong social connotations. To describe something as "populaire" is to say that it relates to or is of the common people (for which the English adjective "working-class" is a rough but not always satisfactory approximation). See also note xviii under "The Great Replacement."

    v. The Ministry of Culture is a cabinet-level ministry under the French Fifth Republic. Established by President Charles de Gaulle in 1959, the Ministry's mission is to defend and promote French culture at home and abroad. In addition to overseeing the French National Archives, the Ministry operates a network of regional cultural centers, promotes architectural programs, and seeks to "democratize" access to culture by sponsoring various festivals and other popular events.

    vi. The French baccalaureate degree, colloquially referred to as "le bac" is basically equivalent to the American high school diploma with the difference that students must pass a comprehensive exit exam to obtain it.

    vii. A French "licence" (a "first-cycle" degree) is equivalent to an American college diploma. A "maitrise" ("second-cycle" degree) corresponds to a master's degree (since 2007, the degree has been referred to as *un master*). The "D.E.U.G." (Diplôme d'études universitaires généralisées) is a defunct two-year, first-cycle degree roughly equivalent to a liberal arts major. The D.E.S.S. (Diplôme d'études supérieures spécialisées), also defunct, was a one-year, third-cycle degree. The D.U.T (Diplôme universitaire de technologie) is extant.

    viii. The term "well-bred" in English perhaps better captures Camus' meaning here, though the connotation of elevation, altitude, or height is lost in translation. More generally, in the same way that the meaning of "well-bred" as regards children is rendered suspect by its lexical (and perhaps more than lexical) proximity to the "breeding" of animals – it is the same root word in one and the other case – so the word élever [to raise] suffers a similar fate due to its lexical (and, again, perhaps more than lexical) proximity to élevage [animal husbandry].

    ix. Gérard Pesson (b. 1958) is a French composer of opera, chamber music, and piano and ensemble works. *Cran d'arrêt du beau temps*, the author's personal journal covering the years 1991 to 1998, was published by Van Dieren, a Parisian publishing house, in 2004.

x. Kyo is a French pop-rock band formed in 1994. The Scissor Sisters are a New York-based American pop-rock band formed in 2001.

xi. In the original French, Camus parenthetically offers two examples of grammatically incorrect statements uttered by an anonymous doctor. The remainder of the paragraph reads: "This very morning on the radio, I heard a distinguished doctor and professor of medicine, the author of several works, speak of 'toute la recherche qu'il avait *fait*,' [all the research he had done] over the course of his life and explain that he had left the public sector, not to earn more money, but so as to be able to do 'toute la recherche que j'avais envie'" [all the research I felt like]. The grammatical errors these statements contain are impossible to render in English, owing in the first case to the phenomenon of gendered declension of past participles and, in the second, to the idiomatic nature of the corresponding expression in English ["to feel like"], the French expression necessitating, when it is formulated in a relative clause, the use of the pronoun *dont*, which has no single English equivalent. The statements in question should read "toute la recherche qu'il avait *faite*" and "toute la recherche *dont* j'avais envie."

xii. In French, "éducation" can refer both to schooling and to the quality of one's upbringing (and thus to the presence or absence of good manners).

xiii. A reference to the Loi Haby (Haby Law) of 1975 that was criticized (and still is) for "dumbing down" curricula in the pursuit of equality of outcomes. The term "one middle school" (*collège unique*) captures the notion of standardization around a "core curriculum" (*tronc commun*).

xiv. Jack Lang (b. 1939) is a French politician and member of the French Socialist Party (*Le Parti socialiste*) who served in various ministerial roles (notably culture and national education) during the Mitterrand and Chirac presidencies. He is currently the president of the Parisian *Institut du monde arabe* (Institute of the Arab World) and is a vocal champion of teaching Arabic in public schools.

xv. "It is like Perette's milk . . ." A reference to La Fontaine's fable, "The Milkmaid and Her Pail" (VII.10). Consumed with daydreams of all that she will buy with the proceeds from selling her milk, the milkmaid Perette stumbles on her way to market, destroying at once the milk pot she is carrying and the imaginary fortune it would bring her.

xvi. The Grand Palais (Great Palace) and Petit Palais (Little Palace) are two Parisian monuments that face each other on the Avenue Winston Churchill, which intersects the Champs-Élysées at the northern edge of each respective palace. Both monuments are used as exhibition halls.

xvii. "Although puzzling questions, [they] are not beyond *all* conjecture . . ." Camus is here alluding to either the epigraph with which Edgard Allen Poe begins his short story, "The Murders in the Rue Morgue," or to the 1658 work by Sir Thomas Browne from which that epigraph is drawn, *Hyrdriotaphia, Urn Burial, or a Discourse of the Sephulchral Urns Lately Found in Norfolk*. See "The Murders in the Rue Morgue," *The Portable Edgar Allen Poe* (New York, Penguin Books, 2006), p. 238.

xviii. "Cerisy-la-Salle" is a reference to Le Centre culturel international de Cerisy-la-Salle (The International Cultural Center of Cerisy-la-Salle), which the small Norman town hosts each year from May to October in the local castle.

Since 1952, the Center has hosted nearly eight hundred conferences on a broad range of intellectual topics. TF1 is a French public television channel.

xix. *Télérama* is a weekly French culture review covering film, theater, music, literature, and other areas of cultural interest. It also provides information about show times and cultural programming. *Pariscope*, a now-defunct Parisian weekly, was a low-cost, small format reference for movie times, exhibition dates, and other details of cultural programming in the Paris region.

xx. Boulangism was a political movement in late-nineteenth-century France centered around Georges Boulanger (1837-1891), a French general and politician who advocated a policy of revanchist nationalism toward Germany in the years after France's defeat in the Franco-Prussian War. The surname "Boulanger" means baker, hence the word play with "baguette" and "croissant."

xxi. "For readers convinced [. . .] that a minister's portfolio [*maroquin*] refers to a government minister 'from a diverse background' . . ." "*Maroquin*" is a type of leather made from goat hide. Since the portfolio traditionally carried by government ministers was often made of this material, "*maroquin*" was long employed metonymically to refer to ministerial posts or portfolios. Camus is here expressing contempt for those who would confuse "*maroquin*" with its homophone, "*marocain*" (that is, Moroccan) and thus conclude that one was speaking, not of a minister's job, but of his ethnic origins.

xxii. Yasmina Reza, *L'Aube le soir ou la nuit* (Paris, Flammarion, 2007). Reza is principally known as a playwright and novelist.

xxiii. Arte is a Franco-German public television channel founded in 1992. France Culture is a French public radio station founded in 1963.

xxiv. *Caroline Chérie* is a 1951 film by Richard Pottier that tells the story of a young female aristocrat at the beginning of the French Revolution. *Mayerling*, a 1968 film directed by Terence Young, follows the tragic destiny of Duke Rudolf, the crown prince of Austria, and his mistress Mary Vetsera, both of whom died in 1889 as the result of an apparent suicide pact. Maciste is a Herculean character created in Italy in 1914 by Gabriele d'Annunzio and Giovanni Pastrone; originally a secondary character, Maciste came in the 1960s to figure in several heroic Italian films set in Antiquity. *French Cancan* is a 1955 French-Italian film by Jean Renoir depicting, among other things, art culture in Paris at the height of Impressionism.

xxv. The author gives examples here that we have not included because they cannot be rendered in English. In the case of syntax, he offers "Si on travaille sur comment gérer cette crise, qu'est qu'y a surtout besoin de bien voir, au fond?" And, for word order, "réfléchir à justement le moyen de leur donner c'qu'i z'ont envie, aux gamins." Readers who are reasonably familiar with French should recognize the aberrant nature of these formulations (especially the second).

xxvi. Antoine Quentin Fouquier de Tinville (1746-1795) was a jurist and notorious public accuser during the Reign of Terror responsible for the execution of more than two thousand people. Fouquier-Tinville was sentenced to death and guillotined in 1795 for his excesses.

xxvii. In contrast to English, the French term for "professor" (professeur) denotes university faculty and schoolteachers alike. Consistent with the more general erosion of distance and hierarchy decried by Camus, it has in recent decades become common to abbreviate this term when speaking of the latter. Middle and high-school teachers are thus now just so many "profs," a term whose less than respectful connotations will be familiar to any aficionado of the American high school cinema of the 1970s ("yo, teach!").

xxviii. Chambord is a chateau in the Loire Valley built between 1519 and 1547. Famous for its distinctly Renaissance architecture, Chambord is arguably the most famous and recognizable of all French chateaus. Leonardo Da Vinci is rumored to have designed the castle's staircase.

xxix. Priority Development Zone (*Zone prioritaire d'aménagement*) is a piece of French administrative nomenclature denoting an urban or peri-urban area singled out for state-subsidized development.

xxx. Nicolás Gómez Dávila (1913-94) was a conservative Colombian philosopher and aphorist.

xxxi. Louis Émile Clément Bernanos (1888-1948) was a French author from the northern, Pas-de-Calais region of France. A Catholic with monarchist leanings (in his youth, Bernanos was active in Action française), he is best known for his novels Under the Sun of Satan (*Sous le soleil de Satan*, 1926) and The Diary of a Country Priest (*Journal d'un cure de campagne*, 1936), both of which center on the spiritual and pastoral struggles of a Catholic priest. La Canebière is an avenue in the southern port-city of Marseille that is in popular culture associated with carousing sailors.

xxxii. Sheila (b. 1945) is a French pop singer whose career spanned several decades starting in the 1960s. Dalida (1933-87) was an Egyptian-born Franco-Italian singer who won international renown in the 1950s and 60s after relocating to Paris. Hit songs by both women, often of a cloying sentimentality, may still be heard in French commercials or as background music in shopping centers. To request that either be played at one's funeral would be a token of bad taste, to say the least.

xxxiii. Giorgio Agamben (b. 1942) is an Italian philosopher whose work has extensively engaged with the conceptual legacy of Carl Schmidt, Michel Foucault, Ludwig Wittgenstein, and Walter Benjamin. The passage quoted by Camus comes from the chapter "Without Classes" in Giorgio Agamben, Michael Hardt (trans.), *The Coming Community* (Minneapolis, University of Minnesota Press, p. 64.

xxxiv. "Cour des Miracles" [court of miracles] refers to the slum districts of early modern Paris where rural migrants congregated. Over time, the term was shorn of its geographical specificity to become a byword for any place mired in poverty, filth, and crime.

xxxv. Bertolt Brecht (1898-1956), German poet and playwright. The lines quoted here come from his satirical poem "Die Lösung" ("The Solution"), written in response to the East German uprising of 1953:

Nach dem Aufstand des 17. Juni
Ließ der Sekretär des Schriftstellerverbands
In der Stalinallee Flugblätter verteilen
Auf denen zu lesen war, daß das Volk
Das Vertrauen der Regierung verscherzt habe
Und es nur durch verdoppelte Arbeit

zurückerobern könne. Wäre es da
Nicht doch einfacher, die Regierung
Löste das Volk auf und
Wählte ein anderes?

xxxvi. Christine Angot (b. 1959) is a French novelist, playwright, and screenwriter best known for her novel Incest (*L'Inceste*), in which she recounts her incestuous relationship with her father, Pierre Angot. Jean-Paul Chambas (b. 1947) is a contemporary French painter whose layered, collage-like work often depicts prominent figures from the most hackneyed and consensual history of literature and art (Rimbaud, Jim Morrison . . .). Michel Onfray (b. 1959) is a French writer, philosopher, magazine editor, and founder of the People's University of Caen (Université populaire de Caen), which offers tuition-free courses in philosophy and other subjects. *Cultures & Dépendances* (Cultures and Dependencies) was a weekly television talk show hosted by the Franco-American journalist Franz-Olivier Giesbert on the France 3 network. Camus' offers this depreciative inventory only to better underscore what he sees as the essential mediocrity of contemporary French culture, particularly compared to "the France of Proust, Cézanne, Bergson, Ravel, and the Collège de France."

xxxvii. Happy Days is a 1961 play in two acts by Samuel Beckett (1906-89) depicting the marital life of Winnie, a woman buried waist-deep in a mound of earth, and her husband Willie, who spends most of the play out of sight behind the mound. At the most general level, the play offers an extended metaphor of futility, including the futility of despair.

The Great Replacement

i. Hérault is a department in the administrative region of Occitania in southern France. Its prefecture is located in the city of Montpellier.

ii. The term *cité*, a cognate of the English-language *city*, has multiple meanings in French. In addition to referring to urban settlements (cities, towns), as in English, it is used to refer to the polity as such and, more recently, the public housing projects where many immigrants live. This passage plays on the ambiguity of the term, particularly as regards its second and third senses: "Je ne parcourais pas des *cités*, comme on dit, et comme on dit mal, pour désigner des zones qui précisément, *cité*, ne parviennent pas à le devenir . . ." Camus, in other words, is underscoring the irony of applying the term *cité* to neighborhoods whose residents singularly fail to meet the basic conditions required of civilization; these places are *cités* in name only.

iii. Rantanplan is the dimwitted canine sidekick of Lucky Luke in the comic book series of the same name created by Belgian illustrator Morris in 1946. Named Rin-Tin-Can or Bushwack in English-language versions of the series, Rantanplan stands apart from the other characters for his stupidity, his life an endless series of misunderstandings from which he never learns.

iv. "It would certainly be unwise to contradict her, in any case." Camus is here alluding to the various laws that in France prohibit "incitement to hatred, violence, or discrimination." To deny that this "veiled woman with a shaky command of our language" was indeed French could very well invite prosecution, fines, even imprisonment.

 v. Sciences Po (Institut d'études politiques de Paris / Paris Institute of Political Studies) is a prestigious French institution of higher learning and part of the highly selective "grande école" system. Founded in 1872 as part of an effort to modernize the education of civil servants, Sciences Po today serves as a major conduit for positions in the French political class and private sector.

 vi. *Faces de craie* is a syllabic inversion of *Français* meaning *chalk faces* – a clever but nonetheless racist reference to the "whiteness" of indigenous Europeans.

 vii. In French: Colombey-les-Deux-Églises and Colombey-les-Deux-Mosquées.

viii. A surname used in reference to King Louis XV.

 ix. See also note vii under "The Communism of the Twentieth Century."

 x. Possibly an allusion to the 2006 film *Indigènes* by Rachid Bouchareb, which follows the adventures and travails of four north African soldiers making their way north through Europe with the Allied army during World War Two.

 xi. The Skin (*La Pelle*) is an autobiographical novel by Curzio Malaparte published in 1949. Set in Naples, Italy, in the final days of the Second World War, it centers on the ambivalent relations between the American forces of "liberation" and the Italian civilian population they have "liberated." Two Women (*La Ciociara*) is a 1957 novel by Alberto Moravia telling the story of a mother and daughter who flee Rome after it is occupied by the Germans, taking refuge in the southern province of Ciociara. Both novels evoke the wave of mass rapes and killings known as the "Marocchinate" and attributed to the "Goumiers," Moroccan auxiliary troops from the French Army of Africa who participated in the Italian campaign as part of the French Expeditionary Corps. Estimates of the number of civilian rape victims during the Marocchinate vary widely, with the Italian government officially recognizing 2600 such cases (600 of whom were men) while some associations claim there were as many as 60,000 victims.

 xii. In Verlan, a type of argot especially popular among the immigrant-origin youth of France's housing projects, "céfrans" is an inversion of "français" specifically used to refer to the nation's (white) native stock population.

xiii. François de Chateaubriand, trans. A.S. Kline, *Mémoires d'Outre-Tombe, Book VII: Travels in New York State*, 1791 (Poetry in Translation, 2015).

xiv. A series of citations illustrating the historical continuity of France that once would have been familiar to any French schoolboy. The Vase of Soissons was a semi-sacred object that, according to Gallo-Roman historian Gregory of Tours (ca. 538-594 AD), was held by the Kingdon of Soissons in Late Antiquity but destroyed by the forces of Frankish King Clovis I following the Battle of Soissons (486 AD). The "morning at Bouvines" refers to the Battle of Bouvines (27 July 1214), which concluded the Anglo-French War of 1213-14, consolidating the French monarchy's hold over the western half of present-day France. "Madame is dying . . . Madame is dead" is in reference to the suspiciously abrupt death of Henriette, Duchesse d'Orléans, sister-in-law of King Louis XIV and an important figure in the royal court. "Messieurs les Anglais, tirez les premiers!" ("May the English gentlemen shoot first!"): according to

Voltaire, the French commanding officer at the Battle of Fontenoy (11 May 1745) addressed his English adversaries with these words, which came to be seen as an emblematic instance of Old Regime gallantry. "We are here by the will of the people and we will only be dispersed by the force of bayonets!" was Mirabeau's famous reply to King Louis XVI's representative after the latter requested that he and other members of the newly formed National Assembly carry on their meeting in separate chambers – in the early days of the French Revolution, a shocking assertion of popular sovereignty. "Que d'eau, que d'eau!" ("so much water, so much water!") was President Patrice de Mac-Mahon's rather feeble response upon viewing the Garonne River in flood in 1875. It became a byword for the lack of imagination and determination so often displayed by politicians. "France has a lost a battle [but has not lost the War]" is a statement commonly (and incorrectly) attributed to General De Gaulle's Appeal of 18 June (1940) urging French soldiers and citizens to resist the Nazi occupation of France. "And the solitary string of the marine trumpets" are the words of "Chantre," a poem that appears in Guillaume Apollinaire's 1913 collection, *Alcools*.

xv.   "Muchiellisme," in reference to Laurent Muchielli (b. 1968), a French sociolo-gist among other things known for his highly-publicized efforts to minimize France's delinquency crisis.

xvi. Racine, *Phaedra*, Act V, Scene 1.

xvii. Georges Bernanos, *La Grande Peur des bien-pensants*, (Paris, Librairie Générale Française, 1998), p. 29.

xviii. "Faut-il souligner que *populaire*, en novlangue, signifie désormais *qui n'appartient pas au peuple* (indigène)." In contrast to its English cognate, "popular," the French adjective "populaire" possesses strong social connota-tions. To describe something as "populaire" is to say that it relates to or is of the common people (for which the English adjective "working-class" is a rough but not always satisfactory approximation). What Camus is saying here, in other words, is that the meaning of the word "populaire" has been inverted or at least adulterated: it is now exclusively used to describe popula-tions that, by virtue of their foreign origin, are precisely not part of the com-mon people (or have replaced them). To preserve this nuance, we have in this instance deliberately opted to translate "populaire" by its faux ami, "popular."

xix. A double play on words doubly lost in translation. The original reads, "*Quartier* tout court ne peut être que *quartiers* sensibles. Seuls les sensibles ont des quartiers. Pour les insensibles pas de quartiers." For the pair "sensible / insensible," we have chosen the more idiomatic "underprivileged / privileged," though "sensitive / insensitive" better captures the humoristic intent of this passage. The term "quartier," meanwhile, which we have translated as "neigh-borhood" but which can also be rendered as "district," lives on in the English expression, "to show/give no quarter." A more literal, less idiomatic transla-tion would thus read: "*Quarter* on its own can only mean sensitive *quarters*. Only the sensitive have quarters. For the insensitive, no quarter" – i.e., show no mercy.

xx.   "La ruquiérisation des esprits," a reference to French author, producer, and talk show host Laurent Ruquier (b. 1963), who for Camus epitomizes the ab-ject celebrity-worship and glib sanctimony of French public broadcasting.

xxi. Oskar Freysinger (b. 1960) is a Swiss politician and member of the national-conservative Swiss People's Party (SVP). Freysinger played a prominent role in organizing the 2009 referendum to ban the construction of minarets in Switzerland. For more on the referendum, see above, "The Communism of the Twenty-First Century," note ii.

Nocence, Instrument of the Great Replacement

i. See note xxxv under "The Great Deculturation."

ii. Robert Redeker (b. 1954) is a French philosopher, school teacher, and the author of twenty-five books, including *Egobody : La fabrique de l'homme nouveau* (Paris, Éditions Fayard, 2010). He is perhaps best known for a September 19th, 2006 editorial in the French center-right daily *Le Figaro*, "Face aux intimidations islamistes, que doit faire le monde libre?" ["Faced with Islamist Intimidation, What Should the Free World Do?"], in which he argued that Islam is inherently violent and sought to impose its rules on France. Redeker's editorial was the subject of bitter controversy and led to death threats against its author, who was placed under police protection.

iii. "Une chance pour l'Espagne." Camus is here alluding to a rhyming platitude of the French immigration debates according to which immigration is "une chance pour la France" ("an opportunity for France"). The expression appears to have been first used by French politician Bernard Stasi (1930-2011) in his 1984 pro-immigration book, *L'immigration, une chance pour la France* (Paris, Robert Laffont, 1984).

iv. "La nocence c'est bien sûr la nuisance, au sens écologique du terme . . ." Camus is here playing on the obvious Latin derivation of the French word "nuisance," often translated as "pollution" ("nuisance sonore" = "noise pollution"). Its English cognate, "nuisance," is not used in this sense.

v. Camus is here alluding to a phenomenon known in French as "les casseurs" (literally, "breakers," but better translated as "hooligans"). The term first came into general currency in February 2006 during demonstrations against a new law regulating first-time employment (le CPE, or *contrat première embauche* / First Employment Contract). On several occasions, the protesters, most of whom were high school or university students, were set upon, assaulted, and robbed by groups of black and Arab young people – "les casseurs" – who had traveled from the suburbs for this purpose. On the Left, the discomfit was palpable: it turned out that these suburban youth saw the student demonstrators, not as allies, but as *prey*. The anti-CPE movement fizzled and died. The tactics of "les casseurs" would in later years be adopted to different ends by so-called "black bloc" anarchists and other iterations of "antifascist" protestor.

The Replaceable Man

i. See note i under "The Second Career of Adolf Hitler."

ii. Camus is here referring to the text, "Nocence, Instrument of The Great Replacement," included in this volume.

iii. Alexis de Tocqueville, Harvey C. Mansfield and Delba Winthrop (trans.),

Democracy in America (Chicago, University of Chicago Press, 2000), pp. 244-245.

iv. Richard Millet (b. 1953) is a French novelist and essayist and a former member of the editorial committee at Gallimard. During his tenure at the prestigious Parisian publishing house, Millet was instrumental in the publication of Jonathan Littell's novel *Les Bienveillantes* (translated into English as *The Kindly Ones*), which won the Prix Goncourt in 2006. Millet was pilloried in the press in 2012 for an essay he published entitled "Éloge littéraire d'Anders Breivik" ("Anders Breivik's Literary Eulogy") that, while condemning the acts of the Norwegian mass murderer, nonetheless argued that his crimes were symptomatic of Norway's reckless embrace of multiculturalism.

v. Christopher Caldwell, *Reflections on the Revolution in Europe* (New York, Doubleday, 2009).

vi. Following publication of his pro-Dreyfusard manifesto *J'Accuse* in January 1898, Émile Zola was put on trial for defamation. In order to ensure that the court's attention not wander from the particulars of Zola's case to other, more compromising considerations – particularly those that might call into question the impartiality of the justice system – the presiding judge, Delegorgue, regularly interrupted the proceedings with the words, "the question will not be asked" ("*la question ne sera pas posée*"). The expression became famous as shorthand for an act of fiat intended to shut down any challenge to institutional authority.

vii. A reference, apparently, to the European sovereign debt crisis of 2009-12, which witnessed soaring interest rates, higher taxes, and cuts to public expenditures. In many countries, the crisis would have knock-on political effects, fueling public mistrust of technocratic governance from Brussels and ramping up support for sovereignist movements, most notably in Germany and the UK.

viii. Since 1976, all those seeking to present themselves as candidates in the French presidential elections must first secure the endorsement of 500 elected officials. In contrast to candidates from the centrist "parties of government," who can count on their party apparatuses to gather the necessary signatures well in advance of the deadline, this requirement often constitutes a major hurdle for the representatives of smaller parties. Such was the case of Renaud Camus, who was obliged to withdraw his name from the 2012 French presidential election after failing to gather the requisite number of endorsements. With Camus out of the race, the Party of In-nocence called upon its supporters to vote for National Front candidate Marine Le Pen instead.

ix. In French, the verb *apprendre* means both *to teach* and *to learn*. "To learn" is sometimes observed in this double sense in non-standard dialects of English ("he learned me good," for example), whereas in French such double use belongs to the standard version of the language.

x. An international conference center located near the National Assembly in Paris.

xi. Familiar figures much beloved by France's progressive media establishment. Laurent Ruquier (b. 1963) is an author, producer, and radio and television celebrity best known for hosting a series of comedic talk shows on the France 2 television network, including *On a tout essayé* (2000-07) and *On n'est pas couché* (2006-20). An essayist, Socialist Party politician, and professor of education at the *Université Lumiére-Lyon 2*, Philippe Meirieu (b. 1949) has been a tireless advocate for many of the educational system "reforms" decried by Camus. Richard Descoings (1958-2012) was a high-ranking French civil servant and director of the prestigious *Institut d'études politiques* (Sciences-Po), from which the French political class is disproportionately drawn. He drew much criticism for his efforts to "Americanize" Sciences-Po, where he oversaw the development of English-language degree programs, courted private enterprise, and instituted outreach programs to facilitate the admission of students from Priority Education Zones (see note xxix under "The Great Deculturation"). His reputation would be tarnished by the revelation of financial and sexual improprieties following his death in a Manhattan hotel room in 2012. Laurent Muchielli (b. 1968) is a sociologist at the National Center for Scientific Research (CNRS) who specializes in security policy and the sociology of delinquency. He is best known for his critical interventions in debates over crime, in which he has contested official estimates of delinquency, which he sees as fueling a "feeling of insecurity" largely unsupported by statistical realities.

xii. Built in 2005, the Viaduc de Millau is located roughly 150km (93 miles) to the west of the Pont du Gard, a 1st-century AD Roman aqueduct and bridge that crosses the river Gardon near the southern French town of Vers-Pont-du-Gard. The worlds' tallest and best-preserved Roman aqueduct, it was added to the list of UNESCO World Heritage sites in 1985.

xiii. See note ii under "Nocence, Instrument of the Great Replacement."

xiv. See note vi under "The Second Career of Adolf Hitler."

xv. Gilles-William Goldnadel (b. 1954) is a prominent Franco-Israeli lawyer, author, conservative journalist, and, for a time, President of the France-Israel Association.

xvi. Gilles-William Goldnadel, *Réflexions sur la question blanche* (Paris, Jean-Claude Gawsewitch, 2011).

Speech before the 17th Chamber

i. 17th Chamber of the Judicial Court of Paris, responsible for overseeing application of the 1881 law on the freedom of the press. Its remit includes judging accusations of "incitement to racial hatred," which has been a crime in France since 1972.

ii. *L'Affiche Rouge* (Red Poster) refers to a notorious propaganda poster distributed by Vichy French and German Occupation authorities in the spring of 1944. Against a red backdrop, it features photos of the arrested and soon to be executed members of the Manouchian Group [see note iv below], with details of their backgrounds offset in captions. Its legend reads, "Liberation by the Army of Crime!" As propaganda, the poster drew upon the foreign origins and communist affiliations of this particular group to discredit the French Resistance more generally.

iii. FTP-MOI is the acronym of *Francs-tireurs et partisans – main d'oeuvre immigrée* (Francs-tireurs and Partisans – Immigrant Workforce), a French

Resistance organization created in Paris in 1941 that wholly consisted of foreign volunteers (many of them Jewish) under the direction of the Communist
International. Among the most active Resistance groups of the war, FTP-
MOI carried out a string of bombings and assassinations against the forces of
occupation.

iv. Missak Manouchian (1906-44) was a Franco-Armenian poet, communist
activist, and survivor of the Armenian genocide. Under the German occupation, Manouchian became military commissioner of FTP-MOI for the Paris
region. In November 1943, he was arrested with many of his comrades by
French collaborationist police. Following a show trial, they were executed by
a German firing squad at Fort Mont-Valérien on February 21st, 1944. The government of Emmanuel Macron has announced that Manouchian's remains
will be transferred to the Panthéon on the eightieth anniversary of his execution (21 February 2024).

v. The "jambon-beurre" (ham-butter) is a sandwich made from sliced ham and
buttered baguette. In this instance, it is being used as a derogatory metonym
for the native French: traditionally the most popular sandwich in France, the
fact that it contains a pork product makes it *haram* (forbidden) for French
Muslims.

vi. Farid Tali, *Prosopopée* (Paris, Éditions P.O.L., 2001).

vii. On May 8th, 1945, French police fired on Algerian Muslims demonstrating
for independence in the French Algerian town of Sétif. Over the days that
followed, independence activists killed 102 French settlers in the surrounding countryside in reprisal. This provoked massive retaliation on the part of
French military and police units, who, with assistance from local irregulars,
killed between 6000 and 30,000 Muslims in the weeks that followed.

viii. On February 8th, 1962, a demonstration was held in the vicinity of Paris'
Charonne metro station to protest the activities of the Secret Army Organization (OAS), an underground terrorist organization seeking to prevent Algerian independence. Although it had been prohibited by the government, the
demonstration went ahead anyway. Under the direction of Maurice Papon
(1910-2007), Prefect of Police for Paris and a Vichy-era Collaborator, the Paris
police force brutally repressed the demonstration, resulting in the death of
9 members of the CGT labor union, most of whom were also members of the
French Communist Party.

ix. The Harkis were native Muslim soldiers who served as auxiliaries to the
French Army during the Algerian War. Regarded as traitors by independent
Algeria and officially excluded by the French government from resettlement
in France (though an estimated 90,000 of them did ultimately make their
way there), the Harkis and their families were the object of mass reprisals.
Estimates of Harki deaths in postwar Algeria vary widely but it is generally
accepted that tens of thousands were killed, with some estimates as high as
150,000. In 2001, the government of President Jacques Chirac proclaimed a
Day of National Recognition for the Harkis.

x. The Basilica of Sacré-Coeur (Sacred Heart) is a Roman Catholic church and
minor basilica located in the northern Paris neighborhood of Montmartre.
Built between 1875 and 1914, the church was conceived as an expression of

repentance in the aftermath of the Franco-Prussian War of 1870, which witnessed the annexation of French territory by Imperial Germany and the collapse of Napoléon III's Second Empire regime. Though the idea for the church preceded the period of revolutionary turmoil known as the Paris Commune (bloodily suppressed in 1871 by the national government in Bordeaux), French leftists have long seen it as a symbol of reactionary triumphalism and called for its destruction.

xi. Frantz Fanon (1925-61) was a psychiatrist, political philosopher, and pan-Africanist from the French colony of Martinique. He was closely associated with the anti-colonial movements of his time and was a member of the Algerian National Liberation Front (FLN). His best-known work remains *The Wretched of the Earth*, which was prefaced by Jean-Paul Sartre and advocates violent resistance to white colonial rule.

xii. Frantz Fanon, *Toward the African Revolution: Political Essays*, trans. Haakon Chevalier. (New York, Grove Press, 1967), p. 43.

xiii. Éditions Maspero was a French publishing house founded in 1959 by François Maspero and Marie-Thérèse Maugis. It quickly distinguished itself as a champion of Third World anti-colonialist movements, publishing work by Frantz Fanon, Che Guevera, and Mongo Beti, among others, and launching the careers of numerous figures of the French New Left, including Régis Debray and Bernard Henri-Lévy. In 1983, it was transformed into *Éditions La Découverte*, now a holding of French media group Vivendi.

xiv. A joke. In French, MRAP is the acronym of both the original organization (*Mouvement contre le Racisme, l'Antisémitisme et pour la Païx*) and its successor (*Mouvement contre le racisme et pour l'Amitié entre les Peuples*). It would also be the acronym of the Movement for the Accelerated Replacement of the People (*Mouvement pour le Remplacement Accéléré du Peuple*) should such an organization exist.

Exchange with Alain Finkielkraut on Migrants

i. In France, the expression, "*faire amalgame*" – literally, to "amalgamate," "lump together," or "conflate" – is often used to discredit those who would argue that contemporary social problems (crime, terrorism, education, etc.) have an ethnic or racial component. This is particularly true for discussions of Islam, where it is understood that this can never be the case.

The Apartment

i. Emmanuel Carrère (b. 1957) is a prominent French author, screenwriter, and film director. In 2016, he published a collection of his journalism, *Il est avantageux d'avoir où aller* (Paris, Folio, 2017).

ii. *La Verità* (The Truth) is a conservative Italian daily published in Milan.

iii. Carrère refers here to the hometown of Joachim Du Bellay, a sixteenth-century poet who, along with other poets of the Pléiade group, was instrumental in valorizing the French language as an artistic competitor to Latin. Present-day Liré is a village of approximately 2500 people in the Maine-et-Loire department in west-central France.

iv. A euphemism – often derided – for the day-to-day experience of ethnically-blended suburban communities. *Vivre-ensemble* is literally translated as "living together" but is better rendered as "social cohesion" or "social harmony," it being understood that such harmony and cohesion are precisely what lack. We retain the French as a lexical item as Camus immediately offers a non-euphemistic translation: the "forced cohabitation of different peoples."

Appeal of Colombey

i. Following the Battle of France (May-June 1940), General Charles De Gaulle, then Under-Secretary of State for Defense and War in the government of Prime Minister Paul Reynaud, fled to England. The following day, 18 June, he delivered his Appeal (sometimes also known as the Appeal from London) on the BBC. In it, he called upon the French people to resist German forces, denounced the new government formed in Bordeaux by Philippe Pétain, sought to rally French troops in North Africa to his cause, and invited any French soldiers who could do so to make for England, where they would form the basis of a reconstituted French Army. De Gaulle's Free French movement would eventually be recognized by the Allies as France's legitimate government in exile and its soldiers would fight alongside Allied forces in the campaigns to liberate occupied Europe. Though few heard it at the time, the Appeal of 18 June is seen in popular memory as inaugurating French resistance to the occupation in mainland France.